The Journey

An American Soldier in World War I

D. Kent Decker

Printed in the United States of America
First Printing, 2017

ISBN: 978-1-5356-0745-2

Acknowledgements

WRITING THIS BOOK HAS BEEN quite an educational adventure to say the least. When my wife's family found their Uncle Dick's letters in the attic, I knew very little about World War One or even the condition of the country during that period. Uncle Dick's comments along the train routes and in the army camps aroused my curiosity to the point where I was motivated to write this book. It took a lot of research and this story would have been incomplete without the help of others. I first want to thank my wife, Kathleen, for her diligent work in tracing the Bakker ancestry, not to mention her patience and understanding that allowed me the time to work on this project over a period of two decades or so. I have to thank the Bakker family for making the letters available and allowing me to write Uncle Dick's story. I thank the elder members of the family: Jeanette Bakker Bruns, Wilma Bakker Beekman, and Earl Habben for taking the time to document their memories of their parents and grandparents.

I thank Robert Laplander for his invaluable inputs to this story and for his permission to reprint his material. Mr. Laplander is considered to be the world's leading authority on the Lost Battalion. His book, *Finding the Lost Battalion*, provided the details of Dick Bakker's last days in battle with the 308th Infantry. This book is a must read for anyone interested in an in-depth account of what happened to these brave men in the Meuse-Argonne offensive. Mr. Laplander also sent me Dick's burial documentation which contained the correspondence between the government and the Bakker family after Dick's death.

There is an abundance of information on World War One via the World Wide Web. The accounts can be conflicting at times, especially when statistics are quoted. I have quoted information from what I believe are reliable sources. One source that provided much useful information on America's involvement in World War One was *The Last Days of Innocence: America at War*, 1917-1918 by Meirion and Suzie Harries, copyright © 1997 by Meirion and Suzie Harries. I am using the cited excerpts herein from *The Last Days of Innocence* by permission from Random House, an imprint and division of Penguin Random House LLC. All rights reserved. Any third party use of this material, outside of this publication, is prohibited. Interested parties must apply directly to Penguin Random House LLC for permission.

Another entertaining read is *The Doughboys, the Story of the AEF*, 1917-1918, by Laurence Stallings. Stallings was wounded in the leg in the Battle of Belleau Wood. The leg was eventually amputated. He became a successful writer after the war. I am reprinting twenty excerpts from *The Doughboys* with permission from HarperCollins Publishers. [THE DOUGHBOYS, THE STORY OF THE AEF, 1917-1918 by LAURENCE STALLINGS. Copyright © 1963 by Laurence Stallings. Reprinted by permission of HarperCollins Publishers.]

I thank all the sources that gave me permission to use the information from their research. These sources are cited in the footnotes and in the bibliography along with the links to the web sites. Permission to reprint quoted material must be obtained from the original source.

Contents

Prologue

WORLD WAR I WAS CALLED "the Great War" and "the war to end all wars," but it was neither. World War I was a devastating war of trenches, barbed wire, grenades, poison gas, machine guns, flame-throwers, heavy artillery, tanks, and U-boats. The roots of air combat were planted in World War I. These new technologies of mechanized warfare far outstripped the battlefield tactics of the era, leading to some of the bloodiest conflicts known to man as scores of infantrymen marched bravely into walls of artillery and machine-gun fire. Private First Class Dick W. Bakker was one of those brave infantrymen. This is the story of his journey from the Minnesota farmlands to the Western Front as American citizens struggled under the demands of a national government that wanted to control every aspect of their lives, from the food that was consumed to the conversations that were allowed.

At a time when a vast industrial expansion led to a large influx of immigration that included fifteen million citizens of German descent, war propaganda aggravated the tensions between the diverse factions of the American society and instigated animosity, distrust, and intolerance throughout. In an effort to maintain social and economic stability, big government was set in motion as the Wilson administration issued a multitude of controlling measures over its citizens. Major industries were nationalized or placed under strict government regulation with set prices and production quotas. Food and fuel were rationed, dissent prohibited, honest criticism forbidden. The country was steeped in turmoil.

Chapter 1

Somewhere in France

"I AM NEAR THE FRONT now and I expect to go within a few days. That may not sound very good to you but I have no fears & am ready to meet death at any time but I expect to be back." Hunkered down in the rain-soaked, forested area around La Croix Gentin, two miles behind the jump-off trenches, Dick Bakker penciled his message on plain lined paper that Wednesday, September 24, 1918, using only the envelope from his army pack for support. "Well if I don't write for a while after this letter you know where I am & I sure won't have any time or chance as you know that but I will write more if I can. As ever, your Son and Bro, Dick W. Bakker, Company E, 308th Infantry, American Expeditionary Forces, France." The letter would not reach the farm near Renville, Minnesota, until late November, a few weeks after the Armistice was signed. Mother Grace would hold it close in the years to come.

Nearby, the Seventy-Seventh Division's officers and NCOs poured over maps of all sizes and shapes in preparation for their next big objective—to break through the Hindenburg Line between the Argonne Forest and the Meuse River. The Argonne, its heights bristling with artillery and heavy machine guns, so threatened the American's left flank that it could not be permitted to remain in German hands. Furthermore, it was the key that had to be turned to open the way to Grand-Pre, Sedan, and the great German communication centers along the Sedan-Mézières railway. The Argonne was the size of Manhattan, with dense foliage never before encountered by the New Yorkers of the Seventy-Seventh. "Huge trees," recalled Lieutenant Arthur McKeogh, "tower protectively above their brood of close-grown saplings, branches interlacing branches, overlaid until no patch of sky is visible, and the light is the sickly half-light of early dawn. The ground hides under a maze of trailing vines, prickly bushes, and rheumatic tree branches, embedded in soggy leaves and rank fern."[1] With the forest's dense underbrush and barbed wire entanglements, it had a reputation as one of the most formidable killing grounds on the Western Front. The Germans, entrenched in the region for four years, knew every inch of the terrain.

The Seventy-Seventh had seen action on August 14 on the Vesle above Bazoches and Fismes, taking heavy casualties after a month of hard fighting. Allied Commander Ferdinand Foch relieved the division on September 16, replacing them with the Italian Garibaldi Division.[2] Replacement troops started pouring in on September 22, including four thousand men from the Fortieth "Sunshine" Division. Dick Bakker was among the replacements. The Fortieth had been re-assigned as the Sixth Depot Division

1 Meirion Harries and Susie Harries. *The Last Days of Innocence: America at War, 1917-1918*. New York: Vintage Books, 1997, 370.

2 Laurence Stallings. *The Doughboys: The Story of the AEF, 19171918*. New York: Harper and Row, 1963, 200.

stationed near Château Fontenay when they arrived in France in late August. Now, these men from the Western states with no combat experience were about to engage in the largest battle in the history of the country under a new command.

They were a strange lot, these boys from the Seventy-Seventh—certainly different from the Westerners of the Fortieth. New York City's own, the Seventy-Seventh was named the "Metropolitan Division" with an insignia of a gold Statue of Liberty on a truncated triangle of flag blue. It spoke forty-two languages, and among its gamblers could be found Chinese from Mott Street playing fan-tan, Jewish boys from Allen Street in stuss games, Italian boys from east of Union Square playing piquet, and Germans from Yorkville on the Upper East Side. There were Turks who spoke a little Hebrew, and Hebrews who spoke a bit of Arabic. Many could speak nothing but Brooklyn English (i.e., from the Don Marquis ballad, "When you call on a Brookalyn goil, say Poil for Pearl and erl for oil"). There were even Kentucky and Tennessee immigrants to New York City who referred to a dud shell as a "possum playin' daid." It was rumored that there were many gangsters among them. The division took on many nicknames, including the "Melting Pot" Division and the "Liberty" Division.[3] These were the men with whom Dick would go to war. He had better get acquainted.

Getting to the designated jump-off point had been a difficult task within itself. General John Joseph "Black Jack" Pershing, AEF Commander, had committed the American First Army to undertake two major operations within the space of roughly

3 Ibid., 198.

three weeks: the first, to pinch out the Saint-Mihiel pocket; the second, to shift forces rapidly north and west and break through the Hindenburg Line. With the sheer number of American troops flexing their muscles on the battlefield, the balance of power had shifted to the Allies by the end of August. No fewer than six Allied armies were pushing the Germans back toward the Hindenburg line at that time, with the British, commanded by Field Marshall Alexander Haig, inflicting major damage to the north. Now convinced that the conflict could be won in 1918, Pershing wanted to position his army in such a way that America could take a major share of the credit for winning the war. This would allow President Woodrow Wilson to exert a greater influence at the peace conference. It was a high-risk gamble with a heavy price to pay.

While the Saint-Mihiel operation had been planned in advance with the necessary support systems in place, the Meuse-Argonne operation was completely out of the American zone and had not been considered by the First Army planners.[4] Fortunately, the Saint-Mihiel operation went off as planned on September 12 and 13. For the Meuse-Argonne operation, Pershing committed nine divisions of the American First Army to attack along a twenty-four-mile front. The attack was scheduled for September 26, limiting preparation for the assault to a mere two weeks of frantic improvisation following the capture of Saint-Mihiel, sixty miles away. The perceived enemy weakness was the shortage of troops; the Germans had only five divisions actually manning

4 Meirion Harries and Susie Harries. *The Last Days of Innocence: America at War, 1917-1918*. New York: Vintage Books, 1997, 331-333.

these splendid defenses, and many of the gun emplacements were empty. Pershing's staff calculated that four German divisions could be brought up within twenty-four hours, two more in forty-eight, and another nine in seventy-two hours, at which time the sector would become impassable.

Consequently, success depended on the element of surprise. French headquarters spread the notion of an American attack in the east, and the First Army staff attempted a ruse with some dispersed radio stations. The First Army used codes based on American rivers such as "Wabash" and "Colorado," but the codes alone could not conceal the mass influx of 600,000 American troops, 3,980 artillery pieces, and 90,000 horses. The only hope of obscuring so vast a movement was to execute it by night.[5]

The hundreds of thousands of Doughboys were hustled along three narrow roads dotted with spent and dying horses every hundred yards. The troops, moving by night, hid in barns, houses, and rain-soaked woods or under camouflage netting by day. With the veteran divisions employed at Saint-Mihiel, the newest and greenest divisions nearest the front arrived first. The American command had little choice in placing the divisions on any particular section of the line; whatever division was nearest a gap of the front was moved there by the closest available route at top speed under the rain-soaked blanket of night, a great movement rushing to achieve surprise of time, position, and mass.

Moving up the vital support for the infantry that would soon plunge into the tangle of undergrowth and barbed wire was perhaps the biggest undertaking of all the impromptu circumstances. To

5 Ibid., 351-353.

arm the nearly four thousand guns of all calibers that had to be in place by September 25 required forty thousand tons of shells. Once these guns began firing, fourteen trainloads of shells were required to feed them daily from twenty-four ammunition depots established at nineteen railheads. The quartermaster needed nine depots; the engineers demanded twelve for supplies and eight for water carts. Chemical warfare required six. Trucks transporting the Doughboys forward twenty thousand at a time needed nine depots for gas and oil. Forage had to be brought forward for the ninety thousand horses. Surgeons needed thirty-four evacuation hospitals. The greatest of all tasks for engineers was the rebuilding of the 164 miles of standard railways out of the existing 215 miles.[6]

However carefully the Allies were hiding by day, their feverish nocturnal maneuvers were easily spotted. The noise of narrow-gauge railways, the unloading of heavy material, loud cries, sirens, and klaxons could be heard throughout the whole night.[7] In the night sky above the Argonne Forest, a German aviator cut his engine and listened, gliding silently just above treetop level. He could see no lights below, but he could hear the bellow of mule skinners, the racket of light tank engines, and the crashing of truck gears. There was no mistaking the bedlam—the Yanks were

6 Laurence Stallings. *The Doughboys: The Story of the AEF, 1917-1918*. New York: Harper and Row, 1963, 226-227.

7 Meirion Harries and Susie Harries. *The Last Days of Innocence: America at War, 1917-1918*. New York: Vintage Books, 1997, 352-353.

coming![8] The local German forces, aware of an impending attack but uncertain as to its size, began preparations.

Nevertheless, Dick Bakker and the Fortieth Division replacements had made it to the Seventy-Seventh's bivouac by September 24 in the midst of the bedlam and chaos. Anticipation gripped the camp. French troops had repulsed three German waves that morning amidst the exchange of artillery fire. Orders flew between command posts at alarming speed as commanders assigned attack and support battalions, each with a machine-gun unit. A reserve battalion, a reserve machine-gun unit, and three Stokes Mortars would follow each support battalion.

No one knew for sure when they would go over the top. The men huddled together by candlelight in the rain-soaked woods talking of their chances, hoping for the best, but admitting that their fate was in the hands of God. Each man made peace with his own God in his own way. Final orders came down on the afternoon of the twenty-fifth. The first phase was to be completed in seventy-two hours, before the Germans could bring up replacement units. Once launched, the strike had to be extraordinarily rapid. Ground gained could not be given up under any circumstances. The troops were ordered to drop packs as a full load of regular equipment was deemed to be unnecessary. Furthermore, it would slow down the soldier. With that, each man left behind his overcoat, poncho, rain slicker, blankets, and shelter tent. His combat gear consisted of rifle, bayonet, steel helmet, and gas mask; short combat pack containing two days of iron rations, four boxes of hard bread, and

8 Laurence Stallings. *The Doughboys: The Story of the AEF, 1917-1918.* New York: Harper and Row, 1963, 223.

two cans of corned beef; mess kit; entrenching tool; cartridge belt with full load of one hundred pounds of ammunition; one-quart canteen; and first aid pouch.

In the evening light, unit leaders whistled the troops to fall in. Final instructions were brief and tense. The message was clear: This is it, the big one. Supply sergeants continued to scurry about, completing last minute details. Nevertheless, some went forward without iron rations, others short of combat gear. The rain had stopped, but the damp air was unseasonably cold. German artillery lobbed stray shells into the vicinity as the massive movement to the jump-off trenches began. Single-file, tens of thousands of troops slogged the two miles through mud and foliage, groping their way through the darkness, rookies and veterans alike. At 6 a.m. sharp, the attack battalions would go over the top. They had no idea the 308th Infantry would become legend.[9]

9 Robert J. Laplander. *Finding the Lost Battalion: Beyond the Rumors, Myths, and Legends of America's Famous WWI Epic*. Waterford: Lulu Press, 2006, 80-86.

Chapter 2

Minnesota

JUST FOUR MONTHS PRIOR, DICK Bakker was managing the Columbia grain elevator in the rural farming community of Renville, Minnesota, a position he had held for three years. Educated to the eighth grade in a one-room country schoolhouse, blonde and blue-eyed Dick, the second son of Walter and Grace Bakker, was engaged to be married to his sweetheart, Tetje Sietsema, a local farm girl he had met at Sunday School.

Dick's grandparents, John and Hendrika Bakker, came to America in 1869 from Emden, Germany, and took up farming in Forreston, Illinois. After thirteen years of farming in Illinois and Grundy County, Iowa, the family moved to Renville County and purchased two hundred acres of farmland. Mr. Bakker became very successful as a land agent in the west central Minnesota area, and eventually accumulated over one thousand acres of land, which was divided among his six living children when he retired. He founded the Emden German Christian Reform church and was influential in developing a strong German community. Later, Mr. Bakker moved on to become a charter member of a second church, the Ebenezer Presbyterian Church, which was situated amongst the farms three and a half miles north of the small town

Dick and Tetje

of Renville. Both the church and its cemetery are well-kept and functioning as an integral part of the community today.

In his younger days, Dick helped to work the family farm. The farm site consisted of a roomy house, a barn for horses and milk cows, a hog house, a chicken house, a machine shed, a corn crib, and a granary that was a part of the barn. A small tool shed stored all the tools and small equipment needed to keep everything in good repair. There was a pump house where a windmill pumped water for the animals and also into a cooler where cream was stored in cans. The Bakker farm, operated in an efficient manner, was self-sufficient in its own right.

Walter, a tall, slim man with a white mustache who often wore a white straw hat, raised a sizeable herd of Black Angus beef cattle and purebred Duroc hogs. He was remembered as quiet, kind, and respected with a friendly personality. One family member noted that Walter had the unusual habit of eating peas and potatoes with a table knife. On the farm, spring brought on the annual tilling of the land for planting crops of oats, wheat, hay, corn, and soybeans. Although tractors were the way of the future in 1918, most farming was done with horses. Walter along with sons John, Bill, Dick, and Helmer were in the fields at the break of dawn during planting time and didn't return until the last rays of the sun disappeared in the west. To save time in the short Minnesota planting season, the Bakker women brought food and water to the fields for both the men and horses.

These early American farmers exhibited a broad range of knowhow and skills long forgotten in the modern age of specialization. During all seasons, through the harsh Minnesota winters that could reach thirty below zero and on through the sweltering heat of summer, the men performed chores morning and night, which included milking the cows and gathering eggs. They fed, watered, and bedded the farm animals that included horses, cows, pigs, and chickens. They cleaned the barn stalls, chicken houses, and pig pens and carried the manure to the fields for fertilizer in the spring. As the need arose, the men repaired equipment, mended fences, mowed the lawn, and painted the farm buildings to keep the farm site in good order. Each year, they butchered a pig and a young steer and preserved and stored the meat. Lard was rendered from the animal fat, and lye soap was made from a concoction of lye, lard, cold water and Borax. The family exerted great effort to use every resource and byproduct available.

While the men worked the fields and tended to the livestock, Grace and daughters Reka, Josie, and Christine were busy doing their own work. Grace was remembered as a very kind, generous, and loving mother who cooked big, tasty meals. She was especially remembered for her cookies with sweet raisin filling and her homemade cranberry relish, hand-ground with apples, oranges, and sugar. Hardy and industrious, these women were creative in their own right, exhibiting skills of sewing, crocheting, knitting, tatting, and cooking. On the sewing machine, "new" outfits were created from old clothes, feed sacks, and donations from relatives. Rugs, draperies, quilts, and bedspreads were created in the same fashion. In later years, the children would look at a quilt made by Mother Grace and recall fond memories of the clothes that they had worn and outgrown. The hub of activities was the kitchen, where the women cooked, baked, canned, ate meals, packed school lunches, prepared food to be delivered to the fields, washed dishes and clothes, and bathed.

There was no day busier than wash day, which was almost always Monday. They had to pump the water, haul it to the house, heat it in a boiler, scrub each garment on the washboard, wring and twist, rinse, and then hang outdoors to dry, sometimes in freezing weather to add a fresh smell and white look. After dinner at noon, they would empty the wash water and tubs, bring in the clean and dry laundry, fold and sort, sprinkle with water and roll up for later ironing—perhaps on Tuesday, dip Sunday shirts in homemade starch before drying (no permanent-press fabric or spray starch), heat flat irons on the stove, and spend the rest of the day ironing.

Cleaning was a major part of the daily routine. Even the outhouse had to be cleaned, a task which was assigned to Christine, the youngest, who was nicknamed "Toots." Toots remained disgruntled about that job till her dying day. The Bakker women didn't always work in the house, though. They gathered eggs, worked in the garden, trimmed flowers and shrubs, and kept the yard looking orderly, as many of the women of the era were inclined to do.

The Bakker Family. From left to right: Helmer, Reka, Bill, Josie, Christine, Dick, Grace, John, Walter

The family went shopping on Saturdays. Grace would bring a list for the clerk, who would gather the items from the store shelves. They brought a few cases of eggs which were used to pay for the groceries. The store had tin coins called "duebills" that could be used as money in the store again for exchange. On winter Sundays, they went to church in a bobsled pulled by a team of horses. One of the boys drove the horses while the other children and Grace were wrapped in blankets to keep warm. Walter stood on the back of the sled with a hand on each side of the box like he was guarding his family.

The Bakker family was not all work and no play. They knew how to entertain themselves, out of necessity perhaps, as commercial radio stations were yet to find their way into this rural community. Mother Grace played the reed organ and the boys played the violin, exhibiting musical skills handed down from generation to generation. Neighbors came over with other instruments such as the accordion and percussion instruments, and the group sang hymns and other songs of the day. They spun yarns and played cards and games like horseshoes, baseball, and cricket. Dick enjoyed riding his horse, Peanuts, and gave Toots "horsey back" rides. This happy, peaceful family was far removed from the devastation that was ravaging Europe. [10]

There was great unrest across the nation due to the war effort, however. Minnesota was no exception. Renville County, located in west central Minnesota, consists primarily of farms and small towns. The county population in 1918 was over twenty-three thousand.[11] The town of Renville had a population of a little over eleven hundred, a typical size for the ten communities in the county.[12] The racial makeup of the county has always consisted

10 Bakker farm life based on the memories of the Bakker family with special contributions from Jeanette Bakker Bruns, Wilma Bakker Beekman, Earl Habben, and Kathleen Habben Decker.

11 "Renville County, Minnesota." Wikipedia. July 3, 2016.

12 "Renville, Minnesota." Wikipedia. July 10, 2016.

almost entirely of white people, with the majority of those coming from German descent.[13] Nevertheless, Renville County almost doubled its sales quota by the end of the third Liberty Bond drive, showing a noteworthy support for the war.[14]

The war declaration was immediately felt at all levels of government. One week after the declaration, articles were published in the local newspaper, the *Renville Star Farmer*, on the need to conserve food. Articles on food shortages and the need to supply food to the troops were published throughout the war. At the Minnesota state level, the Commission of Public Safety was established eight days after the United States declared war. The commission was loosely modeled after the Council of National Defense and was the first such state agency established. The seven-man commission was an interim agency designed to take swift and decisive action toward suppressing disloyal outbreaks and unorderly disturbances in communities where the German element was predominant. The commission was empowered to perform all acts and things necessary or proper so that the military, civil, and industrial resources of the state were most efficiently applied toward maintenance of the defense of the state and nation and toward the successful prosecution of such war. It could seize or condemn property, require anyone to appear before it or its agents, demand that district courts issue subpoenas, examine the conduct of public officials, and advise the governor on actions against such officials.

13 "Renville County, Minnesota." Wikipedia. July 3, 2016.

14 *Renville Star Farmer*, November 1, 1917.

The Commission of Public Safety was deeply concerned with the influence of German in public schools and assigned an eight-person committee to examine German textbooks used in Minnesota. A survey revealed that during 1914 and 1915, German had been taught as a subject in 198 of the state's 221 high schools. Furthermore, nearly two-thirds of the state's private schools spoke German primarily, occasionally using English for instruction. The commission made its intentions clear with the slogan, "One Country, One Flag, One People, and One Speech." By the end of November 1917, the textbook committee had completed its study and created a "white list" of over two hundred acceptable German titles. The commission passed a resolution in which school administrations and teachers were urged to require the use of English as the exclusive medium of instruction, but the committee did not go so far as to ban German as a spoken language. The committee did pass an order "that no person who is not a citizen of the United States shall be qualified to serve as a teacher in any public, private, or parochial school, or in any normal school in which teachers for those schools are trained."[15]

The commission was headed by Governor Joseph A. A. Burnquist and Attorney General Lyndon A. Smith, a banker from Montevideo. The other five commission members were appointed by the governor. The commission addressed problems in a wide area and issued fifty-nine specific orders. These orders concerned war-related subjects such as food production, marketing, labor

15 La Vern J. Rippley. "Conflict in the Classroom: Anti-Germanism in Minnesota Schools, 1917-1919." *Minnesota History Magazine,* Spring 1981, 170-83. Used with permission from the Minnesota Historical Society.

and industrial peace, iron-ore output, fuel, soldiers' welfare, waste prevention, forest fires, and milk prices. The agency processed mail, answered letters, and mailed materials about the war and the effort to win it to state newspapers and persons on its list. The government body published and distributed its own official weekly newspaper, *Minnesota in the War*.

While some historians have called the commission dictatorial and fascist, backers of the agency justified its existence by explaining that nearly a quarter of the state's two million residents were either German-born or of German-Austrian parentage. Frightened by pro-German sympathizers among the substantial German element, the commission created its own army in the form of Home Guard battalions that were made up of men over draft age or those who could prove they were exempt from the draft. By the summer of 1918, there were twenty-one Home Guard battalions operating in Minnesota. This action caused the socialist weekly, the *Minneapolis New Times*, to write, "The commission was at once able to Prussian-ize Minnesota and establish here that military autocracy which we are supposed to be fighting in our war with Germany."[16]

And the commission did not hesitate to wield its power. On July 25, 1917, the residents of New Ulm, a southwest Minnesota town proud of its German heritage, held an anti-draft meeting. The town mayor, Dr. L. A. Fritsche, presided over the meeting. Mayor Fritsche opened the meeting with this statement: "This is a peaceful gathering of American citizens. We have no desire to cause a disaffection of the draft law... We do ask, though, that

16 Ibid.

Congress and the government do not force those drafted to fight in Europe against their will." The meeting had come about due to the fact that many of the local draftees were concerned that they would be fighting against their German relatives whom they knew were in the war. The draftees insisted that they were proud to serve their country at war if only they could serve without fighting. The meeting attracted between six and eight thousand people from nearly every town in the south central part of Minnesota, as reported in the *Brown County Journal*, and gained national attention. The Minnesota Commission of Public Safety sent agents to monitor the meeting.

Albert Pfaender, city attorney and former major of the National Guard, followed Dr. Fritsche and spoke of constitutional rights. The next speaker was Albert Steinhauser, a man who had served as a captain in the United States Army during the Spanish-American War and commanded a National Guard company in the Philippine Islands. He was a practicing Minnesota attorney and served as the superintendent of Brown County Schools, in addition to being editor of four publications. A fourth speaker included Professor Adolf Ackerman, head of the Dr. Martin Luther College, among several others.

The meeting resulted in a severe negative reaction in the surrounding communities and from the state government. Critics claimed the anti-draft speeches were "un-American," "undemocratic," and "autocratic." Governor Burnquist claimed the meeting was "disloyal to America and pro-German." Subsequently, Burnquist removed Dr. Fritsche and Albert Pfaender from their mayoral and city attorney positions on the charge of disloyalty through the powers vested in him as governor. The Minnesota State Medical Association ordered the Brown-Redwood Medical Association to place Dr. Fritsche on trial with the charge of disloyalty. When the Brown-Redwood Medical Association found Dr. Fritsche not guilty, the Minnesota State Medical Association revoked the Brown-Redwood Association's charter. This action created additional lawsuits that resulted in the Brown-Redwood Medical Association's charter being reinstated in 1920, but this was only under the condition that Dr. Fritsche and any doctor associated with him were permanently excluded from the association.

Albert Pfaender was disbarred from the Minnesota State Bar association on the grounds of disloyalty and conduct unbecoming of a member of the association and of a citizen of the state. Professor Ackerman was forced to resign as head of Dr. Martin Luther College. Albert Steinhauser was arrested and charged with publishing words "intended to bring the army and also the navy into contempt, scorn, contumely, and disrepute." Although these charges were either dismissed or not pursued, Steinhauser's military pension, awarded for the injuries he received during his service with the United States Army in the Spanish-American War, was discontinued. He was also expelled from the Minnesota State Editorial Association for his disloyal actions.[17]

A little over sixty miles up the road from New Ulm, a citizens meeting was held in Renville on Monday, August 13,

17 Reprinted with permission from the author, Christopher James Wright. "The Impact of Anti-German Hysteria in New Ulm, Minnesota, and Kitchener, Ontario: A Comparative Study." PhD. diss., Iowa State University, 2011.

1917. It was decided there that a Home Guard organization for their community would be made permanent. The Home Guard was to be under the command of a single person known as "the lieutenant," and the entire organization was to be under the command of the county board or sheriff. The lieutenant was to be named at a later date. At the same meeting, the committee drafted a loyalty pledge, the objective of which was to have each and every citizen of Renville express his or her loyalty to the government and cheerfully show the government that their feelings were in accord with the action it had taken in declaring war on the country's enemies. Furthermore, Renville's objective was to constantly uphold every move the government saw fit to make, in order that the country would soon be able to bring the war to a termination, and that the country would emerge with honor and credit. The following pledge was drawn up and signed by over forty persons:

"As an expression of loyalty to our government and flag, I hereby pledge myself to earnestly, honestly, and loyally aid and support the government, its laws, and duly constituted authorities in bringing the cruel war, now existing, to a successful and honorable termination."[18]

The records indicate that the Renville community was highly supportive of the war effort. Numerous activities were held in Renville's Opera House to instill citizens with the war spirit. The Opera House was a six-hundred-seat hall with a stage that was built in 1892 above the O'Conner Brothers bank. It was the center of town happenings, providing a venue for travelling companies

18 *Renville Star Farmer*, August 16, 1917.

of musicians, actors, comedians, lecturers, and even con men. In addition, it was the home for local events such as benefits, school activities including school plays, dances, parties, band concerts, political meetings, and even wrestling. During World War I, large crowds turned out to hear wounded servicemen tell of front line conditions. Knitting classes, bandage rolling meetings, Red Cross gatherings, Food and Fuel Commission meetings, as well as fund raising events were only a few of the activities that were held in the Opera House.[19]

These doings provide an indication of how deeply the tentacles of the government's war campaign had penetrated into the American landscape, instilling hatred for the German regime from the national and state levels down to a small rural town where the majority of the population was German. Indeed, a few recorded incidents shed light on the animosity towards German sympathizers in the communities surrounding Renville. John Meintz, a well-known and respected retired farmer living in the southwest Minnesota town of Luverne, was dragged from his car and flogged naked with a coiled rope by four masked men, one of whom he recognized as a local minister. Meintz was believed to be a German sympathizer because he had chipped in fifty dollars to help start a Nonpartisan League newspaper, the *Rock County Herald*, and he had refused to kneel before the members of a mob and sign a paper repudiating the "Hun-Partisan League." Meintz,

19 Adrian Bottge and Dan Licklider. *Adrian Looks Back: An Historic Account Gleaned from Early Newspapers of Renville, Minnesota.* Renville: Historic Renville Preservation Committee and the *Renville Star Farmer*, 1988, 98-101.

the son of a Danish father and Holland-Dutch mother, had bought Liberty Bonds in all four drives. He explained that he did not belong to the League, and he only wanted the farmers to have a newspaper of their own in which to tell their story. Nevertheless, Meintz was tarred and feathered at the point of a shotgun and told to get out of town and not come back. The farmer had to make a painful walk to the South Dakota line.

In Renville County, two Cairo Township men were taken into custody by the County Sheriff at their homes and taken to the county seat in Olivia. While there, a crowd gathered and seized the men. They were made to march through the streets waving American flags. They were then made to kiss the flag and give three rousing cheers for the flag and America. The men were confined to the Olivia jail that night and taken to Renville the next morning for their hearing. All this came about through the failure of the men to buy Liberty Bonds and to otherwise aid in the prosecution of the war. The men were fined $109, and each bought $1,500 worth of bonds, gave $100 to the Red Cross, and $100 to the War Work Fund.

A stranger in St. Cloud, Minnesota, was seen taking three spoons of sugar for his coffee. When it was suggested to him that this was not in accordance with the laws of the Food Administration, he stated that it was for this reason that he was doing so. This, with his other seditious remarks, resulted in his making a gift of fifty dollars to the Red Cross and fifty dollars to the Saint Cloud War Chest.[20] Elder members of the Bakker family seemed to recall that a certain German Renville doctor had his house smeared

20 Ibid., 180-182.

with yellow paint. Splashing yellow paint on a person's house or painting the door of their house or business yellow was a tactic used by vigilante groups to "call out" or identify someone, namely Germans, whom they felt was not supporting the war effort.

There is no recollection or documented evidence that any of the Bakker family was involved in seditious activity or that they were involved in any incidents of harassing citizens for not supporting the war effort. First and foremost, they were farmers. By this time, John Bakker, the land agent and church founder, had passed away, but his six surviving children along with their families were upstanding members of the community. Early on, it became evident that full support of the war effort was expected at the sacrifice of personal gain. Any hint of seditious activity would be met with harsh discipline and ridicule. By all accounts, the Bakker family did their part to support the war effort. Seven members of the Bakker family, including Walter and Dick, purchased Liberty Bonds in 1917, as reported in the *Renville Star Farmer*. In the unforeseen months ahead, the throes of war would dig deep into the Bakker family's life.

Chapter 3

Drafted

FOR THREE YEARS, PRESIDENT WOODROW Wilson steadfastly
kept America out of World War I. Consequently, he had not
seen a need to engage in a substantial build-up of the armed
services. When Wilson was forced to declare war in April 1917,
the regular army totaled around 128,000 officers and men;
the National Guard could muster another 80,000 troops for a
combined total of a little over 208,000 men, a minute number
compared to a combat-trained German army of over four
million.[21]

Initially, America was operating with a volunteer army. It
soon became evident that the only way to mobilize a force capable
of defeating the Germans was to resort to conscription. So the
Selective Service Act became law on May 13, 1917, and June 5,
1917, was declared Registration Day. All male citizens between
the age of twenty-one and thirty were required to register at
their local draft board between the hours of 7 a.m. and 7 p.m.

21 "The U.S. Army in WWI, 1917-1918." In *American Military History:*
Volume II, edited by Richard W. Stewart, 7-52. Washington, D.C.: Center of
Military History, 2005, 18.

Across America, the festivities surrounding the proceedings were worthy of a national holiday. Bands played, local dignitaries made speeches, girls cheered, and matrons pinned flags on the enrollees' shirts as they were declared the heroes of the day. Each man's name was placed on the "list of honor" and assigned a number.[22] Such was the mood of the day; America was going to war so that "liberty shall not perish from this earth."

No such festivities occurred in the small villages of Renville County. The young men registered in their local township halls, many of which were located in the countryside. Registration proceedings were conducted under the direction of a captain appointed by the Minnesota Commission of Public Safety. Twenty-three year old Dick Bakker and his brother John registered at the Crooks Township Hall along with their cousin once removed, Amos Bakker. Their registration numbers, as published by the *Renville Star Farmer*, were in sequence which implies that they went together to register. The registration forms were then tallied at the county level, and each registrant was then assigned his number. In Washington, D.C., officials drew numbers out of a bowl to determine which men would be drafted. For example, if the number ten was drawn, then all registrants with the assigned number ten were called from each local draft board.

22 Meirion Harries and Susie Harries. *The Last Days of Innocence: America at War, 1917-1918*. New York: Vintage Books, 1997, 92-94.

Dick Bakker Draft Registration Card

Registrar's Report

In July, the first draftees began reporting as the government began a massive buildup to assemble a formidable army. The need for an army of millions, in turn, created the need for an enormous industry to house, train, supply, and feed them, which had to be hastily implemented. When America declared war, there were around 285,000 Springfield rifles on hand, about 400 field guns, and fewer than 1,500 machine guns of four non-interchangeable types.[23] By the fall of 1917, the Ordnance Department had ordered "for delivery in France" 2,137,025 rifles; 57,000 light Browning automatic rifles; 102,450 heavy machine guns; 5,490 seventy-five millimeter field guns with 2,850,000 high-explosive and 2,750 shrapnel shells; 700 seventy-five millimeter anti-aircraft guns; and 3,315 one-hundred-fifty-five millimeter howitzers with 950,000 high-explosive and 50,000 shrapnel shells. By November 1917, the Quartermaster General's department had placed orders for seventeen million blankets, thirty-three million yards of flannel shirting, and 125 million yards of canvas for tents. By the end of the following year, the armed forces had ordered twenty-nine million pairs of shoes, 82,500 trucks, sixteen thousand automobiles and twenty-seven thousand motorcycles. They also required one horse or mule for every five to seven men, which meant millions of tons of forage, a veterinary service, and hundreds of miles of leather harness.[24] The effect of these activities was to put enormous pressures on money, labor, and natural resources. American

23 Laurence Stallings. *The Doughboys: The Story of the AEF, 1917-1918.* New York: Harper and Row, 1963, 25.

24 Meirion Harries and Susie Harries. *The Last Days of Innocence: America at War, 1917-1918.* New York: Vintage Books, 1997, 145-146.

industry was now being asked to equip the National Army in addition to the essential supplies and staples they were already shipping to the Allies. Furthermore, a core part of the work force was being taken away by conscription.

Meanwhile, the regular army divisions, such as they were, were sent to France. At the end of June, the First Division arrived, fourteen thousand strong,[25] filled with raw volunteer recruits, brimming with enthusiasm buoyed by an American propaganda machine and ready to beat the hated Germans to a pulp so that "liberty would not perish from the earth." Known as the Big Red One, they were showered with kisses and flowers as they marched down the Avenue des Champs-Elysees, bringing new hope to a city that had long lost its soul. The Twenty-Sixth Division made up of New Englanders from the National Guard arrived in early September. By the end of the month, the Second Division arrived with a mish-mash of Marines, regulars, and engineers. The Forty-Second "Rainbow" Division, made up of National Guardsmen from twenty-six states, arrived in late October.[26]

As 1918 rolled in, General Erich Ludendorff, the brains behind the German war strategy, realized that he had to attack before a sizeable American army arrived in Europe. After three years of a virtual standoff that had taken over a million lives, it was time to decide the war. The Tsar had abdicated the Russian throne in March 1917. In December, the Bolsheviks, led by Lenin and Trotsky, signed an armistice with Germany, allowing the German

25 Laurence Stallings. *The Doughboys: The Story of the AEF, 1917-1918*. New York: Harper and Row, 1963, 13.

26 Ibid., 26.

forces to concentrate on the Western Front. The truce with the Bolsheviks allowed Ludendorff to throw an additional one and a half million men at the Allies on the Western Front. There were now four German soldiers for every three of the Allies. As the New Year started, the American Expeditionary Forces in Europe totaled 9,804 officers and 165,080 men.[27]

Knowing the Americans were coming, Ludendorff stepped up his offensive in the spring in an attempt to win the war before the Americans could amass an army in Europe. This action essentially forced the Wilson administration's hand when General Pershing demanded a large troop build-up in order for America to play a decisive role in the Allied victory. By the end of June, 1918, Pershing had endorsed a commitment of one hundred 28,000-man divisions to the Allies by the summer of 1919, a commitment he deemed necessary to win the war.[28] This gigantic figure was well beyond the capability of the country by any stretch of the imagination. Nevertheless, the situation presented an opportunity for America to step onto the world's stage and show their leadership capability, an opportunity that was no doubt appealing to President Wilson in his quest to establish a League of Nations where America could sit at the table and wield her diplomatic power. With the premise that America was "saving the world for democracy," there was no turning back. Considering the sacrifices demanded of the citizens and an economy tied to

27 Meirion Harries and Susie Harries. *The Last Days of Innocence: America at War, 1917-1918*. New York: Vintage Books, 1997, 210.

28 Ibid., 275.

an Allied victory, losing the war was not an option. So the draft board got busy, and the call for troops accelerated. Over one and a half million American men were rushed into service between March and August of 1918 in a frantic scramble to muster an army capable of stopping the Germans.[29] Dick Bakker was one of those called. His brother John would be called later.

On May 28, 1918, Dick Bakker bid goodbye to dad Walter; mother Grace; brothers John, Bill, and Helmer; sisters Reka, Josie, and Christine; and his sweetheart and fiancé, Tetje Sietsema, to answer his country's call to service. Dick received orders to report to the National Guard at the armory in the nearby town of Olivia, Minnesota, at 1 p.m. along with sixty-eight other young men from the county.[30] That night, the recruits were honored with a reception at 8 p.m. in the armory auditorium. The reception was attended by an estimated 1,500 people, many of whom drove several miles through mud and rain to attend. Lynas D. Barnard, Renville county attorney, presided over the reception and introduced the first speaker, District Judge Richard T. Daly of Renville. Judge Daly spoke words of comfort to the parents and other relatives of the drafted boys. His address created a proper spirit among the audience on an occasion that was considered most serious. Following the judge's address, Miss Delilah O'Conner of Sacred Heart gave a dramatic reading in the Italian dialect, which was

29 Leonard P. Ayres. "Four Million Men." In *The War with Germany: A Statistical Summary.*

30 *Renville Star Farmer,* May 23, 1917.

very well received and which brought forth vigorous applause. The young lady was obliged to respond several times to encores to satisfy the audience.

The principal speaker was the Honorable J. L. O'Conner of Milwaukee, formerly Attorney General of Wisconsin. Mr. O'Conner compared the government of America to the government of Germany, pointing out the advantages and opportunities offered to the people here, emphasizing the fact that patriotism consisted in the service and sacrifice of individuals rather than in declarations and proclamations. He pleaded for unity among the people, calling attention to the national debt of gratitude which we owed the people of France, Ireland, Germany and other countries of Europe for the part they had played in the Revolutionary and Civil Wars. He pleaded for tolerance and fairness among nationalities and creeds and showed a broad view of all questions affecting our national life. The address made a profound impression on the audience and was most favorably received.

Following Mr. O'Conner's address, Mike J. Dowling, local teacher and newspaper editor, spoke briefly on the importance of the occasion and concluded by calling the sixty-nine young men of the draft to the platform. While the men took their places, a local band played a pleasing medley with the audience standing.[31] A group picture with the men dressed in suit and tie was taken to be displayed in the next issue of the *Renville Star Farmer*. Each

31 *Olivia Times-Journal*, May 30, 1918.

recruit had a strip of paper pinned to his lapel which served as a temporary name tag and army identification badge.[32] This concluded the speaking program. Afterwards, a motion picture show entitled *The Silent Master* was shown. After the show, a formal dinner was served to the drafted men and their relatives in the armory club rooms while the auditorium hall was cleared for a dance which continued until 2 a.m., when the men were summoned to the depot for their departure. With the festivities concluded, the parents and relatives of the young men made what was undoubtedly a worrisome, long trip home.[33]

In the early morning of May 29, 1918, a fourteen-coach troop train steamed out of the depot in Olivia, Minnesota, and headed for Camp Lewis, carrying more than seven hundred fifty young men from six local Minnesota counties.[34] The train chugged through the night, following the Chicago, Milwaukee, St. Paul, and Pacific line that would take them into the northwest through South Dakota, North Dakota, Montana, and Idaho. Prior to departure, each recruit was handed a kit that consisted of a deck of playing cards, a sewing kit with buttons, a pencil and pad of paper for writing home, and various sundries. Many of these young men from west central Minnesota had never set foot off the farm, let alone experienced the thrill of a train ride. For some, the population of their hometown was less than the number of men on the train. Dick Bakker wrote his first letter home the following

32 Picture provided by Renville Museum.

33 *Olivia Times-Journal*, May 30, 1918.

34 Dick Bakker letter to his parents, May 30, 1918.

afternoon while riding through the Black Hills and Badlands of South Dakota, "I am on my way still to Washington. I'm enjoying this ride very much. We have a real nice bunch from Renville County. We are having such a good time. Our boys all feel happy but for two or three. Slept three hours last night and don't feel a bit tired. The boys are making good use of their Red Cross cards, playing nickel ante poker and big money, too."

The train passed through one small town after another, stopping often to refuel, gather food and supplies, and allow the young men to expel some energy. In his second letter home dated May 30, Dick wrote, "Sold about three barrels of beer to the locals in Deer Lodge. We had a great time there." In the evening of the same day: "We are running on steam now, but were running on electric all day since 4 o'clock this morning." The train had switched from steam-powered engines to electric between Harlowtown, Montana, and Avery, Idaho. The Milwaukee had found that operation of steam locomotives over the mountain passes was difficult, with winter temperatures that reached minus forty degrees Fahrenheit. Electrification was deemed to be the answer, especially with abundant hydro-electric power in the mountains and a ready source of copper at Anaconda, Montana. The first electric train ran in 1915 between Three Forks, Montana, and Deer Lodge, Montana. The electric locomotives, built by General Electric and American Locomotive Company, used a three-thousand-volt direct current (DC) overhead line and proved to be an economic and efficient method of transportation. The locomotives were the first to use a technique called regenerative braking that enhanced the safety of mountain operation, reduced wear on brake shoes, and returned electrical power to the overhead system for use by other trains.[35]

In Montana and Idaho, the rural boys from Minnesota, raised in a land as flat as the pancake griddles atop their wood-burning stoves, got their first view of the majestic Rocky Mountains. Dick relates, "We have been travelling in the mountains all day. Got up this morning at 5:30 and went out on the platform but was quite cold. Could see the snow top mountains for 80 miles away. You would think you were a mile away from them, but we could ride two hours going about 45 to 50 miles an hour. There was snow along the snow fences yet. Seen snow all day long, but the best was when we got in Idaho we went thru a tunnel one mile and ¾ long, could not see a thing and was so damp in there the water was just raining from the cement. Was a real stream of water coming out. We went through over 60 tunnels today. We're going in one every 5 minutes after 7 o'clock, and we could look up on one side about 800 to 1000 feet and look down 500 feet on the other. The number of feet is posted on the side, and we have been riding along the streams for 5 hours at a stretch, and the water so clear can see the bottom all the time. Go about 20 minutes on one side of the valley and then cross the river where it is quite narrow over a bridge about 800 feet high and then go back just as far as where we started from only a whole lot lower. You can imagine that it is up pretty high. Have been running downhill since 4 o'clock. The brakes are squealing all the time. It don't go so fast in the Idaho mountains as in Montana mountains. I never knew there

35 Rodney A. Clark. "The Milwaukee Electrification: A Proud Era Passes." *The Milwaukee Road Magazine*, July/August 1973. March 3, 2009.

were such places in this world as there are. I could talk to you a whole day about it and wouldn't be through yet. This trip is worth hundreds of dollars to everyone on the train. Have had our heads out the windows all day and don't feel a bit tired yet."

The new recruits arrived at Camp Lewis on June 1, 1918, four days after leaving the only world they had ever known: the Minnesota farmlands, the world of their fathers. They had introduced themselves to one another, sharing their thoughts, their memories, their hopes, and their dreams - young men thrown together for a common cause with the expectations that they would set the world right. Now, after a breathtaking roller-coaster ride through the Rocky Mountains, they were about to enter the world of the United States Army and the living hell of World War I. Some would never return. The ones who did would never be the same person that rode with his head out the window, gasping at the wonderment of America the beautiful. The unforeseen road ahead, strewn with death, dismemberment, destruction, and prostitution, was a one-way ticket to adulthood.

Chapter 4

Château-Thierry

IN CONTRAST TO THE FESTIVITIES on Dick Bakker's train, the American Expeditionary forces in France were experiencing serious conflicts. The day before Dick reported for duty, German artillery thundered a devastating barrage onto the French Sixth Army instantly wiping out whole divisions. Following the barrage, three hundred thousand German veterans swept through a thirty-mile front, capturing railway yards, airplanes, stores, 650 guns, 2,000 machine guns, 60,000 prisoners, and 45,000 hospital beds.[36] The attack was such a success that Ludendorff decided to continue forward in the hopes of capturing the Marne Valley and opening a road to Paris. With the Germans advancing toward the Marne River and the bridge at Château-Thierry, Allied Commander Ferdinand Foch, wise in the ways of Ludendorff's tactics, refused to send his reserves in the belief that Ludendorff was pulling a feint. So the task of filling the gaps left by the devastated French troops was given to Pershing. With the Big Red One at Cantigny, and the Twenty-Sixth Division holding down Seicheprey, the closest

36 Laurence Stallings. *The Doughboys: The Story of the AEF, 1917-1918.* New York: Harper and Row, 1963, 78.

division to Château-Thierry was the Third Division which was still in the early stages of its training.

Nevertheless, on May 31, the American Third Division raced north on roads clogged by retreating French troops and refugees telling them that all was lost and it was too little too late. The Third Division's motorized machine gun battalion arrived at Château-Thierry just as the German juggernaut was approaching the northern edge of the town. A squad of fifteen men led by Lieutenant John Bissell raced across the bridge to access the situation at the north end of the town where the remainder of the French troops was trying to slow down the Germans. The rest of the battalion dug in along the south bank of the Marne. By the next evening, the Germans had reached the river and were fighting their way across the road bridge when the French blew it up, annihilating both attackers and defenders. Fortunately, Lieutenant Bissell and his buddies were able to later escape to safety across a railroad bridge. In the meantime, the rest of the Third Division had arrived and dispersed themselves among the defending French troops along a ten-mile stretch on the south side of the Marne.[37] The initial German advance was repulsed, but German intelligence soon identified the American positions, and the troops took a heavy shelling over the next two days. There were spies everywhere.

At the same time, the American Second Division was being carried towards the battle arena on a caravan of staked flatbed trucks being driven by little brown men from French Indo-China

---

[37] Meirion Harries and Susie Harries. *The Last Days of Innocence: America at War, 1917-1918.* New York: Vintage Books, 1997, 247.

who spoke no English and could only be identified by their thumbprints. Just before dusk on May 31, the caravan arrived at the deserted railhead town of Meaux, with the troops covered with white dust from the road and thirsty from the June heat. As the trucks turned up the road towards Château-Thierry, the troops came face-to-face with an endless stream of refugees fleeing the German assault. Private Leo Bailey later wrote of the experience, "There were people of all ages except men of military ages; there were children riding on the creaking wagons, held in place by their feeble grandparents; everyone who was able to do so was compelled to walk. There were carts drawn by every conceivable animal: cows, oxen, dogs, and horses. The other cattle were driven along by the side of the wagons. The procession was noiseless, for the marchers were too miserable to more than glance at us as we passed and probably thought: *a few more for the Boches to devour.* Alongside the road, too tired to go farther, was a leathery-faced old woman with all her remaining property piled on a wheelbarrow... Each procession occupied half of the hot, white road from which there rose a cloud of bitter dust—the young going up to slaughter and be slaughtered; the old and their youth fleeing from the *furor Teutonicus.* Each half pitied the other, and the fresher half swore to avenge the feebler."[38]

The troops moved on toward the distant roar of artillery, and eventually the trucks would go no further, so they marched through the night with little sleep, carrying seventy-two-pound packs with rifles, machine guns, ammunition, and bandoliers. The

38 Laurence Stallings. *The Doughboys: The Story of the AEF, 1917-1918.* New York: Harper and Row, 1963, 84-85.

stench of mustard gas became stronger as they marched, causing some to retch and even faint. Through all this, they continually encountered fleeing French soldiers telling them of the oncoming swarm of German soldiers and the futility of their effort. They stopped to rest in abandoned French villages and watched fleeing French soldiers looting, ripping open parlor sofas in search of hoarded gold, throwing furniture from windows, stuffing their musettes with laces and linens, and battering in the doors of wine cellars. "If we don't loot it, the Germans will," the French replied.[39]

But the Second Division would not be denied, especially the marines who believed they were the toughest fighting force on the face of the earth. The Third Division had stopped the Germans at the Marne around Château-Thierry, but the superior German regiments were pushing around them to the west. The twenty-five thousand men of the Second Division arrived at the battlefront midday on June 1 among widespread chaos as the Germans ripped gaping holes in the remainder of the French lines. Hungry and exhausted, the Americans jumped into the gaps left by the French, sometimes of their own recognizance without orders, and established a battle line just south of Belleau Wood. Fighting with sheer determination and effective marksmanship, the Americans repulsed wave after wave of the oncoming German legions. By end of day, scores of German soldiers lay strewn throughout the poppies and wheat fields, sliced to ribbons by artillery and machine gun fire. Faced with heavy losses, the Germans retreated. Ludendorff's march to Paris was halted...for the moment.

39 Ibid., 87.

Chapter 5

Selling the War

THE DIFFERENCE BETWEEN THE FESTIVE mood on Dick Bakker's train and the reality of combat on the Western Front can be partly explained by the government campaign to sell the American war effort. The trigger that aroused the country's emotions in World War I was Germany's unconditional submarine warfare that resulted in American deaths. This, combined with an intercepted telegram to the Mexican government from German Foreign Minister Arthur Zimmerman requesting an alliance against the United States that would allow Mexico to regain territory lost in the Mexican-American War, threatened America's existence and way of life. The killing of American citizens aroused anger and a call for revenge. The outrage was further fueled by Germany's brutal rampage through the neutral country of Belgium at the start of the war. However, there were still many who opposed the war, requiring the Woodrow Wilson administration to launch an extensive propaganda campaign to motivate citizens to back the war effort both personally and financially and accept the sacrifices necessary to support a successful army. The propaganda strategy was designed to avoid a backlash of resentment against the first Selective Service Act of its kind since the Civil War; to instill a national pride in fighting for the cause of liberty and humanity; to build hatred for the German enemy; and to lay guilt at the feet of those who did not support the cause.

One week after the war declaration, President Wilson created the Committee on Public Information (CPI), an independent government agency, to administer the propaganda campaign. Wilson chose George Creel, a progressive and influential journalist, to head the agency. Creel, the son of a Confederate officer from Independence, Missouri, was a liberal, crusading journalist with a wickedly sharp pen and an impressive list of conservative enemies. With curly dark hair and burning eyes, Creel was a fiery orator who had supported Wilson in the 1916 presidential campaign. Wilson was greatly attracted to Creel's blend of idealism and outrageousness. Creel maintained that he could see the President anytime by simply entering the White House and loudly cursing Henry Cabot Lodge.

Creel's men gathered material from government departments and shaped it into handouts that could be classified as early prototypes of a press release. Publication of these handouts was not mandatory, but there were no alternative sources of news. The remoteness of the war gave Creel the huge advantage of being able to control virtually all the information that came into the country from the battlefront. America was cut off from Europe to the extent that all war news had to pass through official channels. All private and commercial radio stations operating in the United States were either shut down or taken over by the government. Since no American troops were in action in the early months of the war, none were coming back wounded to describe the horrors of trench warfare and its psychological impacts. The American

Expeditionary Forces censored mail, and the navy controlled the trans-Atlantic cable.[40] Furthermore, it became illegal for a private citizen to possess an operational radio transmitter or receiver.[41]

In an attempt to limit dissent and interference with military operations, Congress passed the Espionage Act on June 15, 1917. The Espionage Act made it a crime to convey information with intent to interfere with the operation or success of the armed forces of the United States or to promote the success of its enemies, which was punishable by death or by imprisonment for not more than thirty years or both. It also made it illegal to convey false reports or false statements with intent to interfere with the operation or success of the military or naval forces of the United States; to promote the success of its enemies when the United States is at war; to cause or attempt to cause insubordination, disloyalty, mutiny, or refusal of duty in the military or naval forces of the United States; or to willfully obstruct the recruiting or enlistment service of the United States. Violation of the Espionage Act was punishable by a maximum fine of ten thousand dollars or by imprisonment for not more than twenty years or both. The Act also gave the Postmaster General authority to impound or to refuse to mail publications that he determined to be in violation of its prohibitions. The Act forbade the transfer of any naval vessel

40 Meirion Harries and Susie Harries. *The Last Days of Innocence: America at War, 1917-1918.* New York: Vintage Books, 1997, 165-166.

41 Thomas H. White. "Radio During World War One (1914-1919)." Early Radio History.

equipped for combat to any nation engaged in a conflict in which the United States was neutral.[42]

Congress then passed the Trading with the Enemy Act in October 1917, which authorized the government to control and censure all incoming information from foreign countries, including mail, cable, radio, or any other means. The Trading with the Enemy Act gave the President the power to oversee or restrict any and all trade between the United States and its enemies in times of war.[43]

While the Espionage Act made it illegal to interfere with the war effort, some lawmakers felt the law was inadequate in allowing the government to curb public disorder and mob violence that resulted from unpopular wartime speeches. On May 16, 1918, Congress passed the Sedition Act. Aimed at socialists, pacifists and other anti-war activists, the Sedition Act forbade the use of "disloyal, profane, scurrilous, or abusive language" about the United States government, its flag, or its armed forces; or the use of language that caused others to view the American government or its institutions with contempt. The act also allowed the Postmaster General to refuse to deliver mail that met those same standards for punishable speech or opinion. Those who were found guilty of such actions, the act stated, could be punished by a fine of not more than ten thousand dollars or imprisonment for not more than twenty years or both. This was the same penalty that had been imposed for acts of espionage in the earlier legislation. Though President Wilson and Congress regarded the Sedition

42 "Espionage Act of 1917." Wikipedia. September 4, 2016.

43 "Trading with the Enemy Act of 1917." Wikipedia. September 15, 2016.

Act as crucial in order to stifle the spread of dissent within the country in that time of war, legal scholars considered the act to be contrary to the letter and spirit of the U.S. Constitution, namely to the First Amendment of the Bill of Rights which guarantees freedom of speech.[44]

With the passing of the Espionage Act and later the Sedition Act, the government was given the legal authority to control what citizens said in public. Furthermore, it had the power to suppress the content of any written publication. Postmaster General Albert Burleson was given the power to ban offensive material from circulating through the mail.[45] Given these controls, the CPI launched their highly successful propaganda campaign extolling the virtues of democracy and building hatred for the German enemy. The CPI used every means of communication at their disposal including hard-hitting posters and even movie stars to deliver their message.

The CPI employed seventy-five thousand trained professional speakers known as "four-minute men" who would deliver rousing, four-minute patriotic messages in churches, music halls, movie theaters, schools, and other public places.[46] Billboards, newspapers, and walls of government buildings were plastered with posters of German atrocities that brandished grim messages of the need for action. An example of the harsh rhetoric used to instill passion into

44 "Sedition Act of 1918." Wikipedia. July 15, 2016.

45 Meirion Harries and Susie Harries. *The Last Days of Innocence: America at War, 1917-1918*. New York: Vintage Books, 1997, 167.

46 Ibid., 172.

the souls of every American citizen is revealed by a poster showing a child with severed hands standing on a flat stone with "kultur" etched in the stone. A village burns in the background. The poster reads, "They MUTILATE, For Humanity's sake, Enlist."[47]

World War 1 Recruitment Poster, Courtesy of the Pritzker Museum & Library

Opposition to the war was suppressed along with any oratory that argued for Germany's position in the conflict. Like many American families, Dick Bakker's parents mailed him the local

47 G. N. Beringer. *They mutilate: for humanities sake enlist*, United States Army, 1918. Pritzker Military Museum and Library (https://www.pritzkermilitary.org/explore/museum/digital-collection/view/oclc/813230382)

papers. In one letter from France, Dick wrote, "I have been reading in the Renville papers about things over here, but they don't hit the nail by a long-ways. They don't know until they see it with their own eyes, see."

The CPI appealed to the citizens' honor and patriotic duty to fight for a free, democratic world and laid guilt on those who were not willing to fight and support the war financially. The deeds of the soldier were glorified while negative aspects of the war were suppressed, which no doubt included the horrific conditions in the trenches. The success of the CPI propaganda campaign is demonstrated by the fervent backlash against American citizens of German descent and those who opposed the war. With American casualties starting to mount in Europe and the CPI ramping up their extensive propaganda campaign, it was inevitable that feelings towards Germans would spill over into violence. Many citizens mistrusted Germans and questioned their loyalty. This feeling of mistrust was shared by all levels of the U.S. government, from President Wilson down to local city officials. Rumors ran rampant as the CPI showed hate movies such as *The Kaiser, the Beast of Berlin* and circulated publications such as *Why America Fights Germany* that asserted an invasion of America would result in the same atrocities as occurred when Germany marched through Belgium to start the war. It was rumored that Germans were putting ground glass into food and poison on Red Cross bandages. Light refracted from William Randolph Hearst's stained glass windows was thought to be a signal to German submarines lurking beneath the Hudson River.

It is a fact that German agents were operating within the country, so the espionage concerns were not without foundation. On the other hand, the vast majority of German-American citizens were peaceful, hardworking people, like the Bakker family, whose only aspiration was to earn a respectable living. Nevertheless, all things German came under attack as paranoia and spy fever reached epic levels. Many German language newspapers were shut down. The *New York Times* refused to circulate German publications fearing that there were coded messages hidden in the print. German language was banned in many schools, including colleges and universities, and the books were burned. The names of cities and streets were changed from German to English. German Americans changed their names to hide their German ties. Musicians refused to play Bach and Beethoven. Frankfurters became "Liberty sausages," dachshunds became "Liberty dogs," sauerkraut was "Liberty cabbage," hamburgers became "Salisbury steak," and German measles became "Liberty measles." Governors of several states issued proclamations that made English the only legal language to be used in public. Newspapers, schoolbooks, and ethnic church services had to be in English.[48]

As the anti-German hysteria mounted, the impetus to seek out German spies increased and the protection of civil liberties all but vanished. Harassment of German Americans became commonplace. The standards that were applied to the measurement of loyalty were buying bonds, registering for the draft, and adhering to the requests for conservation of food

[48] Meirion Harries and Susie Harries. *The Last Days of Innocence: America at War, 1917-1918*. New York: Vintage Books, 1997, 294-295.

and fuel. President Wilson appealed for unity, obedience, and unquestioned loyalty as the American economy went from a flourishing industrial expansion rich in resources to a war-driven market that devoured men and materials like a giant, ravaged Pac-Man. It was a time of great trepidation, but life in the training camps was a world within itself.

Chapter 6

Camp Lewis, Shortages and Rationing

CAMP LEWIS, NAMED AFTER CAPTAIN Meriwether Lewis of the Lewis and Clark Expedition, was one of sixteen cantonments that were hastily erected after the declaration of war. These cantonments were preludes to our modern military bases. Other National Army cantonments built as a result of the war declaration were Custer (Battle Creek, Michigan), Devens (Ayer, Massachusetts), Dodge (Des Moines, Iowa), Dix (Wrightstown, New Jersey), Funston (Fort Riley, Kansas), Gordon (Atlanta, Georgia), Grant (Rockford, Illinois), Jackson (Columbia, South Carolina), Lee (Petersburg, Virginia), Meade (Admiral, Maryland), Pike (Little Rock, Arkansas), Sherman (Chillicothe, Ohio), Taylor (Louisville, Kentucky), Travis (San Antonio, Texas), and Upton (Yaphank, Long Island, New York).

In addition, National Guard camps were built where troops were quartered in hastily erected tents with wood floors and wooden buildings for kitchens and mess halls. National Guard camps were built at Beauregard (Alexandria, Louisiana), Bowie (Fort Worth, Texas), Cody (Deming, New Mexico), Doniphan (Fort Sill, Oklahoma), Frémont (Palo Alto, California), Green (Charlotte, North Carolina), Hancock (Augusta, Georgia), Kearny (Linda Vista, California), Logan (Houston, Texas), MacArthur

(Waco, Texas), McClellan (Anniston, Alabama), Mills (Long Island, New York), Sevier (Greenville, South Carolina), Shelby (Hattiesburg, Mississippi), Sheridan (Montgomery, Alabama), Wadsworth (Spartanburg, South Carolina), and Wheeler (Macon, Georgia).

Camp Lewis was a seventy thousand-acre, 104-square-mile complex located on the south side of American Lake near Tacoma, Washington. The cantonment, constructed in ninety days in 1917, consisted of 1,757 buildings and 422 other structures, all lighted and heated. The buildings were arranged in a "U" shape with a large parade and drill grounds in the center. Camp headquarters stood at one end of the parade grounds while the snowcapped Mt. Rainier loomed large and majestic at the open end.

The cantonment was a community within itself with streets named after the American states. Troops arrived and departed from a railroad station serviced by a spur line from the railroad. There was a post office, a fire department, road maintenance, and a camp police force. A motor pool serviced Dodge touring cars, ambulances, and trucks. Two blacksmith shops took care of horses and mules. A large hospital complex administered physicals, tended to the sick, and provided facilities for soldiers quarantined after vaccination. Canteens provided a limited supply of goods, snacks, and cigarettes. There were churches for the major denominations, including a Knights of Columbus building. The barracks housed over fifty thousand men. Latrines, much admired by the country-raised soldiers, were separate buildings with flushable toilets and hot and cold running water for showers.

Early on, officials discovered that the troops got into trouble if they were allowed to take leave in Seattle. To reduce the problems, an amusement park was constructed across from the main gate, complete with carnival rides, movie theaters, vaudeville programs, and dancing lessons. Several YMCA buildings sponsored boxing and wrestling matches as well as social programs for the soldiers. The YMCA provided materials for writing home, and volunteers even wrote letters for those soldiers who couldn't write. Athletic fields were constructed on the camp where the troops played baseball, football, and other sports. The army encouraged sports to enhance a soldier's health, make him more fit for battle, and build bonds with his teammates. The army viewed sporting events as a non-hostile form of combat with rules and regulations that served to develop the essential qualities of the officer and leader. The camp put together baseball and football teams that included professional players who had been drafted or enlisted on their own. Earlier that year, the Camp Lewis football team was defeated 19-7 in the Rose Bowl by a Marine Corps team from the Mare Island Naval Shipyards in Vallejo, California.[49] Since most of the college football players were in the army, the Tournament of Roses committee decided to stage the game with military units. The game was played in Tournament Park near Cal Tech in Pasadena as the present Rose Bowl Stadium would not be built until 1923. The parade Grand Marshal was Dr. Zachary Taylor Malaby, who served in the medical corps in the Philippines and in the Spanish-American War. There was no rose queen that year.

49 Material provided by Friends of the Fort Lewis Military Museum.

The war effort had a pronounced effect on sports activities worldwide. Many sporting events were cancelled, including Wimbledon, Tour De France, World figure-skating and speed-skating championships, all major golf championships, and all major motor racing events. The Rose Bowl committee requested approval from the White House before staging the event. The major league baseball season was cut short in 1918 and ended on Labor Day, September 2. The World Series that immediately followed was won by the Boston Red Sox four games to two over the Chicago Cubs. The immortal George Herman "Babe" Ruth won two games on the mound for the Red Sox. During the season, Ruth won thirteen games on the mound for the Sox. He played the outfield when not pitching, and batted three hundred while hitting a league-leading eleven home runs.[50] Game one marked the first documented occurrence of "The Star-Spangled Banner" being performed at a major league game although there are claims that the anthem was played at various baseball games in the eighteen hundreds. During the seventh-inning stretch, the band began playing the song as a patriotic gesture to America's involvement in the war. "The Star-Spangled Banner" was recognized for official use by the navy in 1889, and by President Woodrow Wilson in 1916, and was made the national anthem by a congressional resolution on March 3, 1931, which was signed by President Herbert Hoover.[51]

Upon arrival to Camp Lewis, the new recruits were greeted by uniformed officers, marshaled into columns, and marched to their

50 "1918 World Series." Baseball Almanac.

51 "The Star-Spangled Banner." Wikipedia. September 27, 2016.

barracks. The barracks consisted of a large second-story dormitory with iron cots and a kitchen, mess hall, storerooms, and captain's office on the first floor. The first order of business was inspection for vermin and venereal diseases, followed by the first of a series of vaccinations for smallpox, typhoid, and other contagious diseases. Those who drew the short straw were put on kitchen patrol (KP) duty. "Dear folks at home, just got back from vaccination," Dick Bakker wrote the day after he arrived. "Got in camp about six o'clock Friday evening. Have got quite a bad cold. Sixteen of us have been working in the kitchen all forenoon, washing dishes and cleaning the table and setting the table for dinner. They have been unloading men in here all week. It is raining off and on here today. We have very nice places to sleep in wooden buildings. All new and plenty to eat. We have no meatless or wheatless days here. Quite a few feinted when they were vaccinated. Six or seven from our load. It is real sandy. It is all gravel on our grounds. We will be under quarantine about three weeks. I think we will get our uniforms by Monday. We just come from the YMCA. It is about ¾ of a mile to walk. My arm is getting sore and stiff already. We have plenty of room to run on here. There are so many things to write about. I don't know what to write first. Will write more later when we get a little more time."

Dick's mention of meatless and wheatless days alluded to a food-rationing program set up by the government. Feeding the army quickly became a huge problem for the administration. German U-Boats had cut off the shipping lanes from Argentina, Australia, and Russia, causing dire shortages to the Allies whose own output was severely hampered by the fact that most of their men were fighting the war. With a large amount of American grain and beef already being shipped to the Allies, it became immediately evident that rationing would have to be implemented in order to keep both Armies from starving. Wilson established the Federal Food Administration to regulate the production and consumption of the American food supply. He nominated Herbert Hoover to head the administration.

Hoover set about fixing and manipulating prices in order to encourage production of the products needed for the war. The easiest foodstuffs to ship to the front were wheat, sugar, and meat. So the propaganda machines were once again cranked up to encourage Americans to alter their diets and eat foods such as fish and eggs that could not easily be shipped abroad. Hoover then initiated wheatless and meatless days—wheatless Mondays and Wednesdays, with one wheatless meal for the rest of the week, and meatless Tuesdays, with one meatless meal every other day.[52] These sacrifices were asked so that "our heroic young men who were fighting for liberty" could enjoy a decent meal at the battlefront. Needless to say, these policies did not sit well with American farmers and ranchers who were accustomed to eating the very crops and livestock that they had grown. The price controls created imbalances that agitated the farmers and ranchers even further as the demand for resources increased the rate of inflation.

52 Meirion Harries and Susie Harries. *The Last Days of Innocence: America at War, 1917-1918*. New York: Vintage Books, 1997, 158.

But the entire American population was coping with rationing in one form or the other. World War I was the first war in which motorized vehicles played a major role, both in the combat arena and in the land and sea support systems required to deliver the necessary personnel, supplies, and equipment to the Western Front. Consequently, oil and coal became precious commodities, leading to shortages and rationing. To combat the shortages, President Wilson created the Federal Fuel Administration under the authority of Harry A. Garfield on August 23, 1917, as part of the Food and Fuel Control Act, also known as the Lever Act. Garfield was the eldest son of President James A. Garfield. The agency exercised control over the production, distribution, and price of coal and oil.[53]

Coal was the dominant source of fuel driving the country's industry. Garfield appointed state and local administrators to assess consumption needs, and by November, industries had been classified as to the relative importance of their output or service to the war effort. Only those producing food supplies or munitions of war or performing some vitally necessary service were allocated a supply of fuel. Every conceivable measure was taken that would help to conserve the supply of fuel. Non-essential industries were closed; all business offices and stores were forced to shorten their hours of business; street and interior lighting were reduced to a minimum; and all electric display advertising and winter lighting were discontinued in an effort to reduce the consumption of fuel. Baseburners were considered the most economical heaters, and these received the preference in the distribution of hard coal.

53 "Federal Fuel Administration." Wikipedia. March 13, 2016.

Users of hot-air furnaces were not allowed to exceed fifty percent of their regular requirements in hard coal. Only for special types of hot water and steam boilers was hard coal allowed. Fuel economy was preached at every opportunity, and a great amount of newspaper publicity was secured along this line. In order to simplify the transportation problem, zoning systems were adopted, thus avoiding a large number of duplicating shipments in opposite directions, as well as unnecessary long hauls. Also, the government requisitioned supplies of anthracite and other smokeless coals for use in transports and ocean freight-carrying vessels that passed through the submarine danger zone, thus reducing their risk of being sighted and attacked by submarines.

The snow storms and blizzards of the harsh 1917-18 winter caused widespread suffering as a result of the coal shortages and the railroad shut-downs. The shortages became so extreme that terrified citizens in Ohio tore up railroad tracks to keep coal from being shipped to the east coast. Recognizing the emergency situation, Garfield convinced Wilson to give coal a top shipping priority. He went on to shut down all bituminous coal-consuming factories east of the Mississippi that were not essential to the war effort for five days in January. He then ordered the factories to be closed on Mondays for the next two months. Not to be outdone by the Food Administration, Garfield put forth the idea of heatless Thursdays, in which homes were not to be heated with coal.[54]

54 Livingston County, Michigan, Memorial library, Reprinted with permission from Pam@MemorialLibrary.com

The Fuel Administration also initiated Daylight Savings Time, which began March 31, per the Standard Time Act of 1918,[55] an approach that no doubt would have pleased Benjamin Franklin, the proponent of "Early to bed, early to rise."

The second major objective of the Fuel Administration was to keep the oil supply flowing. By the time America entered the war, it was already supplying eighty percent of the Allies' petroleum needs. The Motor Transport Corps of the United States Army shipped 110,911 vehicles, including motor trucks, passenger cars, ambulances, motorcycles, bicycles, and sidecars, to the American Expeditionary Forces from the beginning of the war to December 1, 1918.[56]

The American automobile industry had grown to a billion-dollar business by 1917 with 550 companies employing over 280,000 workers in thirty-two states. Motor vehicle production for the calendar year was 1,814,988 vehicles, of which nearly all were passenger cars. There were 4,842,139 motor vehicles registered in the country with prices ranging from four hundred dollars to over six thousand dollars for limousines.[57] The Ford Motor Company, founded by Henry Ford, was the major motor vehicle manufacturer.

With the need for oil conservation, Garfield created the Oil Division within the Fuel Administration and appointed Mark Requa as director. Requa, a close friend of Herbert Hoover, was

55 "Federal Fuel Administration." Wikipedia. March 13, 2016.

56 "Chapter 26: 1918." Early American Automobiles.

57 *The New York Times*, January 6, 1918.

a successful petroleum and mining engineer and entrepreneur from California and Nevada who was serving as a staff member in Hoover's Food Administration. Prior to his government appointments, Requa had formed his own oil company in California's Coalinga field, managed the Nevada Consolidated Copper Company, and acted as President of the Eureka and Palisades Railroad. Requa's task was to coordinate oil production and direct the industry to serve the nation's military needs. In an ironic twist of fate, the administration needed cooperation from a company that had a history of contentious relationships with the government: the Standard Oil Company of New Jersey, formerly the Standard Oil Company, founded by John D. Rockefeller. In 1882, Standard Oil's attorneys put all of its many companies into a trust, which was essentially a corporation of corporations, thus centralizing control of operations. The enormous size and wealth of the trust allowed Standard Oil to monopolize the oil industry across state borders, gaining an aura of invincibility while always prevailing against competitors, critics, and political enemies. When other companies began emulating Standard Oil's business model, Congress passed the Sherman Antitrust Act of 1890.[58]

Once the United States entered the war, the increased demand for petroleum products put on hold the focus on antitrust actions and breakup of monopolies. The emphasis now was on cooperation, efficiency, conservation, and maximization of production. Requa went about issuing directives for the pooling of oil supplies and supervising their distribution through a system of priorities and licenses. He promoted efficient, sound conservation

58 "John D. Rockefeller." Wikipedia. September 29, 2016.

D. Kent Decker

policies and honored any voluntary cooperative policies that he deemed beneficial to the war effort. This new emphasis on industry cooperation was in direct conflict with the earlier Supreme Court ruling against Standard Oil, which was aimed at preventing this type of collusion.

On the consumer side, the Fuel Administration requested gasless Sundays on a volunteer basis, in which motorists residing in states east of the Mississippi were to refrain from using gasoline for pleasure purposes. Exempt from this public request were tractors and motor trucks employed in actual transportation of freight; physicians' vehicles used in performance of professional duties; ambulances, fire apparatus, police patrol wagons, undertaker wagons, and funeral conveyances; gasoline-powered railway equipment; telephone and public service repair outfits; and motor vehicles on errands of necessity in rural communities where transportation by steam or electricity was not available. *The Automobile Journal*, in its September 1918 issue, estimated that motorists saved an approximate seven and a half million gallons of gasoline on the first gasless Sunday, September 1, in an indication that American citizens were still willing to sacrifice for the cause some seventeen months into the war effort.[59]

With the present emphasis on the development of electric vehicles, it is interesting to note that the Anderson Electric Car Company produced a car called the Detroit Electric in 1917. The vehicle operated from fourteen 6-volt batteries with a top speed of twenty miles per hour and an advertised range of eighty miles per charge. It could be charged to full capacity overnight. The vehicle

59 Automobile Journal 66 (September 1918). doi: Google eBooks. 30-31.

was marketed to women because it did not emit exhaust fumes, nor did it require cranking. Another aspect of the marketing strategy played on the citizens' patriotism in that the car did not use gasoline that was in short supply to support the war effort. Sales were steady during and after the war years due to higher gasoline prices, but the company went out of business in 1939 as a result of improvements in gasoline engine vehicles, ending an idea that was perhaps ninety years ahead of its time.[60]

But Dick Bakker was not concerned with shortages and rationing. "I am getting along very good now, but didn't feel very good Sunday," Dick wrote on Tuesday, June 4. "Missed two meals. Was quite sick from the vaccination. Will get two more. Had one examination yesterday and one today and passed O.K. both times. Quite a few fell out. Seahinsen didn't pass and one from Olivia and one from Sacred Heart and quite a few more I don't know. Our uniforms are to be here tonite." The uniforms were originally promised on Monday; it was the fourth day in camp, and they still had no uniforms. "Our clothes we are wearing can never be cleaned by the way they look. When we are examined, we throw our clothes on the floor and everybody walking over them. It is all in such a rush. We don't get time to dress. They examine from 1200 to 1500 men a day and every day steady and then you can imagine how many there are coming in here."

The American war effort was in high gear: It was an all-out effort to put soldiers at the Western Front. As the number of recruits accelerated, the system was literally bursting at the seams.

60 "Detroit Electric." Wikipedia. September 30, 2016.

"There are supposed to be 150 in each, but there are 306 in our barrack on account of so many coming in every day," Dick noted.

After vaccination, the recruits were trained in close-order drill. While drill was viewed as a waste of time by many soldiers, it had its purpose to the army. Drill movements were constantly repeated until they became so firmly engraved in the mind that they produced predictable, conditioned reflexes which had nothing to do with conscious thought. In the bedlam and confusion of battle, the army wanted precise responses to leaders' orders that overcame natural instincts. Drill was, and still is, the tool that produced these results. It was an impatient, intolerant system that punished those who could not conform. "They drill us very hard here," Dick wrote. "We get more every day. It makes us tired so we feel like laying down when we get back but we will get used to that in a little while. I tell you we have to learn something here and pretty quick too. Great many of the boys don't catch on very quick and they send them on K.P. for five days for not obeying. I have not reported to the Orderly Room yet. Don't expect to either. It is quite easy for me but some cannot get swing of it."

Camp Lewis was a beehive of activity. While the troops trained in close-order drill on the parade grounds, the sounds of Springfield rifles and machine guns could be heard on the firing range. Horse-drawn field artillery trained in columns. The art of trench warfare was taught in the outlying areas. There was a bunker used as a gas chamber to train the troops in the appliance of their gas masks. Amongst these sounds of war, a marching band on the parade grounds aroused the troops with inspirational songs of the era. "We can hear the guns roar all day long," Dick wrote.

"It is busy here day and night. Noise of every kind. The trucks they use to haul people around hold 23 people and they go night and day. All other trucks that haul coal and other supplies, they just shake the ground when they go by. They go night and day too. The band comes out three times a day on the marching grounds. The best band I ever heard and all military bands just as there are on our phonograph. The grounds are just covered with companies as far as you can see."

Downtime due to vaccinations was not scheduled in the training regimen. "Had my second shot in the arm yesterday," Dick wrote on June 9, after a week of drill. "Feel pretty sick. Been in bed all day. The vaccination is working as I have two big stiff arms. I see my name on the Bulletin for guard tomorrow but don't know whether I will be able to do so. Will Jacobs was in bed all day, too."

But time heals all wounds, and the troops' appetites returned once the effects of the shots wore off. With rigorous daily workouts, no one ever called these farm boys late for supper. On the evening of June 12, a hungry Dick Bakker wrote, "I feel better today than ever before. Can eat and eat and never get full. Will go to the YMCA after a little. We can get everything we want. They have the best cake there I ever ate with fresh strawberries for filling and a half a pint of milk for 15 cents or cake and ice cream for 15 cents also or coffee instead of milk." Four days later, he was still eating. "Was over to the Y.M.C.A. and the canteen post exchange and had some cake and ice cream. I can eat all the time here and never get full. We go up after supper every night. We sit six inches from the table and eat till we touch the table and then we go and drink a pint of milk and half a cake and a few pieces of candy cane or an apple and bottle of pop Then we feel like laying down. Then we go to bed and wake up hungry as ever." A day later, "Just weighed tonight and weighed 148 and when I came here I weighed 143 so I am gaining." So the troops were eating well, at least in Camp Lewis, if that was any consolation to the folks at home who were enduring meatless and wheatless days.

It is always amazing how well one can adapt to a new routine, especially when there is no choice, and Dick Bakker was no exception. On June 16: "I just as soon stay here for a while as to move to a warmer climate. It is such fine climate here. I have one blanket on doubled, and one single and my raincoat and my overcoat over too, and in the morning I get cold in bed. Yet it is so easy to get up here. When the bugle calls we got to get up at once. We have to be clean shaved and hair cut short all the time or we get K.P. for a few days and that is no snap. If your rifle is dirty in any way, only a little dust on, we get K.P. Quite a few got K.P. Saturday morning for dirty rifles. I know all the orders of the arms so I can do them correct. It is quite easy for me to catch on. Quite a few get K.P. every other day for a week for not holding their gun right in Reveille and Retreat. It's got to be everything up to the dot. It is 8:40 now. No talking after nine o'clock. We can stay out till eleven o'clock if we want to, but I can sleep here all the time anyway."

Dick received his first letter from home, written by Tetje, on June 12, two weeks after he had left Minnesota. He received his first letter from his family on June 16, reflecting the speed of communications in the country during that time period.

Between eating, sleeping, marching, and cleaning his rifle, Dick found time to attend to some personal matters. Once his uniform had arrived, Dick mailed home his civilian clothes, which consisted of a suit, hat, raincoat, and a pair of shoes. He also bought a pennant of Camp Lewis for a dollar and mailed it to Tetje. Dick wrote to his parents, telling them to sell his horse, Peanuts, for twenty-five dollars or whatever they could get. "I have no more use for him now," he wrote.

One can only speculate as to why he made this request, but these actions indicate that Dick was now viewing himself as a soldier as opposed to a civilian. While the military oath is sometimes viewed as a meaningless ceremony from those on the outside, the ritual arouses a powerful sense of obligation in the recruit and establishes a bond between him and his branch of service. Along with the mental ratification marked by the oath, the recruit is made to look and feel like a soldier with the issue of a uniform and the application of a military haircut. These practices promote cohesion and a sense of group allegiance. The radical change of appearance helps to impress on the recruit his change of status: It is an external symbol of the psychological transformation produced by the oath.[61] From that standpoint, Dick severed a link to his farm life when he sent home his civilian clothes. He was now focused on fulfilling his duty as a soldier in the United States Army. Understandably, Dick would have some apprehensions

61 Richard Holmes. *Acts of War: The Behavior of Men in Battle*. New York: Free Press, 1986, 34.

looking forward. In that light, he took out a $10,000 life insurance policy that cost $6.50 per month taken out of his wages. Even in those days, the salesmen never missed a beat.

With the pomp and circumstance of seemingly endless drill formations on the parade ground punctuated by the inspirational songs of the military band, it is easy to see why the rural farm boy was caught up in the military spirit. By his own account, Dick was one of the better recruits at handling his rifle, which undoubtedly provided him with a sense of self-confidence and belonging.

The Ninety-First Division that trained at Camp Lewis during this time was known as the Wild West Division. They wore a green pine tree patch with the battle cry: "Powder River! Let'er buck!" It contained some of the finest and most accomplished cowboys from the western states. Periodically, they would put on rodeos at the horse arena on Sunday afternoons. Dick Bakker was fortunate enough to attend one of these events. "Went to the horse show this afternoon and there were about 35,000 people. The most people I ever saw."

On Wednesday, June 19, less than three weeks after he had arrived at Camp Lewis, Dick Bakker departed on a sixteen-coach train carrying five hundred troops headed for Camp Kearny near San Diego, California.[62] The military band, the finest band that Dick had ever heard, gave them a rousing send-off as they shook hands from the coach windows and said goodbye to their friends in a gesture of fellowship and respect. These young men had become brothers during a brief period of history in which they proudly trained together for freedom, for God, for country. Many

62 Letter from Dick Bakker to his parents.

of them would never see each other again. The entire Ninety-First Division departed the camp between June 21 and June 24, headed for the East Coast and on to France. Soon after, in July, the Thirteenth Infantry Division was formed at Camp Lewis as the continuous stream of troop trains chugged in with fresh recruits conscripted by the Selective Service Act. A new group of soldiers slept in the bunk houses, their arms smarting from the sting of the vaccination needle. The war machine rolled on.

Chapter 7

The Trip South, Parlor Songs and Railroads

DICK BAKKER WAS NOW HEADING south through the state of Washington, oblivious to the carnage that was World War I. Until he shipped out of Camp Lewis, Dick had no idea where he we would be going. The American government, worried about sabotage, kept the details of troop movements a guarded secret and even put out false information to confuse the issue. This fact is born out in the letters that Dick wrote to his family. On June 4: "We are to stay here a little more than a month and then we will move to another camp or to the East Coast to go across. We get 3 months of training in France behind the lines." Eleven days later on Saturday, June 15, he wrote, "We are going to move Tuesday I am quite sure to Indianapolis, Indiana, or Frisco, California." Then, on Sunday, June 16: "You better not write to me any more over here for some of us will move Tuesday afternoon but don't know where we are going." Again on Monday, June 17: "I think we will have a six-day trip the way I heard, we will know where we are going after we have rode a few days." He shipped out Wednesday on the Northern Pacific Railway. His destination was Camp Kearny near San Diego. The trip took three days and three nights without sleepers.

As the train meandered through the countryside of western Washington along the route of the Northern Pacific, the Minnesota farm boy noted the irrigated grain fields and the patches of fern "as thick as the hair on a dog." Passing through towns and villages, the troops were treated as heroes. "We stopped on the way one time this afternoon and the girls gave us the prettiest flowers you ever saw and loaded us with magazines and we surely did give them the cheers," Dick wrote. "We sure have a good time on our way where we go." The train churned into mountainous areas thick with tall timber and passed near forest fires bellowing smoke that limited their vision to less than a mile. With the windows open in the warm June climate, Dick marveled at the cinders falling on his paper. Dick noted that he had not had a cigarette since he had been in camp. His main reason: "When a fellow has a package of cigarettes everyone wants one and you will only get one from the package yourself." Some things never change.

The train passed through a tunnel "dark as night" and dropped down into the town of Kelso, continuing south along the picturesque Columbia River. Thoroughly enjoying the ride, Dick noted the rocky bluffs of the wide river with the majestic evergreens along its banks. "I haven't seen a cottonwood since I left," the Minnesotan wrote. The train passed a dairy farm with Holstein cows, and a little later, Dick spied a coyote scurrying into the underbrush. Around 7 p.m., they crossed the Columbia and entered the town of Kalama, passing boaters and swimmers taking advantage of the cool river water. It was a scenic tour that any AAA agent would be proud to map out for a club member—compliments of the United States Government.

Not every soldier was enjoying the ride. As the train chugged through Kalama, Dick wrote, "We had to stop to get one of our men. He jumped out of the window and we got him all right. We have every door guarded all the time. Everyone has his turn 1 hour at a time. Haven't been yet. Will be on during the nite sometime. The one who tries to get away from the Army, he is out of luck all the time. I have never had the least notion to skip. Wouldn't try for the whole world." Obviously, this man was not the first to attempt to flee. Like the motto it later adopted, the army was prepared.

The train continued through the towns of Martin's Bluff, Woodland, and Ridgefield, where there was considerable logging activity. As he rode, Dick observed horses, alfalfa fields, and a large cherry tree loaded with cherries. He wrote down his observations in a letter to his parents as he rode along. The letterhead had an American flag on the left side and a circle enclosing a triangle on the right side, a logo used by the YMCA. The heading in the center read:

War Work Council
ARMY AND NAVY
YOUNG MEN'S CHRISTIAN ASSOCIATION
"With the colors"

That night, the train rumbled into Portland, Oregon, and crossed the Columbia on a double-deck bridge that Dick estimated to be a mile long. With the streetcars and autos passing overhead, Dick's train passed another on the double track's lower deck. From the bridge, Dick marveled at the many boats in the Portland Columbia River shipyards, well-lit with strings of electric lights and well-guarded, reflecting the paranoia gripping the country in the wake of the war. The Pacific Northwest steel and wood shipbuilding industry had flourished since the start of the war in 1914, first producing ships for Britain, Norway, and France. When America entered the war in 1917, the Emergency Fleet Corporation, a wartime federal agency, commissioned steamships from the Columbia River Shipbuilding Corporation and other regional corporations. This brought large amounts of government money into the area, and the industry now employed over fifty thousand people.[63]

This large employment base included skilled workers who belonged to unions that made up the American Federation of Labor (AFL) and unskilled workers who belonged to more combative and militant unions such as the Industrial Workers of the World (IWW), more commonly known as the Wobblies. The IWW was in the midst of a very successful lumber industry strike in the Northwest when the United States entered the war in 1917. The abundant spruce in the region was used for aircraft building and in the cantonments as well as for shipbuilding. The dire need for this material caused the federal government to create the U.S. Army Spruce Division and place twenty-seven thousand soldiers in the lumber camps and sawmills. The government also created a large union called the Loyal Legion of Loggers and Lumbermen and succeeded in breaking the IWW strike.[64]

These activities created tension and mistrust among the various factions of the industry. In addition, all German Americans

63 Kathy Tucker. "Shipbuilders Will Help." Oregon History Project. 2002.

64 Gail Wells. "Union Activity and World War I." Oregon History Project. 2006.

who were not naturalized citizens were classified as enemy aliens. Fear of anti-American activities caused President Wilson to issue Proclamation Number 416 that forbid German Americans to go within one hundred yards of the waterfront or a half-mile of an armory.[65] These suspicions led to the well-guarded and well-lit shipyards observed by Dick Bakker as he passed over the river.

After crossing the river, the train stopped, and the troops were let out for a rigorous two-mile march through Portland before proceeding on through the night into the Oregon countryside. The troops were now traveling on the Southern Pacific Railway. The next morning, Thursday, June 20, the train arrived in the small town of Roseburg, Oregon, where the troops again were let out for a march, this time through the town. In the early morning light, the townspeople peered out their windows at the marching soldiers who sang, "Pull your shades down, Marianne, if you want to keep a secret from your future man. Pull your shades down, Marianne."

Camp Lewis had developed a daily singing program under the direction of Robert Lloyd, the camp musical coordinator. Dick Bakker wrote home, "We learned all kinds of songs here like *Over There* & *On That Long Long Trail with You* & *We Won't be Back Till It's Over Over There*." Lloyd, who had volunteered for WWI service as a retired music teacher, believed that a tune made the men better soldiers. He convinced the Camp Lewis commander that singing would improve the men's lungs and lessen their chances of getting tuberculosis. He argued that singing was

---

65 Trudy Flores and Sarah Griffith. "Circle Theater and Pershing's Crusaders." Oregon History Project. 2002.

guaranteed to help officers and NCOs shout commands. Lloyd wrote new songs and arranged Broadway hits for the soldiers; he even directed choruses as large as ten thousand men.[66]

War songs designed to rouse the patriotic fervor of every citizen were very much a part of the American culture during World War I. Between mid-1914 and mid-1919, 35,600 American patriotic songs were copyrighted, and 7,300 were published. The messages delivered by the songs changed as America's position in the war changed. Before America entered the war, songs that were anti-war in nature such as "I Didn't Raise My Boy to be a Soldier" appeared. The lyrics preached to mothers worldwide that if they united in the cause, they could put an end to the fighting and save the lives of millions of young soldiers. An equally pacifist song entitled "Stay Down Here Where You Belong" was written by the famous composer Irving Berlin. Other songs, like "When the Lusitania Went Down," were written with messages preparing American citizens for the inevitable entry into the war.[67]

Once America entered the war, the song messages became more supportive for the national cause. The day after Wilson's declaration of war against Germany, George M. Cohan composed "Over There," a march containing lyrics that stressed patriotism and a sense of national identity. It was one of the most successful American pro-war propaganda songs, enthusiastically inspiring the American spirit of confidence about the ability of American troops to end the war and return home safely. Since it was a march, it was easily sung and enjoyed, and it proved to be an

66 Material provided by friends of the Fort Lewis Military Museum.

67 K.A. Wells. "Music as War Propaganda." Parlor Songs. 2004.

effective propaganda tool at the onset of the war for recruiting and homeland support. It was publicly advertised that the royalties from this song were donated to war charities, so this music was even more valuable as a pro-war tool. Being an all-American venture, one sheet music cover (one of several) was drawn by famous American artist Norman Rockwell, and it showed soldiers happily joined in song, sending the positive message of the effects of song on the troops, both from the standpoint of morale and of unity by singing together. "Over There" had gained so much popularity that Enrico Caruso, a world-famous singer, recorded it in both French and English, another good propaganda move. The song sold two million copies of sheet music and one million recordings by the time the war was over and would later become a legendary song in American folklore. The message from "Over There" was so effective that Cohan was later awarded a special Congressional Medal of Honor.[68]

The government, led by the CPI, was quick to utilize the patriotic songs as part of their propaganda machine. Songs written by government composers identified only as "Army Song Leaders" were used by the four-minute men in their speeches. Song writers encouraged people to spend evenings singing war songs, and it became the patriotic thing to do at this time of the war. Citizens were urged to join together in patriotic songs at home, in theaters, in arranged songfests, at community sings, and at Liberty Bond rallies. The CPI issued songbooks of patriotic music which were distributed to audiences in music halls to stimulate communal singing and build home-front morale. Special song leaders

68 Ibid.

dispatched by the government visited the theaters to promote this activity. Government song leaders also paid visits to the troops and supplied them with patriotic songbooks, encouraging soldiers to sing many of the popular, well-known marches and war songs. Many of those who entertained the troops attempted to alter the moods conveyed in the trench songs by making them into parodies, thus overriding their bitterness with a more carefree and optimistic attitude. John Philip Sousa, an American composer, was recruited to train young bandsmen at the Great Lakes Naval Training Center. After completing this stint, he continued to provide patriotic inspiration with his music at Liberty Loan rallies and Red Cross relief drives. Irving Berlin was recruited into the military in 1917, and a commanding officer requested that he write and produce an all-soldier show to raise $35,000 for a much-needed Service Center for the soldiers. Besides starring in the review, *Yip, Yip, Yaphank*, which was staged in 1918, Berlin wrote all the songs, sketches, dialogue, and dance routines. In one scene he played a whiny K.P. singing, "I scrub the dishes against my wishes to make this world safe for democracy." In another scene, dragging himself out of his cot in response to reveille, Berlin sang "Oh, How I Hate to Get Up in the Morning," which became one of the most successful comedy songs of WWI.[69]

All in all, the patriotic songs were an effective propaganda tool for promoting the war effort and government programs while boosting morale and rousing national pride. Some would claim that this music made a significant contribution toward winning the war. At a minimum, it provided a new means by which

69 Ibid.

music composers and publishers could further their personal and economic goals and political agendas. Indeed, many of them made a handsome profit off the war songs and the associated sheet music. All this, of course, was of no concern to the young farm boy, Dick Bakker, as he enjoyed his march through the streets of Roseburg, Oregon.

With the troops fully exercised, the train continued south through the picturesque Cascade Mountains of Oregon. In the afternoon, the train stopped in Ashland, Oregon, and the troops were let out for thirty minutes to roam the town while the brakes were refurbished. "Just sent or mailed a book from the scenery from Portland to San Francisco," Dick wrote. "It is just the way it looks but not like seeing the clear life." At this point, the train was split into two sections of six cars and nine cars in preparation for the mountainous journey ahead. Each train was pulled by two oil burning engines. "We are going uphill all the time averaging about ten miles an hour," Dick wrote. "We have some great scenery here. It is quite hot this afternoon. We were quite low and this afternoon we are getting up higher and is getting cooler. We are going thru a tunnel pretty soon and then another one 3000 foot long and we got to close the windows or we will smother from the oil burned smoke. We are going in a zig-zag around the mountains. We can look down a thousand feet or more from where we came. Just gone over a bridge between two bluffs. It makes a man shiver to look out the window. The train looks just like a fly."

Dick continued his letter as he rode, sometimes in shaky handwriting, "The locomotive is nearly stopping. If they were burning coal, it would fly all out the smoke stack. Three locomotives on our load now. Don't know if we are at the top or not. It took two hours to go fourteen and a half miles."

A while later, "Just went through another tunnel 4000 feet long. We are going downhill, now. Just crossed a wooden bridge between two bluffs. It cracked like it was going to break. The grain here looks very slim. Don't see a patch larger than 10 acres and is all irrigated. The corn is about 2 feet high and all kinds of trees and such great big orchards of peach trees but they are not ripe yet."

At 4:45 that afternoon: "Just stopping now. We make some pretty short curves. We go in about 700 directions here. We can see the engine on one end and the rear of the cars across from us, so you can think we are going quite zig zag. They cut most of the grain for hay for it dried up. Lot of barley ready to cut but one man can keep up with four 8 foot cut binders here. Just let a double header by."

Dick's letter highlights the inadequate capabilities of the locomotives in the early twentieth century. The need to efficiently move men and materials in a timely fashion during the war period put a tremendous strain on the nation's transportation system whose main component was the railroads. Many of the nation's roadways were unfit for heavy freight traffic, and the evolution of the airplane as a cargo transport was still in its infancy. To add to the problem, thousands of rail workers were drafted as a result of the Selective Service Act, creating labor shortages on top of material and capital shortages.

By 1916, the Interstate Commerce Commission had complete control over the shipping rates that railroads could charge their customers. Railroad companies were required to justify rate increases, which were not always granted. The tight regulatory controls combined with the advancement of competing technologies, such as electric trolley cars, gasoline powered automobiles, and an expanding network of telephones that reduced the need for travel, led to reduced investment in railroads. In addition, railroad unions threatened strike action for shorter hours and better pay, which resulted in the Adamson Act that set the eight-hour day as the standard. The result of these activities was that rail firms had difficulty in securing sufficient funds to keep pace with rising costs. Consequently, locomotives were outdated and underpowered. Many railroads were still using wooden passenger cars as well as lower-capacity thirty-ton freight cars, even though forty-ton steel-reinforced freight cars were available. Furthermore, ton-miles increased significantly—by 32 percent—in 1916 as the allied nations began to purchase American natural resources to sustain their war effort. Serious congestion occurred in the yards, terminals, and ports of the Northeast and New England as the demand for goods in Europe increased. As things deteriorated, the Interstate Commerce Commission reported in January of 1917, "The present conditions of car distribution throughout the United States have no parallel in our history... Mills have shut down, prices have advanced, perishable articles of great value have been destroyed... Transportation service has been thrown into unprecedented confusion."[70]

When the winter of 1917-1918 roared in like a lion, it created a major transportation crisis. With the country's rail system at a

70 "Early Twentieth Century Railroads." HowStuffWorks. May 19, 2008.

virtual standstill, President Wilson issued an order on December 26, 1917, to nationalize the railroad industry under the direction of the United States Railroad Administration (USRA). On March 21, 1918, the Railway Administration Act became law, and Wilson's 1917 nationalization order was affirmed. Wilson appointed his son-in-law, Secretary of the Treasury William Gibbs McAdoo, as Director General of the newly formed USRA.

The USRA organized the railroads into three divisions: East, West, and South. Duplicate passenger services were killed off, costly and employee-heavy sleeping car services were cut back, and extra fares were applied to discourage their use. Uniform passenger ticketing was instituted, and competing services on different former railroads were cut back, a move that essentially ignored the Sherman Antitrust Act. Terminals, facilities, and shops were shared. Over 100,000 railroad cars and 1,930 steam locomotives were ordered to replace much outdated equipment at a cost of $380 million—all up-to-date and standardized USRA designs. Both wages and rates for both passenger and freight traffic were raised by the USRA during 1918 to avert strikes.[71] Yet there were still locomotives in use in the summer of 1918 that were under-powered as Dick's letter points out.

As Dick's train journeyed south toward Camp Kearny, it passed numerous trains heading north. "There are trains going way on top on one side and down on the other side and all going the same way," Dick wrote. "Just left another double header and we slapped hands when they passed by through the windows." Did the "high-five" originate in World War I?

71 "United States Railroad Administration." Wikipedia. August 20, 2016.

After crossing into California, Dick wrote, "Just stopped in another town, Hornbrook, a wet town but didn't dare to go near the joint. Going to get off next station and go over to the springs. Six thirty now, feeling fine so far, just crossing the river. We are eight and a half miles from the California line." Hornbrook, California, a small town in Siskiyou County, was a hub for the Southern Pacific Railway at that time. The hub consisted of a switching yard and a roundhouse. Dick makes no mention of changing trains during their brief stop. His mention of Hornbrook as a "wet town" reflects the activities of the Prohibition Movement during the early twentieth century. At the beginning of 1918, nineteen states were dry states, including Washington and Oregon, through which the train had just passed.[72] After three weeks at Camp Lewis, was there a stampede to the nearest saloon followed by a hearty celebration that rivaled the one previously mentioned in Deer Lodge, Montana?

On November 18, 1918, the United States Congress passed a temporary Wartime Prohibition Act, which banned the sale of alcoholic beverages having an alcohol content of greater than 2.75 percent. This act, which was intended to save grain for the war effort, was passed after the armistice was signed on November 11, 1918. The Wartime Prohibition Act took effect June 30, 1919, and July 1, 1919, became widely known as the "Thirsty-First". Congress passed the Eighteenth Amendment, the National Prohibition Act, also known as the Volstead Act, on October 28, 1919, which went into effect in 1920 and banned the sale,

72 "Dry State." Wikipedia. September 7, 2016.

production, and transportation of alcoholic beverages throughout the country.[73]

As the train continued south, the locals somehow knew when the trains would be arriving in spite of the army's attempt at secrecy. "There are no young men left in all the towns we stopped," Dick observed. "Nothing but girls and the last one were mostly Indians. Partly, they were very pretty girls for Indians. The flowers in this letter, I received from the girls in Ashland. Did you get any letters from Montana? The girls wanted our address so we gave our home address to get our camp address from home. Will write tomorrow. DWB." After three weeks in a crowded camp full of young men, the girls were looking pretty.

73 "Prohibition in the United States." Wikipedia. September 28, 2016.

Chapter 8

Belleau Wood

As Dick Bakker enjoyed the pretty girls, the American Expeditionary Forces along the Marne were fighting one of the ugliest battles of the war. After the standoff at Château-Thierry, the next few days were essentially a standoff as the two sides assessed the situation. The Germans had pushed the Western Front to within fifty miles of Paris and were ready to resume the attack once fresh troops and supplies were brought forward. The entire population of France knew that Ludendorff was knocking on the doors of Paris. With Ludendorff's long-range artillery shelling the capital, the French Army retreating, the French government preparing to flee, and droves of refugees walking the streets, the morale of the French people was devastated. The onus was on the Americans to prove their worth and restore the will of the French. The situation was crucial. The Allies needed a victory.[74]

With this in mind, the Allied Command ordered a counterattack to reclaim Belleau Wood, five miles north of Château-Thierry on the Marne River, and Hill 142 next to it on the west. Belleau Wood was approximately one thousand yards wide and three thousand yards long from north to south. It was surrounded

74 Meirion Harries and Susie Harries. *The Last Days of Innocence: America at War, 1917-1918*. New York: Vintage Books, 1997, 260.

on all sides by pastures and poppy-strewn wheat fields. The woods were a jungle of large trees and tangled undergrowth combined with large boulders, ridges, and ravines that provided the perfect cover for a defensive stand. Unknown to the Americans, the Germans were entrenched with barbed wire, sharpshooter pits, heavy mortars, artillery, and machine gun emplacements. The final American orders came down the morning of June 6 with little time for preparations, but no one was about to disobey an order from Blackjack Pershing. The attack on Hill 142 began at 3:45 a.m.

The initial marine battalion, led by Major Julius Turrill, was mowed down like cattle as the troops advanced through the wheat fields. Rather than sensibly withdrawing, Turrill's men became the first to demonstrate the chilling marine theory that the only sure way to overcome machine-gun positions of this kind was to rush them. Time and time again, the marines surged over the German gunners, pushing through the wheat fields and woods, and leaving behind a trail of dead and dying Germans and Americans. The Hill 142 objective was met that day, and further east, the village of Bouresches was captured. The attack on Belleau Wood began at 5 p.m. The Third Battalion Fifth Marines, under Major Benjamin Berry, rose up and, in waves of four ranks, like any Civil War formation, advanced across a wheat field already alive with shrapnel and machine-gun fire. The enemy fire brought them down mangled and bleeding, still in those ranks. The survivors scrambled to the edge of the wood. In the southwest, a battalion led by Major Berton Sibley made it to the edge of the wood but was soon battered with heavy machine-gun fire. As darkness fell under the continuous pounding of German artillery, the wheat fields lay strewn with dead and dying marines. That first day, the division lost 1,087 men, 222 of them killed.[75]

The battle raged on for another eighteen days. As troops advanced in waves across the wheat fields, the Germans opened fire with machine guns and mortars, ripping away arms and legs and leaving the first wave of dying soldiers to block the progress of the oncoming support troops. There was no quit in these proud marines, and they scratched and clawed their way into the wood as the hail of bullets took the lives of those beside them. Once inside the wood, all hell broke loose as the marines became engaged in hand-to-hand combat. All sense of military discipline disappeared as every man fought for survival in a kill-or-be-killed jungle of gunfire, mortars, grenades, and bayonets. Grenades and machine-gun fire from both sides killed friend and foe alike as every man fought to stay alive. Those on the ground were bayoneted to make sure they were dead.

Conditions in the field were abhorrent. After two weeks of continual fighting, the troops were exhausted and falling asleep under bombardment, their minds numb from constant shelling. They were forced to watch their mutilated comrades suffer from injuries that ranged from amputation, hemorrhage, and fractures to mustard gas burns, lacerations, and infection. Hunkered down in a lice-infested wood, wearing the same clothes, they were dirty, ill-fed, sick, and always thirsty. Food was brought to the battlefield in rolling wagons and prepared behind the lines. Runners carried hot stew to the troops on the front line in large clay vessels the

75 Ibid., 254-259.

French called "marmites." At times, the shelling was so heavy that the runners could not deliver the stew for a day or two. By the time the troops received the food, it was cold and soured in the pot, but they were so hungry they gobbled it down among the putrefying stench of decay and excrement and the bloated corpses of their companions who had died before they could get medical treatment.

Troops crawled through the wheat fields at night, freezing in place when German flares lit the sky. The men inched forward on their bellies among the wounded and dying, driven by the command that they would not fail. They gritted their teeth and stood their ground in a deluge of gunfire, unable to attend to their bleeding comrades with their extremities blown off and shrapnel piercing their flesh. Bone-chilling screams of blood-drained, delirious men filled their ears. Their buddies' blood drenched their hands and faces. Entire companies were wiped out. Others were quickly sent in to replace them lest the lines be broken.

On June 24, the artillery was called in. The front lines were pulled back while the big guns rained shells on the German positions. By dark, the wood was reduced to kindling. The next day, the attack resumed and, at last, the marines were able to take the wood, but even in the final battle, it was not easy. Many of the German gunners, well-fortified behind rocks and thick undergrowth, were still alive with the mindset that it was still a fight to the death. Step by step, the marines overtook the machine-gun nests, looking behind every rock and probing every corpse to make sure it was dead. On June 26, the marines declared that Belleau Wood was in Allied hands at the cost of 100 officers and

5,500 men killed, wounded, or missing. No soldier would ever forget the horrifying sights of June 1918 in Belleau Wood: bodies decapitated; torsos eviscerated; joints shattered; eyes put out; jaws shot away; hands, feet, arms, and legs blown off and scattered on the ground; men blistered and blinded by gas, sweating and gibbering in shell shock.[76] Belleau Wood was a living hell that would long haunt the souls of those who survived...but Ludendorff was far from through.

76 Ibid., 271.

Chapter 9

Camp Kearny, Air Ships

THE TROOP TRAIN RUMBLED ON into California, traveling through the fertile central valley and its many farms. "Saw plenty of orange and fig and walnut trees on the way," the Minnesota farm boy noted. "The oranges were nearly ripe and just loaded full. There were many thousands of acres of them." The train reached Southern California and travelled along the coast for two hours, giving the troops a scenic view of the Pacific shore. "We were as close to the shore as 20 steps," Dick wrote. At 11:30 a.m. on Saturday, June 22, the train arrived at Camp Kearny.

Camp Kearny, established July 18, 1917, was a National Guard camp created by the government to train troops for the war. It was named in honor of Major General Stephen Watts Kearny who led the Army of the West to San Diego in 1846 during the Mexican-American War. Kearny's career began during the War of 1812 and progressed through much of America's expansion westward. He married General Clarke's (of Lewis and Clarke) stepdaughter and subsequently explored the Yellowstone and Oregon Trails. His victory at the Battle of San Pasqual near Escondido was the earliest U.S. military connection to the area near the camp. Kearny was later appointed temporary governor of California.[77]

Camp Kearny was located eleven and a half miles north of San Diego on 12,721 acres.[78] Originally, the area was part of an enormous rancho owned by Don Santiago Arguello, the former Mexican Army commandante of San Diego's presidio with cattle grazing over most of the land. The camp was purchased for $4.5 million and cost another $1.25 million to build. The camp included an immense parade ground with about twelve hundred buildings grouped around the parade ground. However, most of Camp Kearny's soldiers lived in tents, as more than sixty-five thousand men trooped through the camp on their way to World War I battlegrounds. There were 696 buildings classified as "main buildings" which included ten warehouses, each 160 feet by 39 feet, and 140 mess halls each in which 250 men could be fed at one time. There was an infirmary, a gas station, a post office, and a carrier pigeon depot. A very large building housed the Liberty Theatre, where troops could watch silent movies and relieve some of the daily stress. Organizations such as the YMCA, Knights of Columbus, and the Library Association set up branches at the camp to assist in maintaining the morale of the troops.

Some thirty-five hundred men contributed to the construction of the camp. In addition, the city of San Diego spent more than $150,000 in building roads to the camp and supplying it with

77 Thomas Q. O'Hara. Marine Corps Air Station Miramar. Charleston: Arcadia Publishing, 2005, 2.

78 "Historic California Posts: Camp Kearny (San Diego County)." California Military History.

a water system, including the laying of forty thousand feet of twelve-inch pipe from Mission Valley to the camp and building to large reservoirs. The San Diego Gas and Electric Company spent $165,000 in laying gas mains and providing for the transmission of electricity to the camp for light and power. The Pacific Telephone Company spent a large sum of money in providing an adequate communications system for the camp. The Santa Fe Railroad built a spur system to the camp from its main line at a cost of around $200,000.[79]

In the summer of 1918, the main unit that trained at the camp were the troops of the Fortieth Division, which became known as "the Sunshine Division" as a compliment to the excellent Southern California climate where outdoor training could be performed year-round. Dubbing the divisions with nicknames was a policy encouraged by the War Department as a method for instilling good, wholesome rivalry and improving troop morale. The division was commanded by Major General Frederick S. Strong.

The Fortieth was mostly comprised of National Guard units from the states of the Southwest. The division consisted of a Headquarters Company, the Seventy-Ninth Infantry Brigade, the Eightieth Infantry Brigade, and the Sixty-Fifth Field Artillery Brigade. The Seventy-Ninth Brigade was made up of the 157th Infantry under Colonel Patrick J. Hamrock, which included the First Colorado Infantry and the First Colorado Cavalry, the

79 McGrew, Clarence Alan. *City of San Diego and San Diego County: The Birthplace of California.* Chicago: American Historical Society, 1922, 220-221.

158th Infantry that was built around the First Arizona Infantry, and the 144th Machine Gun Battalion. The 158th was known as "the dry regiment" due to a solemn promise of its officers not to touch intoxicants until peace was declared. The Sixty-Fifth Field Artillery was made up of three field artillery regiments, a trench mortar battery, an engineer regiment, a field signal battalion, a military police battalion, an ammunition train, a supply train, and a sanitary train comprised of medical, ambulance, and hospital companies. The 143rd Field Artillery contained recruits from Oakland and Southern California. The 144th Field Artillery, known as "The Grizzlies," was headed by Colonel Thornwall Mullaly and contained many well-known Californians. The 145th Field Artillery contained a Utah regiment largely from Salt Lake City.[80] The Eightieth Infantry Brigade was made up of the 159th Infantry Regiment, the 160th Infantry Regiment that included men from the Seventh and Second California Infantry, and the 145th Machine Gun Battalion. Dick Bakker became a part of the 160th Infantry. His letters home were signed:

> D. W. Bakker
> Co F 160 Inf.
> Camp Kearny
> California.

The 159th Infantry was composed of the Fifth California Infantry and parts of the Second Infantry. A member of the 159th Infantry was a twenty-two-year old actor named Buster Keaton. Buster would go on to entertain the troops with a group of twenty-two men that were known as "The Sunshine Players."

80 Ibid., 221-222.

They performed a popular routine that Buster called "My Snake Dance," in which he was dressed as an Egyptian dancer using a length of link sausage.[81]

Up the road in Hollywood, the silver screen displayed the talents of Douglas Fairbanks and Mary Pickford while "Fatty" Arbuckle and Cecil B. DeMille produced and directed. Charlie Chaplin perfected his persona as The Little Tramp. The year before, the Vamp, Theda Bera, had starred in Cleopatra, the most elaborate film produced to date. Ms. Bera's ornate, and sometimes revealing, costumes would later get the movie banned in certain theaters. Local orchestras and pianists enhanced the movies as "talkies" would not appear until the next decade.

But Hollywood was not a topic in Dick Bakker's letters as he entered Camp Kearny. He had some serious training ahead of him. Unfortunately, he got off to a bad start. Dick reveals in his letter home on Sunday, June 23, "I was quite sick when I got here. There were quite a number of them that were sick. They all put it on the last breakfast we had on the train. Had cramps and stiff all over. Took me to the doctor. Couldn't stand up at all."

Feeding a large number of soldiers two to three times a day was a difficult task in those days due to a shortage of clean washing and preparation facilities; the lack of refrigeration, running water, and fuel supplies; and contamination due to dust, dirt, rain, and bugs. A favorite drink was called "bug juice" because at many field dining facilities, the open twenty-five-gallon vat containing the colored liquid substance provided for drinking had a thin layer

81 Martha R. Jett. "Buster Keaton in World War I." The Doughboy Center. 2000.

of dead bugs floating on the surface. The result was often stomach cramps and diarrhea.[82]

After his brief stint in the Pacific Northwest, the small-town Minnesota farm boy wrote his first impression of the Southern California camp. "It is quite dry here. The ground is red here and sandy. We all have tents here. Five men in a tent with wooden floors in it. I like that better than the barracks. I like the people here better than in Camp Lewis. This is not such a big camp as C. L. but the main railroad trains are running all the time. They say it don't rain here at all this time of year. The sprinklers are running now. I think I will go wash up. Missed three meals. Don't know whether I will eat dinner or not. We can see the air ships cutting along here too."

While Dick wrote that he saw "air ships" from the camp, there is no evidence from the literature that air ships, commonly called dirigibles or blimps, were flown out of the San Diego area in the summer of 1918. When the United States entered World War I in 1917, the navy ordered sixteen non-rigid airships—nine from Goodyear in Akron, Ohio, five from Goodrich in Chicago, and two from Connecticut Aircraft. Goodyear had started an airship facility at Wingfoot Lake near Akron, but its hangar was not completed yet, and Goodyear had to erect its first airship, the B-1, at the White City Amusement Park in Chicago in conjunction with Goodrich. The B-1 first flew on May 24, 1917, and five days later, it was flown nonstop from its Chicago location to Wingfoot Lake. During these early years, the navy trained army and navy

82 Thomas Q. O'Hara. Marine Corps Air Station Miramar. Charleston: Arcadia Publishing, 2005, 13-14.

airship pilots at Goodyear's Wingfoot facility. By the end of the war, the navy operated twenty "B-type" blimps (84,000 cubic feet; single engine) from east coast bases, mostly on training missions but also on patrol operations.[83] The navy also ordered ten "C-type" blimps (181,000 cubic feet; twin engine) that were delivered late in 1918, too late for war use; these were used mostly as experimental vehicles.[84]

The Germans, French, and Italians all used airships for scouting and tactical bombing roles early in the war, and all sides soon learned that the airship was too vulnerable for operations over the front. Germany used airships made by the Zeppelin Company, which was founded by Count Ferdinand von Zeppelin, a retired German Army officer. Many in the German military believed they had found the ideal weapon with which to counteract British naval superiority and strike at Britain itself. More realistic airship advocates believed the Zeppelin's value was as a long-range scout/attack craft for naval operations. Raids on England began in January 1915 and peaked in 1916. Following losses to the British defenses, only a few raids were made from 1917 to 1918, the last occurring in August 1918. Zeppelins proved to be terrifying but inaccurate weapons. Navigation, target selection, and bomb-aiming proved to be difficult under the best of conditions, and the cloud cover that was frequently encountered by the airships reduced accuracy even further. The physical damage done by airships over the course of the war was insignificant, and the deaths that they caused amounted to a few

83 "B-class Blimp." Wikipedia. June 5, 2016.

84 "C-class Blimp." Wikipedia. September 5, 2016.

hundred. Nevertheless, the raid caused a significant diversion of British resources to defense efforts. The airships were initially immune to attack by aircraft and antiaircraft guns; as the pressure in their envelopes was only just higher than ambient air, holes had little effect. But following the introduction of a combination of incendiary and explosive ammunition in 1916, their flammable hydrogen lifting-gas made them vulnerable to the defending airplanes. Several were shot down in flames by British defenders, and many others were destroyed in accidents. The British Army had abandoned airship development in favor of airplanes by the start of the war, but the Royal Navy had recognized the need for small airships to counteract the submarine and mine threat in coastal waters. During the war, the British operated over two hundred non-rigid airships. British blimps were used for scouting, mine clearance, and convoy patrol duties.[85]

In his letter, the Minnesota farm boy was most likely referring to airplanes. During that period, both the army and navy were training pilots out of San Diego's North Island. In 1911, the famous aviator, Glenn Curtiss, opened a flying school on the island and began teaching military and civilian pilots how to fly. The first seaplane flight was demonstrated during that period. In 1914, another famous aviator, Glenn Martin, demonstrated his "pusher" aircraft over the island. This flight included the first parachute jump in the San Diego area, made by a ninety-pound civilian woman named Tiny Broadwick. In 1917, the government appropriated the land of North Island and commissioned two airfields, Rockwell Field (Army) and Naval Air Station (NAS)

85 "Airship." Wikipedia. September 30, 2016.

San Diego (Navy). The navy started with a small tent-covered city known as "Camp Trouble," but both bases grew quickly, as permanent buildings were soon constructed. By 1918, the army at Rockwell Field had 497 airplanes and over one hundred officers. NAS San Diego boasted 76 officers, 110 student officers, and 1,571 enlisted men.[86]

The United States had established the Aeronautical Division of the U.S. Army Signal Corps in 1907 which became part of the Aviation Section of the Signal Corps established in July 1914, a predecessor to the United States Air Force. The Aeronautical Division purchased its first aircraft in 1909 from the Wright brothers, the Wright A Military Flyer. The division set up schools to train aviators and initiated a rating system to qualify pilots. In the next few years, the Aeronautical Division purchased and tested experimental airplanes from the Wright brothers, Glenn Curtiss, and Burgess Company and Curtis, Inc., a company that had received a license to build Wright aircraft.[87]

The U.S. Navy developed an early interest in aviation, leading to an appointed aviation officer by 1910. Significantly, on November 14, 1910, one of Curtiss' pilots, Eugene Ely, made the first takeoff from a warship, the cruiser *Birmingham*, anchored near Hampton Roads, Virginia, in the Curtiss Hudson Flyer. On January 18, 1911, he made the first carrier landing onto a 125-foot platform on the warship *Pennsylvania*, anchored in San Francisco

86 Aldrich, Mark, and Pescador, Katrina, *Images of Aviation, San Diego's North Island 1911-1941*, Arcadia Publishing, 2007, pg 7

87 "Aeronautical Division, U.S. Signal Corps." Wikipedia. September 23, 2016.

Bay.[88] With these achievements, the navy ordered Lieutenant Theodore Ellyson to Curtiss' aviation camp. In 1911, the U.S. Navy bought its first airplane, a Curtiss A-1 Triad, thereby launching the roots of naval aviation.[89]

In 1917 when America declared war, the military leaders in Washington envisioned the grandest air armada the world had ever seen. The First Aero Squadron accompanied the Big Red One to France in August 1917 and began training at the Avord French aviation school.[90] The figurehead of the American aviation effort was Colonel William "Billy" Mitchell, a brash and outspoken Spanish-American War veteran fascinated with aviation who had learned to fly on weekends at his own expense. He served in the Aviation Section of the Army Signal Corp.

In July 1917, the House of Representatives passed a $640 million appropriation bill for aircraft design, development, and production. This act was the largest piece of legislation in the country's history. Unfortunately, the aircraft manufacturing process at that time required hand craftsmanship that was prohibitive to rapid mass production. In addition, America lacked the experience and resources to reliably produce the aircraft. Consequently, the limited number of American-manufactured aircraft that were delivered to France proved to be unsafe in the field. As a result, more than eighty percent of all U.S. Air Service pilots were flying French-manufactured aircraft

88 "Eugene Burton Ely." Wikipedia. February 4, 2016.

89 100 Years of Naval Aviation." Air and Space Magazine, March 2011.

90 "1st Reconnaissance Squadron." Wikipedia. September 17, 2016.

by the end of the war.[91] Although the Americans were the last to enter the conflict, their pilots became one of the more successful flying groups. Led by Captain Eddie Rickenbacker with twenty-six confirmed victories and Lieutenant Frank Luke with twenty-one, the Americans racked up a notable victory total during the summer and autumn of 1918.[92]

Meanwhile, training at Camp Kearny was intense as the United States continued its mad scramble to put troops into action on the European Front. "Received our rifles the other day and go out drilling with arms every day," Dick wrote on Thursday, June 27. "Have to know all parts of the rifle. There are 86 parts on the army rifle. Got to be cleaned every day. Received our bayonets, too."

The rifle to which Dick referred was most likely the M1917 U.S. Enfield although the exact parts count of eighty-six parts could not be verified. As with most of the other needed resources and equipment, the country was immediately faced with a serious shortage of service rifles when President Wilson declared war. The official military service rifle was the .30-06 M1903 Springfield which was adopted in 1903. The Springfield was a clip-loaded, five-round magazine-fed, bolt-action rifle that could fire at a rate of twenty shots per minute. It was 44⅞ inches long and weighed eight pounds, eleven ounces. A bayonet could be attached; the M1905 bayonet blade was sixteen inches long

91 Raul Colon. "The American Air Effort." Century of Flight. 2009.

92 Raul Colon. "The End of the German Air Offensive on the Western Front." Century of Flight. January 25, 2009.

and weighed one pound.[93] In April 1917, the government had approximately 600,000 Springfields on hand, along with some 160,000 obsolescent Krag-Jørgensen rifles, numbers vastly insufficient to meet the projected demand. The Springfields were manufactured at the Springfield Armory in Springfield, Massachusetts, and the Rock Island Arsenal in Illinois. When U.S. Ordnance Department personnel consulted with Springfield and Rock Island engineers for ways to reduce production time and cost for M1903 manufacture without a substantial redesign, it became apparent that the M1903 could not be mass-produced by these two national arsenals in a timely fashion to meet demand. The Ordnance Department had no choice but to procure an alternate rifle.

This activity resulted in the manufacture of the M1917 Enfield, a modification of the "Pattern 1914" Enfield rifles that American plants had produced under contract to Great Britain prior to America's entrance into the war. The M1917 had to be modified so that it could fire the same standard military .30-06 cartridge as the Springfield. The workforces and production machinery used to manufacture the Pattern 1914 were still in place; thus, the firms could almost immediately go into production for the U.S. government. The manufacturers were: Winchester Repeating Arms Co., New Haven, Connecticut; Remington Arms Company, Ilion, New York; and Eddystone Rifle Plant, operated by Midvale Steel & Ordnance Co., an affiliate of Remington located in Eddystone, Pennsylvania. These rifles were commonly known as "Eddystones."

93 "M1903 Springfield." Wikipedia. September 27, 2016.

The M1917 was 46.3 inches in overall length with a 26 inch barrel. It weighed eight pounds, three ounces and had a magazine capacity of six rounds. The rear sight had a folding leaf adjustable for elevation but not windage. The stock and two-piece handguard were made of oil-finished black walnut with grasping grooves milled into both sides of the fore-end. Most of the external metal parts were blued.[94] The vast majority of the American infantry trained with the Enfield due to its availability.

"Well we have to be broke in in one third the time that the last bunch was trained in," Dick went on to write. "We have to get up one half hour earlier on account of that. We get up every morning at 4:30 and have breakfast at 5:00." In his first target test, Dick received a score of twenty out of twenty-five at two hundred yards. He was proud of that. On July 10, he wrote, "Was on the range yesterday. Qualified alright the first time. Had to make 105 points to qualify, and I made 124 out of 150 and today we had different positions. Had to make 95 and I made 104. My name is on the bulletin to go again tomorrow. I think we will go every day this week." Two days later: "Were on the range all day. Had our dinner on the field. Don't know if we will go tomorrow. I qualified every day. Only two done so yesterday, a fellow from Sleepy Eye and me from our company."

That same day, Dick relates the consequences of the firing range. "My watch is on the bum now. It does not run at all now. It run good all the time and kept good time too. The bumps from the rifle probably put it out of commission. Some guys have their

94 Reprinted with permission of the author, Bruce N. Canfield. "The Model 1917 U.S. Enfield." American Rifleman. April 19, 2012.

shoulders black and green from the bumps." Later in a letter to his mother, he said, "My watch is on the bum. I think I will send it home for it costs too much to fix here although it would not cost much to get it fixed there. Most everyone has a wrist watch and everyone has a broken watch too. It is too much rough work for it to stick out on the arm. Nearly everyone had the crystal broke but I haven't broke mine yet. Don't wear it while it don't run."

But sore shoulders and broken watches were of little consequence to the United States Army that summer of 1918 as the demands only increased. "We were on the range today," Dick wrote on July 16. "Had Table No. 7. One more to make. Qualified on every one so far. Most of them have to shoot each table over 3 to 4 times. We shot 500 and 600 yards today. The bulls eye gets to look pretty small at that distance. It is about again as far as from the house to the road. We need 50 out of 100 to qualify. I got 55. My name is not on the bulletin for tomorrow so I don't know what I will do. I will have to do something. I don't worry any that I won't have anything to do. They sure drill us hard while we are here yet." Nevertheless, Dick enjoyed the target practice. "That range business is sport," he wrote.

As in Camp Lewis, Dick was not sure when they would ship out. "I don't think we will be here very long as they are getting us ready in a hurry. We are getting harder boiled every day." The intense activities led to casualties, both physical and psychological. "There was a guy run over with a truck Sunday morning and he was dead Sunday. They shipped him out Sunday and the same day a guy cut his throat with a razor only a little ways from here.

The boys all took a hike when he was lying on the floor. I heard from the sergeant there was another case like that today."

And there was the Southern California habitat. "We are going in the hills and brush some day and catch centipedes. They are about 5 to 8 inches long and have 100 legs and are poisonous too. They killed quite a few rattlesnakes here. Our officer killed one with 14 rattles. There are quite a few of those spiders too. Pour a little water in the hole and stick in a little stick and he will bite himself on the stick and pull him out. We were out there a little while this morning."

The rigorous training inflamed an old sprain in Dick's left ankle which he had incurred prior to his army service. "Well it is past 6:30 now. Just called us out for examination. They caught me on my foot to nite. I never told or said anything about my foot that I sprained in Prinsburg on the Fourth of July. It bothered me quite a little when I go out drilling for a long stretch. I came up to the doctor and he said does your foot ever bother you. I was surprised and I told him yes. I thought he had a pretty keen eye. I asked him which one to see which one he meant and he told me the right one alright. He put my name down and I think I will have to report again in a few days. I looked at my foot when I got out. Couldn't see very much on it. Only it was puffed a little below the left outside ankle." Since Dick was writing this letter on June 27, the original sprain in Prinsburg must have occurred a year earlier.

On July 5, he was again examined. "I was called to the foot specialist today and he put something on my papers but I don't know what. It is blowing out on the left ankle. It bothers quite a little sometimes. Never thought about anything on my foot." Dick never mentioned his foot problem again. There was no mention of any sort of treatment. Either the sprain got better, or Dick decided to live with it.

Dick lamented on differences between Camp Kearny and Camp Lewis. "We have three moving picture shows and Vaudeville and a skating rink, but what I miss is the Depot Brigade Band. That sure was a band. We don't have much music here in Camp Kearny. We got up with music and went to bed with music, but I never got tired of that. They sure had the music at Camp Lewis. Nearly all day long." The sprained ankle did not stop Dick from trying something new. "Was on the skating rink for the first time but didn't tumble once. Many a one fell and one broke his wrist. Looks pretty dangerous. Go about 15 mile an hour. After I was on the floor 15 minutes I could hold my end up. There are from 100 to 300 on the floor. The floor is just like glass. Music all the time. Go one way for a while and then reverse. Going like 60 all the time."

"It gets dark here about one and a half hours earlier than in Washington and doesn't get light so early either," the Minnesota native observed. "We get up at 5:15 and we need lamps to see. It is cloudy every forenoon till about nine or ten o'clock. The sun is straight overhead at noon. That seems funny at first."

On July 2, Dick received his monthly pay. "We had payday today. I got $26.40. Have $23 left from the start. Haven't spent as much here as in Camp Lewis. It took quite a lot there."

The Fourth of July was a holiday at the camp. The troops were allowed to go to San Diego, but Dick decided to stay. "We are going to have a holiday here Thursday and if we want to go we will have to get a pass to nite from the Lieutenant but I don't think I will go because it will be so crowded there and we can't see nothing. Some of my tent chums and I are going to try and go Saturday nite and stay there till Sunday nite. Then we can see more."

On July 5, the camp staged a grand ceremony in a rousing salute to Independence Day. "We had a Regimental Parade to nite with the colors. You just should have seen it. We had four bands on the parade grounds and the officers were on horseback. There were quite a few thousand out there. I just would like to have a picture of that. The boys had played so long that they had blisters on their hands and busted them on the end." Again, on July 10: "Had a parade with the colors and band last nite at five o'clock. The other companies were all around our company and we had to do the marching and distinct acts. We have got quite a swift company only there are about six or seven in the bunch that are very slow and that knocks the whole bunch." Would it be safe to assume that the slow ones were made well aware of their shortcomings?

The primary method of correspondence continued to be the handwritten letter, which Dick often wrote at night after his evening meal or before he went to bed. In return, Dick received many letters of support from his large family including brothers, sisters, aunts, uncles, and cousins as well as his girlfriend, Tetje. On July 10 he wrote, "Received a letter from you yesterday and also from George Roelofs. Got two letters and two cards from Camp Lewis and a card from Aunt Senia. Some of the letters come pretty slow. Had one from Aunt Cobie and Nettie also."

A mother never stops cooking for her son. "I will thank you for that box of candy that you sent me. It is better than what we get here." And there was more. "Received the $20 yesterday and many thanks for same." It is not clear why his parents felt the need to send Dick money. He did not request money in his letters or indicate a need as the army provided ample room and board, and the Bakkers certainly did not have money to spare. Perhaps it was merely the parents' concern about their child in an unknown and dangerous world. His mother asked if he would get a furlough, hoping that she would get to see him before he went abroad, but that was not to be in the hurried summer of 1918.

A networking mechanism formed that kept track of the wellbeing and whereabouts of the local boys in the service through the family letter exchanges, letters between the boys themselves, local newspapers, and word of mouth. Dick continued to receive his local paper, the *Star Farmer*, which carried the news of the local boys in the war. Then, as now, people bond together when fighting a common enemy. "Heard that Henry Raske was sick. He is still in Camp Dodge. So George Groen and Hermann Freiborg are on their way to France. I didn't get an answer from Hermann, so I thought he was on his way. Too bad. George dreaded to go. It is hard for a boy like that." No one was spared the bad news: "Suppose Palmer Adwell's folks are pretty sad about him being killed. He was a nice little scout. I have played quite a few games of pool with him. Well there will be many more if the war keeps on like it is doing. I just as soon go today as later on. I am waiting to be moved again. When I see those long trains come and go, I feel just like getting out and go again." Later he wrote, "There was a fellow here to see me. He was a friend of H. M. His name was Jans. He knew Swanette also but I told him it did not do him any good see. I don't think Henry likes camp life very good. Jans let me read his letter he got from him. I sooner be away farther than where he is to home. His folks and friends come to see him often and then he feels lost."

After the daily drills, the troops' education continued. "Just got back. Seven-twenty now. He lectured on first aid package. That is a package we carry on our belt every day. It consists of bandages and safety pins for wound in the battle front. It keeps the wounds clean." Other lectures focused on the consequences of succumbing to the vices that often tempted the young American men, namely alcohol, drugs, and prostitution. From past wars, the administration was fully aware that brothels as well as illegal drug and alcohol activities soon sprang up around troop encampments such as those erected for World War I, bringing on public resentment and outcry. From the beginning, a program was put in place to improve the soldier's welfare during his leisure hours. This program was responsible for installing organizations such as the YMCA and the Knights of Columbus on each of the bases and setting up sports and entertainment programs so that the troops would be encouraged to stay on the bases during their leisure time.

As they were so inclined, the War Department launched yet another propaganda campaign to educate the young soldier, whom they deemed to be remarkably ignorant about sex. The resulting posters were once again hard-hitting and aimed at the young men's sense of guilt and fear. One poster read, "A German bullet is cleaner than a whore." Another announced, "You wouldn't use another man's toothbrush. Why use his whore?" [95] The troops were especially vulnerable in war-ravaged Europe, where the liquor flowed freely, cocaine was sold like candy, and the ladies of the night waged their own war of survival. Since August 1914, the British Armed Forces and the French had registered one million venereal casualties of which 200,000 were syphilitic.[96] Initially, when General Pershing heard of young American boys being infected at a high rate in the town of Saint-Nazaire, the Iron Commander made a personal visit to the town and administered the blunt of his wrath upon the mayor. The town woke up to find armed Doughboys with fixed bayonets standing in front of brothels and saloons while military police dogged streetwalkers. Pershing put Hugh Hampton Young, a genitourinary surgeon from John Hopkins, in charge of keeping the troops healthy. Condoms were given to troops going on leave, and catching venereal disease was a made a punishable offense. As a result, the venereal rate fell to eleven new cases per year among a thousand Doughboys, an incidence never before known in any great army or civilian population in western Christendom.[97]

There is no evidence that Dick Bakker, the straight-laced Minnesota farm boy, ever succumbed to these temptations. The army training program was quite successful in keeping him occupied on the base. His only vice: "I smoked one cigarette while

95 Meirion Harries and Susie Harries. *The Last Days of Innocence: America at War, 1917-1918*. New York: Vintage Books, 1997, 139.

96 Laurence Stallings. *The Doughboys: The Story of the AEF, 1917-1918*. New York: Harper and Row, 1963, 180.

97 Ibid., 181.

in camp. I got that from a Red Cross girl or lady in Bakersfield, California. I did not want to pass it up see." Confessions of a country boy...

There were shortages at Camp Kearny as there were at Camp Lewis. Dick writes, "Will have off Saturday afternoon. Don't think I am going to San Diego for I have no cotton pants yet nor good shoes. I didn't send my blanket home. I thought I better keep it for I got only 2 blankets at Camp Lewis and the others got three. That was a mistake." Finally, on July 10, eighteen days after he arrived: "Well, I got two more pair of cotton pants and my identification tags. They left out the D in my first name so I sent it back but have got it on now." They gave him an identification tag that said "ick Bakker?" Apparently, no one was checking for accuracy.

Dick had pictures taken at each of the camps and sent them home. On July 10, he wrote, "I think I will have my picture taken pretty soon and then I will send one. I might look strange with my hair cut short." Later, to his mother: "Was over to the studio to see my proofs. They are fair. Have six with blouse and hat on and six without and one enlarged with it for seven dollars. I will send the poorest one home. The proof that I think is the poorest anyhow. They will be ready by the 25th. Will send the address. If I should go before they are ready then you can write to him. I paid him out. He said he will send them, Hartsook Studio, Pacific Center, Camp Kearny, California." The proofs were indeed ready on the twenty-fifth. From a letter dated July 26: "Sending home some more pictures yet. Give P. Freiborgs one of the postal pictures if you have one left. Give M.J.B one of the folders and H. Jalso and Heye and Reka one of the folders too. Give Grandma one and I wrote to Tetje she could get two if she wanted them and so do that. Don't give them all away." These pictures have been preserved and are still kept by the Bakker family today as treasured mementos of this brave soldier.

Private First Class Dick W. Bakker

World War I was well-photographed. Film photography had advanced to the point where cameras were lightweight enough that the field photographers could keep pace with troop movements. While color film was available, most of the pictures were taken in black and white. However, a great portion of the battlefield shots were censured at the time for fear that they would divulge troop positions and critical information to the enemy. After the war, many of these photographs were released and published.

World War I was the first war in which aerial photography was widely utilized. At the start of the war, airplanes flew reconnaissance missions with an observer who drew sketches and took notes of enemy positions. However, it was found that the observers did not always report situations accurately and that photographs were much more reliable. One humorous incidence relates that a German aerial observer reported back that an English unit was running around haphazardly in total disarray. Later, it was revealed that he was observing a soccer game!

A soldier's duties were many. "Was on detail of fatigue to fix gas masks but when we got there, they had too many men already so we were dismissed and then I done up my washing this afternoon. Think I will send it to the laundry after this." On Sunday, July 21: "Am on guard duty today but don't have to walk post. On guard at the Finance Division guarding the safes and papers for the government. Have my five-shooter loaded all the time. Is a fine place here. Off at 5:30 this evening, came on 5:30 Saturday evening."

The five-shooter to which Dick referred was most likely the Smith and Wesson model known as the "Lemon Squeezer" or the "Safety Hammerless." The piece was a double-action, top-breaking revolver that was chambered in either a 0.32 S&W or 0.38 S&W calibers. They were produced with two-inch, three-inch, and three-and-a-half-inch barrels. Production began in the late 1880s and was discontinued just before World War II. Minor changes were made over the years, resulting in several different design models.[98]

As could be expected, the question of the day was when the division was scheduled to ship out for France. Rumors ran rampant as soldiers tried to piece together clues that would give them the answer. From Dick's letter of July 10: "All the canteens will be closed by August 1st so we cannot get any candy on anything in that line." He further wrote, "By the way, I heard from a lieutenant yesterday we will be going to England in August." On July 12: "I think we will be going pretty soon to England. It is on the bulletin today all boys that are off for furlough to come to camp at once. So you can imagine it won't be long. The last we heard we are going to England."

Again on July 16 in a letter addressed only to Mother Grace: "I think we will be going about within 12 days by the way I heard. Today everyone had to dispose of the suitcases if they had any at once and we moved in other tents to nite. Are getting some more new men today. I think we will have to make another hike yet before we go. I will write if I can when we go if I get beware of it soon enough. I think we will get some gas training yet too. We have to go all the time. I haven't heard lately where we are going. The papers stated from San Diego that they wanted men in Russia and probably men from Camp Kearny and Camp Lewis would be going so I don't know where we will be going. Uncle Sam changes his mind quick. When he calls we have to go quick and I am ready to face anything that turns up I any way so don't worry about me for I can help myself in every respectful way of mind and manner and courage. Also that is the whole game of life.

98 "Smith & Wesson Safety Hammerless." Wikipedia. July 28, 2016.

A soldier in war time is alright for it has to be but soldier in peace time I would not be see. I know we will have some hardships over there but am willing to take them at any moment." Thoughtful words, indeed, to a worried mother.

On July 21, Dick wrote, "Was working with the quartermasters yesterday. They are sorting all the clothes and packing them. They are working double-time here all the time. Are boxing up today also. Don't know if I will go to church to nite for I did not get to bed at all till 1:30 last nite when I was relieved. There was a pretty sober bunch around here yesterday afternoon. All the girls and parents that were here. They always are on liberty days. There were quite a few tears rolling I tell you. They know we are going across pretty sudden." Sending loved ones to war. Gut wrenching.

The Fortieth Division started departing Camp Kearny for the east coast and France on July 23, 1918, on a series of trains each leaving quietly, sometimes in the middle of the night, with no public notice or fanfare.[99] Dick Bakker's train departed on July 28. In a letter home, Dick noted that at least one train left after his. Records indicate that the Seventy-Ninth Brigade was the last to leave during the period from July 29 to July 31. As was the practice at Camp Lewis, troop movements were concealed from the public as a precaution to prevent sabotage or violence from those opposed to the war. Even the San Diego newspapers cooperated by writing as if the division was still at Camp Kearny. But in stark reality, Private First Class Dick W. Bakker was headed for combat...with two months' training.

99 *History of the Fortieth (Sunshine) Division; Containing a Brief History of All Units Under the Command of Major General Frederick S. Strong, 1917-1919.* Los Angeles: C.S. Hutson, 1920. September 2, 2008.

Chapter 10

Across Country

July 28, 1918

"On the way to the east coast somewhere. Left Camp Kearny at 12 o'clock. Have been riding along the Pacific shore for quite a while. Some locals just threw some oranges into the windows when we stopped. Is very dry here but a cold breeze from the Pacific. We have lots to carry along. Was on guard duty last night. Guarded the kitchen car. You know there is a lot of food stuffs in those cars. Corn looks pretty dry here. We have sleepers this time and am glad of it too. You will get my new address in a few days when we know where we are going from here. The cactuses are standing thick on the hillsides here. Will write some more tomorrow. As ever, your Son and Bro, DWBakker."

Dick Bakker was no longer the wide-eyed recruit that rode with his head out the window in the Rocky Mountains of Idaho and Montana. With his basic training completed, Dick was now a member of an infantry team headed for an unknown combat mission. He had excelled on the firing range, calmly shooting at a four-foot-square target with an eight-inch bull's-eye at distances up to six hundred yards. His M1903 Springfield was now as familiar to the farm boy as a garden rake. But a stationery bull's-eye does not resemble a live human enemy in battle.

Studies suggest that most men question their performance as they approach combat for the first time. "Hero or coward?" is the unspoken question that mulls in every soldier's mind. Military basic training develops exceptionally strong bonds between team members. Dick Bakker slept in a tent with four other soldiers. It is likely that these five were an assigned team. As a rule, two teams comprise a squad. They trained, ate, slept, and took their leaves together. They were constant companions for two months, supporting each other during the hardships of drill. Undoubtedly, there was some kind of graduation ritual before departure that welcomed them into the fraternity of infantrymen. As fraternity brothers, these were the men that Dick Bakker would trust at his side in battle. Conversely, to let them down was unthinkable.

It would be reasonable to assume that the train ride was a time for reflection and anticipation for Dick Bakker as he began his journey to France. There were many questions to ponder: How will I fare in battle? Will there be exploits that earn ribbons and decorations? Will I be commended for bravery in hometown newspapers? Will I be able to perform at the levels expected of me? Will I earn the respect of my team members and leaders? Will I be able to take a human life? Most likely, some form of these questions materialized in Dick Bakker's mind more than once as he endured a long slow train ride to the east coast.

If any fears were churning inside, the stress never appeared in Dick's letters, although he did hint at a touch of homesickness. "Received 5 letters on the train today. Got that $10 bill also. One from Uncle John and Aunt and one from Reka and one from Tetje and one from John R. Two from home. Will send those pictures home for I can not keep them anyhow. I saw Ike Habben last night. I did not know he was there. He was there a week. He looks good and was surprised to see me. Sounds natural to ride in the man trains again. Don't know which route we will take or are going. Have quite a long ride over 3000 miles. On the way would like to ride through Old Minn once again."

The task of transporting a twenty-eight-thousand-man division across country was no trivial effort in those days, given the condition of the railroads and the shortage of resources. With the division departure spread over at least eight days, it would be reasonable to assume that each train was transporting a few thousand troops with their associated food, water, supplies, equipment, ammunition, and weapons. For the most part, units were transported intact under the direction and watch of their commanding officers. The nominal size of an infantry regiment was thirty-eight hundred men. From that standpoint, it is likely that Dick's train was transporting the 160th Infantry Regiment. This size load would have been near maximum capacity for a reasonably sized train of that era. In spite of the administration's efforts to conceal troop movements, troop trains were fairly conspicuous, as evidenced by locals tossing oranges through Dick Bakker's window and girls waiting with flowers and magazines on Dick's ride from Camp Lewis to Camp Kearny. Any spy with reasonable capabilities would have been able to provide information on troop movements.

The train was following the Southern Transcon, a main line between Southern California and Chicago that was originally constructed by the Atchison, Topeka, and Santa Fe Railway in the eighteen-eighties. From San Diego, the train travelled up the Pacific coast through Santa Ana, San Bernardino, and the Cajon Pass to Barstow. Dick was riding along the Pacific Coast when he wrote his first letter. He observed corn fields and cactus in the hills, which indicates that he was writing the letter in daylight hours. With a distance of a little over one hundred miles between San Bernardino and San Diego, it would be reasonable to assume that the train could make the trip in two to three hours. Dick stated that they left Camp Kearny at midnight. Doing the math, this timetable seems to imply that the troops spent four to five hours loading the train with the vast amount of equipment and supplies required to maintain an army regiment, taking roll, getting car and guard duty assignments, and doing whatever was necessary to cover their activities before departing.

From Barstow, the train meandered through the Mojave Desert, crossing the Colorado River into Arizona at Needles, California. Dick observed, "It was hot there and rough. Not many people." Indeed, the Southwest deserts in the months of July and August can blister one's soul, especially if one is riding without air conditioning! After crossing the Colorado, the train climbed into the high desert regions of Arizona, passing through Flagstaff and across the Continental Divide on into Albuquerque. One would have to believe that water was a cherished resource during those first few days of the trip with several thousand thirsty troopers.

From Albuquerque, the train turned north through Santa Fe into the mountains and crossed into Colorado through a tunnel that Dick described as a mile and a half long. The tunnel to which Dick referred would be the Raton Tunnel that connects Raton,

New Mexico, with Trinidad, Colorado. There were actually two tunnels at the time Dick's train passed through Raton Pass, a part of the old Santa Fe Trail. The first tunnel had been dug in the late 1800s when the rail line was first established. The second tunnel had been added in 1908 to enhance the flow of rail traffic. Both tunnels were actually about a half-mile long at an altitude of a little over seventy-six hundred feet.[100] Trains approaching the tunnels from either side encountered steep grades, which undoubtedly would have required several engines to pull the fully loaded troop train through the tunnel. Most likely, the train was divided into sections, as was the case of Dick Bakker's train travelling through the Oregon Mountains. Perhaps the slow moving train made the tunnel seem "a mile and a half long" to Dick Bakker.

After making it through the Raton Pass, the train went on through Colorado. "When we got farther in Colorado, it sure was a pretty country and the people in Colorado were the best we struck so far." The train continued on through Kansas, stopping in Kansas City. "They were threshing and plowing there. Had a bath in Kansas City in the plunge." A plunge bath is defined as one where a person's body is fully submerged in water. The plunge bath facilities of that era must have resembled our modern swimming pools. One can only imagine the melee that occurred when a few thousand troops stormed the plunge bath facility after several days on a train through the dusty Southwest deserts and mountains.

With clean, refreshed troops, the train continued into Missouri. Dick wrote, "That was a good state. A good corn crop

100 "Southern Transcon." Wikipedia. June 7, 2016.

there." From Missouri, the train travelled briefly through Iowa, crossing the Mississippi River at Fort Madison and continuing on through Galesburg and into Chicago. Dick's view of Illinois: "They had big crop there, corn and oats." The train arrived in Chicago on the first of August, approximately four days after leaving San Diego. The average distance travelled per day would have been around five hundred miles, assuming a travelling distance of two thousand miles between Chicago and San Diego. Per Dick's letters, the train stopped every fifty miles or so, and the troops were let out every morning and evening for exercise. Assuming a daily stoppage time of around seven hours, the average train speed was in the neighborhood of thirty miles per hour. Undoubtedly, traversing the Rocky Mountains took a great deal of time with the underpowered locomotives of that era. Dick noted that the train picked up speed once they hit the central plains. While these calculations are rough approximations, it does give one a sense of the speed of travel. It was not exactly the *Super Chief*.

The Southern Transcon route terminated at the Dearborn Street Station in the heart of downtown Chicago near Lake Michigan. Dearborn Street was the oldest Chicago passenger terminal, having served the city since the 1880s, with seven different railroads operating from the terminal in that summer of 1918, the most prominent being the Santa Fe. The troops were let out for three hours, where Dick went for a good walk. The country boy's comment on Chicago: "It sure is a big city." Before leaving, Dick wrote a few lines to his parents on a postcard provided by the Red Cross describing his trip to that point. Dick also noted that he received some cigarettes and some candy as part of the Red Cross package. The postcard was the first correspondence that Dick had sent his parents since the first day on the train. Unlike his previous train rides, there was no mention of having a frivolous good time such as playing poker or marching through towns singing songs to the locals.

Chicago was the closest location to Dick's family on his trip across country. With the speed of mail in that time period, Dick was long gone before they received the postcard. One can only speculate if the family would have tried to meet him in Chicago if they had known his destination ahead of time, given that it was the height of the farming season in Minnesota. By August first, the crops were in, and the wheat crop, the precious commodity for shipping overseas, was near ready for harvesting. Field work consisted mainly of cultivating the crops to keep the weeds down. In the meantime, the men readied equipment for the fall harvest while performing their daily chores. There was never a dull moment during farming season.

After the three hour stop in Chicago, the troops boarded a train operated as part of the Grand Trunk Railway (GTR) and continued their trip to the east coast. The GTR began operations in 1852 and operated more than 1,100 miles of lines in the United States and another 8,000 lines in Canada by the early twentieth century.[101] Today, the GTR is known as the Grand Trunk Western Railroad, a subsidiary of the Canadian National Railway. After leaving Chicago, the train chugged through the northern part of Indiana and on into Michigan. Ever the farm boy, Dick noted that

101 "The Grand Trunk Western Railroad." American Rails.

the crops were good in Indiana but only fair in Michigan. The train rumbled through Battle Creek, where Dick wrote home that he saw the corn flake company along the route. Indeed, the corn flake company now known as Kellogg's was thriving quite nicely in that summer of 1918, producing Corn Flakes, Bran Flakes, and All-Bran. Formed in 1906 by Will Keith Kellogg as the Battle Creek Toasted Corn Flake Company, the firm was successfully operating throughout the United States and Canada. The company outlasted over forty cereal companies that were launched in the United States during that period.[102]

In the same letter, Dick noted that he saw the Red River Special Threshing Machine factory. The Red River Special was being built by the Nichols and Shepard Company in Battle Creek and was advertised as the only threshing machine that actually beat the grain out of the straw whereas other threshing machines just shook the straw on the principle that the grain would fall out. The marketing pitch was that the farmer would collect substantially more grain with the Red River Special. An efficient threshing machine was undoubtedly in high demand during the World War I period with the government enforcing wheatless days and prices rising rapidly due to shortages and inflation.

John Nichols and David Shepard developed their first threshing machine in the 1850s; it used a vibrator to separate the grain from the straw. Nichols and Shepard received a patent for the vibrator concept in 1862 and introduced their Red River Special line of threshers around 1900. They became quite popular. By the

102 Richard Cavendish. "The Battle of the Cornflakes." *History Today*, February 2006.

summer of 1918, the Nichols and Shepard factory in Battle Creek covered approximately forty acres, manufacturing the Red River Special thresher along with a variety of other farm implements. The company had branch offices in most of the grain-growing states and in Canada. The Nichols and Shepard Company was acquired by the Oliver Farm Equipment Company in 1929.[103]

The train continued through Michigan, reaching the town of Port Huron, where the steam engines were replaced with electric-powered locomotives. The troops were then pulled through a tunnel beneath the St. Clair River into the town of Sarnia, Ontario. The St. Clair Tunnel, now a U.S. National Historic Landmark, first opened in 1891 and was considered an engineering marvel in its day. The GTR began using electric locomotives in 1908 over concerns of suffocation should a train stall in the tunnel.[104] Dick described the tunnel as three miles long when in fact it was a little over a mile long, leading one to believe that perhaps he was not the best judge of distance.

Back on steam-powered locomotives, the train continued on through Canada stopping at the town of London, Ontario, where the troops toured a munitions factory. As part of the British Empire, Canada went to war in August 1914, when Germany ignored Britain's ultimatum to remove their troops from Belgium. The Canadian economy went through similar issues as the United States in the financing and manufacturing of munitions, supplies, and equipment to support the war effort. Between 1913 and 1918, Canada's national debt rose from $463 million to $2.46 billion.

103 "Nichols and Shephard." Wikipedia. September 7, 2016.

104 "St. Clair Tunnel." Wikipedia. September 7, 2016.

Shortages occurred, which caused the Canadian Government to administer rationing while inflation ran rampant. Vast exports of wheat, timber, and munitions helped to sustain the economy. During the war period, munitions became Canada's biggest business headed by a British agency titled Imperial Munitions Board (IMB). Early in the war, Britain incurred a shortage of artillery shells, which resulted in Canada implementing munitions factories to fulfill the need.[105] With the men serving in the army, the shell factories were staffed almost entirely with women who worked in the machine shop and performed many of the heavy-lifting tasks normally assigned to men.

The train steamed on through Canada and crossed back into the United States, stopping at the city of Niagara Falls, New York, where the troops were let out for exercise. Overall, Dick was impressed with his trip through Canada. "A fine country and quite a bit of fruit, too." Dick wrote of his hike to the falls, "That was the prettiest scenery I have seen yet so far. We walked about two miles to the falls. It rained light when we came within a quarter of a mile. From the speed it fell on the rocks, it sure was worth seeing and a very pretty city."

Dick also noted that he saw the Shredded Wheat Company. Shredded Wheat was the invention of Henry Perky of Denver, Colorado. In 1892, he took his idea of a product made of boiled wheat to his friend, William H. Ford, a machinist by trade, in Watertown, NY. Here they developed a machine for making biscuits, which Perky called "little whole wheat mattresses." The

105 Desmond Morton. "First World War (WWI)." The Canadian Encyclopedia. June 17, 2015.

biscuits were then baked, creating a dry cereal which would keep. Perky's original intention was to sell the machines, not the biscuits. He returned to Denver and began distributing the biscuits from a horse-drawn wagon in an attempt to popularize the idea. The company he formed was known at the time as The Cereal Machine Company. The biscuits proved more popular than the machines, however, so Perky moved back East and opened his first bakery in Boston and then in Worcester, Massachusetts, in 1895, retaining the name of The Cereal Machine Company and adding the name of The Shredded Wheat Company. By 1901, drawn by the idea of an inexpensive form of power for baking and the natural draw of a popular tourist attraction, he moved his company to Niagara Falls, New York. There it was first known as The Natural Food Company. The factory itself was called "The Palace of Light" and was white-tiled, air-conditioned, well-lit, and equipped with showers, lunchrooms, and auditoriums for the employees. In 1908, the company again took the name of The Shredded Wheat Company, and another factory was built in Niagara Falls, New York. A third plant, known as The Canadian Shredded Wheat Company, was added in Niagara Falls, Ontario, by 1911. By 1915 The Pacific Coast Shredded Wheat Company had been added in Oakland, California, and by 1925, a factory in England, outside London in Welwyn Garden City, had joined the family. The company was called the Shredded Wheat Company until it was bought by Nabisco in 1928.[106]

With refreshed troops, the train continued south through New York, passing over the Erie Canal and dropping into the

106 "Henry Perky." Wikipedia. September 26, 2016.

coal-mining region of Pennsylvania. By this time, they were riding on one of the New York Central rail lines. Dick noted that he saw some of the Great Lakes as they travelled, most likely Lake Erie and possibly Lake Ontario. Dick's impression of the Pennsylvania coal mining country: "Was dirty and smoky there. The rivers were dirty all over. There were some great mountains and manufacturing companies. Saw quite a few streams of melted iron through the open windows and in the railroad yards. The girls had overalls on and working like men."

Similar to their counterparts in Canada, the women observed by Dick were part of a work force thrust into American industry to keep the war machine rolling as the nation's young men marched off to war. Not only did women maintain their households, but they also played roles to help support the war. Many prior taboos and restrictions thrown up to keep women out of large-scale production industries were broken down. In 1918, nearly three million new women workers were employed in food, textile, and war industries as women took over the production lines in factories. Women worked as streetcar and train conductors, police officers, mechanics, radio operators, and even barbers as well as in steel mills, logging camps, and shipyards. Farm women, nicknamed "farmerettes" by the press, ran the family farms and grew much needed food in support of the Food Administration.[107] Some women worked long hours, six or seven days a week in factories that included chemicals and munitions. Some endured hazardous

107 Joyce Bryant. "How War Changed the Role of Women in the United States." Reprinted with permission from Yale-New Haven Teachers Institute, Yale University.

conditions, handling explosives and dangerous chemicals with very little training. Women who didn't work outside the home supported the war effort by volunteering to knit clothes, roll bandages, and put together hampers for the soldier. The *Renville Star Farmer* ran announcements for Red Cross sewing and knitting meetings as well as women's food campaign meetings during the war period.

World War I was the first war in which American women were permitted to join the armed forces. Some thirteen thousand, known as "Yeomanettes," enlisted in the navy to do clerical work stateside. Nearly three hundred entered the Marine Corps as clerks and won the name "Marinettes." More than 230 women traveled to France as part of the U.S. Army Signal Corps. There, they served as telephone operators for the American Expeditionary force. Known as the "Hello Girls," these women operated the Army Signal Corps' telephone switchboards and supported communications among General Pershing's troops and with other allied forces in France. A small group of bilingual women took on the duty of coping with operators of the French telephone system, who rarely spoke English. Overall, about twenty thousand women worked for the military. But they were not the only ones to travel overseas. Some eleven thousand women, although not actual members of the armed forces, served abroad in various capacities.[108]

The war machine was in high gear, fueled by American patriots in all walks of life. Dick Bakker's train rambled through Pennsylvania and on into New Jersey, arriving at Jersey City

108 Ibid.

around 6 p.m. on Friday, August 2. There, the troops were let out for six hours. "That sure was a great place and so many little children," Dick wrote. "They were just crazy to walk with us from 3 to 10 years and just twinkled with kids. We had a good time and was a large city." The next morning the troops awakened at 4 a.m., and the train proceeded to the waterfront, where they unloaded onto a ship that ferried them to Brooklyn. From there, they again loaded their extensive gear onto a train which transported them to Camp Mills, Long Island. A tired group of soldiers arrived at Camp Mills at 5 p.m. on August 3 after a long day, especially for Dick who had been on guard duty the previous night and the day before. The trip from Camp Kearny took six days. Undoubtedly, the unknown journey ahead was foremost on their minds as they whiled away the hours confined to a slow moving train; it was a stressful, tiring trip, indeed. But there was no time for rest in the hurried summer of 1918. America was at war. By this time, the Allies had stopped a major German offensive at the Marne River and were now on the attack across a front from Chateau-Thierry to Soissons, but the Germans were inflicting heavy casualties on their pursuers. The American divisions were in dire need of replacements to fill the depleted ranks. And Dick Bakker and the Fortieth Division were on their way to France.

Chapter 11

Across the Atlantic, the Shipping Crisis

ON AUGUST 6, 1918, DICK Bakker wrote his final letter on American soil:

Tuesday, Aug 6 – 1918
Co. F, 160th Inf. 3129880
A.E.F. 90 Postmaster
New York City, N.Y.

Dear Folks at home,

Use this address until you get my new address. Am sending my razor home to nite. I think it will reach home alright. Was awful hot today. Was working nearly all nite last nite & nite before. Don't think I will write many more letters after this one. Are leaving about the time & mentioned some time ago & wrote H & R about it too. Will write when I get there. Can not write very often from there. Am feeling fine & we are all willing to go. Glad to get away from here. Say or greet all the folks & Uncle George & Grandma also & have no time to write now days. Will be on another place again tomorrow. Did not get any letters today. Got

Lillians letter yesterday & 2 from Tetje also & one from Kathryn also. Don't think we will get any more mail after this. Looks like rain now. It rains here quite a lot. Wish you all kind of good luck there & do your bit in every way for every little helps. Leave me feeling OK in every way. Got a new razor today.

Your Son & Bro,

DWBakker

The Fortieth Division's stay at Camp Mills was brief while they were inspected and equipped for overseas duty. Camp Mills was located on Long Island about ten miles from the eastern boundary of New York City on the Hempstead Plains near Garden City. It was named in honor of Major General Albert L. Mills, who was awarded the Medal of Honor for gallantry during the Spanish-American War. Camp Mills was one of three camps under control of the New York Port of Embarkation at Hoboken, New Jersey, whose major function was the preparation of army units for their deployment to Europe. By July 1918, it consisted of about 1,200 buildings with a capacity of forty-six thousand, including space for forty thousand transients (about half in barracks, half in tents), a five hundred-inmate detention camp, and 5,500 members of a permanent garrison. Facilities at Camp Mills included a hospital, warehouses, a bakery, a delousing plant, and other facilities. Once at Camp Mills, the units waited until they could be scheduled for embarkation, whereupon they traveled by trains on the Long Island Railroad to board ferryboats for the overseas piers in Brooklyn or Hoboken. At the piers they

D. Kent Decker

were loaded onto troop ships that transported troops primarily to the ports of Liverpool, England, or Brest, France.[109]

On August 6 at 9 a.m., the same day that Dick Bakker wrote his last letter on American soil, the Eightieth Brigade Commander, Brigadier General Hall, and his Adjutant, Major Raymond I. Foumer, reported to the Commanding General, Port of Embarkation, Hoboken, New Jersey, pursuant to Confidential Orders No. A- 147, Camp Orders: L-420 Port Orders. The officers were assigned to Ship No. 343 (British Steamship Cretic), which was boarded at 11 A.M. from Pier No. 39 in Hoboken, New Jersey.

The next day, August 7, 1918, the remainder of the Eightieth Brigade along with their equipment and supplies boarded the following named twelve ships from various countries as coordinated by the Shipping Board: *Cretic, Osterley, Balmoral Castle, Teiresias, Otranto, Empress of Russia, Guyam, Louisville, Mantor, Lapland, Metegama,* and *Nestor.* The following day, August 8, 1918, pursuant to telegraphic instructions from the War Department to Commanding General, Port of Embarkation, Hoboken, New Jersey, the Eightieth Infantry Brigade left port for overseas duty at 3 p.m. aboard a convoy of these twelve ships escorted by the U. S. Cruiser *Rochester* and U. S. Destroyer No. 73.[110] Dick Bakker and his buddies in Company F, 160th Infantry, spent a total of four busy days at Camp Mills. It was fortuitous

109 "Camp Mills." Wikipedia. September 2, 2016.

110 *History of the Fortieth (Sunshine) Division; Containing a Brief History of All Units Under the Command of Major General Frederick S. Strong, 1917-1919.* Los Angeles: C.S. Hutson, 1920. September 2, 2008.

that Dick found time to write the folks at home. He would not get a chance to write for another twenty-four days.

The convoy system had been introduced by Britain in May 1917 to counteract the German U-boat threat. By the time Dick Bakker crossed the Atlantic, the U-boat threat had been greatly minimized, but precautions were still strictly enforced as the U-boats struck from beneath the sea without warning. Between May 1917 and November 1918, a total of 1.1 million American troops were transported across the Atlantic in convoy, and only 637 were drowned as a result of German attacks.[111] However, the availability of ships to transport men and equipment across the Atlantic was yet another shortage of epic proportions.

At the turn of the century, the United States relied heavily on foreign vessels to meet their shipping needs. When the war in Europe broke out in 1914, those countries diverted their Merchant Marine full-time to supply their own armies. The declaration of war resulted in the withdrawal of about six million gross tons of ships by Germany and Austria, and one million gross tons by France and Russia. Little more than ten percent of the United States' water-borne foreign commerce (measured in dollars) was carried in American bottoms.[112] It quickly became evident that national legislation was needed to increase the country's merchant marine fleet, but Congress could not agree on an acceptable bill until 1916, when they passed the Shipping Act which created the

111 "This Day in History: May 24, 1917." History.com.

112 Edward N. Hurley. *The Bridge to France.* Philadelphia: J.B. Lippincott, 1927.

Shipping Board. The Shipping Act was a peacetime legislation that was not intended to meet the needs of the war into which the country was about to be plunged. It read: "An Act to establish a United States Shipping Board for the purpose of encouraging, developing, and creating a naval auxiliary and naval reserve and a Merchant Marine to meet the requirements of the commerce of the United States with its territories and possessions and with foreign countries; to regulate carriers by water engaged in the foreign and interstate commerce of the United States for other purposes." The Board was to consist of five commissioners to be appointed by the President with the advice and consent of the Senate and was granted broad powers to construct, equip, or acquire vessels suitable for commerce and military and naval purposes. Most important of all, it was given the power to form one or more corporations for the purchase, construction, equipment, lease, charter, maintenance, and operation of merchant vessels in the commerce of the United States under certain conditions. It could subscribe for the stock of these corporations, protect government interests, and sell stock to the public with the approval of the President. The Board had powers which gave it complete control over American ships and shipping.

When the United States declared war on April 6, 1917, the Shipping Board immediately established the Shipping Board Emergency Fleet Corporation, a government-run entity, to carry out the task of providing the tonnage the army would need in order to maintain an immense force overseas. The Emergency Fleet Corporation was funded with $50 million to initiate activities. On June 15, Congress passed the Emergency Shipping Fund Act which bestowed on President Wilson the far-reaching authority to requisition, construct, and operate ships, which he then delegated to the Fleet Corporation.

Wilson appointed Edward N. Hurley as Chairman of the Shipping Board on July 17. Hurley, a Chicago business man of Irish descent, had served on the Federal Trade Commission and the Red Cross War Council as well as the War Trade Board for the Department of Commerce. Hurley quickly assessed the shipping situation and realized that he had to take drastic action if the United States was to win the war. Hurley realized that transportation was the life-blood artery of the army, the navy, and essential industries. The United States needed raw materials required for producing military supplies. Farmers demanded nitrates from Chile, and so did explosives manufacturers. Steel plants wanted manganese ore from Brazil and chrome from Australia. The world had to be scoured for essential raw materials, which had to be carried in ships under American control. Every industry was crying for coal, which of necessity had to be carried by water as far as possible because of railway congestion.[113] Furthermore, there were fewer than fifty thousand shipyard workers in American yards. Production could not possibly meet wartime demands and attrition.[114]

Under the direction of Hurley, the Shipping Board exercised all possible means to acquire tonnage. Besides requisitioning ships under construction, no matter for whom they were being built,

113 Ibid.

114 "United States Shipping Board Merchant Fleet Corporation." Wikipedia. July 25, 2016.

they also seized interned enemy vessels; commandeered American ships in service; secured enemy tonnage from foreign countries; chartered or commandeered foreign vessels in American ports; purchased ships under construction in foreign yards; and let contracts in foreign countries for building ships.

The enormity of Hurley's task cannot be overstated. To meet their goals, the Shipping Board was required to take control of every aspect of the shipping industry, from creation and financing of new facilities to operations and delivery to the Western Front. Entirely new yards had to be built at an expense so huge that it could not be defrayed by private companies. In the end, the Fleet Corporation had to build the yards with government money and to act as their banker. When the United States entered the war, there were in the United States only 37 yards with 142 ways building steel vessels, and 24 yards with 73 ways building wood vessels of over three thousand tons. About seventy-five percent of the steel-ship ways already had hulls for the navy upon them.[115]

As the mad scramble to assemble an adequate Merchant Marine fleet came into fruition, operation of the fleet became yet another task of epic proportions. Congestion at the ports in France, as well as at New York and other American ports, coupled with the fact that the War Department, the Navy Department, and the Shipping Board were endeavoring to operate separate fleets, created a situation that was chaotic. Regardless of the number of ships that were built, unless they were efficiently

115 Edward N. Hurley. *The Bridge to France*. Philadelphia: J.B. Lippincott, 1927.

operated through proper loading, prompt departure from port, and a reduction in round-trip time to France, it would be impossible to feed and supply even a small expeditionary force. In addition, the Shipping Board had to ensure that civilians were receiving necessary food and supplies. If that weren't enough, shipping schedules of neutral countries had to be coordinated as they were bringing vital food and materials for both the civilian and war industries. Hurley decided to appoint a Shipping Control Committee to supervise and coordinate operation of the combined fleets. Hurley appointed P. A. S. Franklin, President of the International Mercantile Marine Company, as chairman of the Shipping Control Committee on February 11, 1918. He was the recognized authority on ocean transportation in America, and his opinions on shipping matters and world trade commanded respect at home and abroad.

Franklin's first act was to put all shipping into what was called "liquid" form so that no governmental department or person had the right to claim any ship as its or his own. Thereafter, ships ceased to be identified with the army, the navy, the Fuel Administration, or even the Shipping Board. They became international tonnage. The Government Departments were requested to state how many tons they had to lift within a given period, and the Shipping Control Committee thereupon found the ships to carry them. This basic idea of a "liquid fleet" proved to be quite successful. Manufacturers of essentials in the United States were assured of a steadier stream of raw material. It became possible to meet the most pressing demand with ships that happened to be in port. When a ship arrived, it was assigned at once to another necessary voyage, whether or not it previously had carried a cargo for the Fuel Administration or any other governmental agency. The requirements of the various departments were laid upon Franklin's desk in the order of their priority, and the most urgent received immediate consideration. The turn-around, which had been as high as thirty-eight days in France and thirty-four days in the United States, fell to nineteen days in France and twenty-three days in the United States. It continued to decline in the United States to fifteen days in April, rising slightly to twenty days in November. In the meantime, the amount of tonnage handled increased nearly four-fold. This efficient method of operating ships to France saved America the equivalent of hundreds of ships.[116]

And so it went. Order was established in a hectic and chaotic world in which the Shipping Board was able to deliver the resources to allow the Allies to win the war. One can only imagine the bookkeeping nightmare that occurred at a time when statistics were logged on paper and delivered by hand without the modern computer and communications networks. They had to not only keep track of the multitude of ships and match the availability of ships to resources ready for shipping, but they also had to deal with the laws and bureaucracies of the various governments and independent companies while keeping accurate time schedules. Fortuitously, the Emergency Fleet Corporation was organized and managed as if it were a private enterprise, which allowed the Shipping Board to avoid much of the inefficiencies

116 Ibid.

and bureaucracy of government agencies. The Board therefore had the mechanism of a private enterprise and yet maintained government control.

Once a ship was ready for boarding, each soldier was given an instruction booklet published by the National War Work Council of the YMCA. The booklet described the ship's construction and facilities as well as the procedures, rules, and regulations for the voyage. When arriving at the gangway, each soldier was handed a slip of paper known as a "billet." The billet was to be kept with the soldier at all times as it proved his right to be on board that ship. It told the soldier where to live, sleep, and eat while on board. The billet listed the name of the ship, compartment, hatch, deck, and bunk number for each specific soldier. It also listed the parade station nearest the hatch and the ship's weather deck. In addition, it contained a few short instructions on how to get about on that particular ship, for there were hardly any two ships that were constructed alike internally.

During the voyage, each soldier filled out a postcard provided by the Red Cross that was mailed back to their family once they arrived at their destination across the Atlantic to let the family know that they were safe. The front of the card was labeled "SOLDIERS' MAIL NO POSTAGE NECESSARY" along with the family name and address. The back of the card stated, "THE SHIP ON WHICH I SAILED HAS ARRIVED SAFELY OVERSEAS," along with the soldier's name and organization.

Once on board, the soldier was directed to the place where he would live, eat, and sleep during his time onboard, known as the "berthing space." Bunks were approximately six feet by three feet, made from canvas and iron pipe, and stacked three and four high. Each bunk had a life preserver that could be used as a pillow. The bunk and life preserver had matching numbers which also had to match the bunk number on the soldier's billet. Washrooms near the berthing space were equipped with washbasins. Fresh water was rationed as it was a scarce commodity onboard these ships. Soldiers were to bring their own shaving kits; note that Dick Bakker bought a new razor before he left. Soldiers were encouraged to get a haircut before leaving as barbershop facilities were limited on board. Instructions were given as to how to use the fire hoses and extinguishers in case of fire. Smoking was prohibited in the berthing places because of the fire danger and the "sickening smell." Perhaps this was the first "no smoking zone" enforced by the government. One could wonder why it took so long to catch on with the rest of the country.

Meals were ladled to the soldier's mess pan from kettles of hot food in much the same manner as they were served at camp. When the meal was over, soldiers rinsed their mess kit in long tubs of hot water. Receptacles were provided for rubbish which was collected at certain times of the day, taken to the fire room, and burned. Throwing refuse overboard was strictly prohibited while the ship was at sea. Any soldier caught throwing anything overboard was subject to arrest by guards distributed about the decks. The captain of a submarine could clearly trace a ship's path by the distinct trail of refuse thrown overboard. An astute captain could tell almost to the minute when the refuse was dropped because of its character, and he could tell the number of ships that had passed from the number of trails left behind. It was thought that the captain could tell the approximate size of the ship by the amount floating at different intervals.

Smoking was allowed during the day, only out on the open decks, but the smokers were not allowed to throw their cigar butts overboard. Certain places were provided for smoking and entertainment in the evening, but absolutely no smoking was allowed on the open decks at night. The ship was to be made as nearly invisible as possible at night. It was stated as fact that the glow of a cigarette could be seen at a distance of one-half mile, hence the precautionary measure, for anything that designated the whereabouts of the ship at night made her a target for the first submarine that happened along. Any officer or enlisted man who disobeyed the regulation was dealt with summarily and usually finished the balance of the voyage under guard and therefore under suspicion. Soldiers were encouraged to arrest any person seen about the open decks showing a light of any character. Matches and flashlights (then called "electric lamps") were strictly prohibited and were to be turned over to the proper authority immediately upon arrival on board. Only patent cigar lighters provided for use by the troops could be used.

Each ship was equipped with lookout stations that were equally divided into sectors. Lookout stations were manned 24/7 with soldiers taking assigned turns. A lookout was not to leave his station under any circumstance until properly relieved. Lookouts were directed to immediately report the movements of other ships and anything floating in the water, no matter how trivial. Each station was equipped with a semicircle divided into degrees with a moveable pointer such that the lookout could accurately phone the exact bearing of the suspicious object to central control. Soldiers were directed that every person onboard should consider himself a self-appointed lookout at all times. Eternal vigilance was the price of safety.[117]

The ships left the port of embarkation with no fanfare or noisy demonstration, slipping quietly away from the pier and disappearing over the horizon so as to attract as little attention as possible. One can only imagine the gamut of emotions that flashed through the soldiers' minds as they watched their homeland fade into the evening mist, heading for an unknown destination in a world fraught with danger. Perhaps there was the dread of a bullet, or a torpedo, or a gas attack; perhaps there was a teardrop down the cheek, a twinge of sadness, a longing for loved ones left behind, a yearning for one last goodbye; perhaps there were visions of bravery, of valor, of heroic deeds; perhaps there was a sense of pride to answer the call, the call to save democracy.

The convoy arrived at Liverpool, England, at 8 a.m., August 20, 1918. The twelve-day voyage from Hoboken to Port of Debarkation at Liverpool was made without accident so far as was known. The course taken was unknown; the weather was generally fair and the sea calm, except in northern waters. The troops debarked and marched four miles over the cobblestone streets of Liverpool to the American Rest Camp at Knotty Ash, each soldier burdened with his own heavy equipment, rifles, extra

117 Joe Hartwell. "Troopships, Battleships, Subs, Cruisers, Destroyers." WWI Ships Histories. August 14, 2013.

rations, and miscellaneous supplies.[118] Knotty Ash was a tent city that had sprung up overnight to meet the emergencies of war. The tents were conical in shape and designed to hold eight men, but up to twenty were jammed in at any given time. Each man's mattress consisted of a pad a couple inches thick that was narrow at one end and wide at the other such that the men had to sleep with their feet towards the center pole. The camp, surrounded by stone and picket fences, accommodated ten thousand troops. The Red Cross had opened U.S. Army Camp Hospital No. 40 at Knotty Ash in the spring of 1918. The five hundred-bed hospital was staffed with forty-five nurses who primarily attended wounded soldiers returning from the Western Front. Knotty Ash was anything but a rest camp for the vast majority of the soldiers passing through on their way to or from the battle front. Little beggars followed the soldiers, calling out, "Hey! Yank, 'ave you got any cents (sense)?"[119]

Dick Bakker and the Eightieth Brigade entrained at Knotty Ash at 3:30 p.m. the next day, August 21, en route to Port of Debarkation, France. The Eightieth arrived at Winchester, England, at 2 a.m., August 22, and marched two miles to Romsey Rest Camp. Originally operated by the British, Romsey was a way station for American soldiers, similar to Knotty Ash. It had accommodations for seven thousand troops. The Red Cross, with

118 *History of the Fortieth (Sunshine) Division; Containing a Brief History of All Units Under the Command of Major General Frederick S. Strong, 1917-1919.* Los Angeles: C.S. Hutson, 1920. September 2, 2008.

119 T. Ben. Meldrum. *A History of the 362nd Infantry.* Ogden: A.L. Scoville Press, 1920.

the help of the army, had built United States Hospital No. 34 at the site. The permanent brick building was complete with long, sunny wards, operating and x-ray rooms, diet kitchens, a milk pasteurizing plant, and gas and electric equipment. The facility was operated with a permanent staff of seventeen nurses.[120]

After one day at Romsey, the Eightieth Brigade left the rest camp at 8 a.m. on August 23 to entrain at the Winchester, England, station at 9 a.m. During their one-day stay at Romsey, Dick Bakker and his buddies were allowed to visit Winchester Cathedral and the surrounding area. In a letter written later in France, Dick related the experience to the folks at home. "At England we visited an old church or cathedral, what they might call it. We went thru it and an old man explained it to us. The first part that was built was in 1093 and they have been keeping it in repair and building more to it. It was 555 feet long and there were 6 kings buried in that cathedral. They were buried in a lead casket and covered with carved wood and a great many more bodies were buried in that cathedral. There was a big boat there from Belgium that was over a thousand years old and hundreds of statues were there and there was a well in the basement that was made there when the first part was put up. It is all stone the whole church and there are flags hanging from the early wars. If you would touch them they would fall apart. We also saw an old college which was all broke down that was very old too. There was one church a small distance from this one that had a church that was built before Christ. I would have liked to have seen that."

120 Lavinia L. Dock *History of American Red Cross Nursing*. New York: MacMillan, 1922.

The train carrying the Eightieth Brigade arrived at Southampton, England, at 10 a.m. on August 23 where the troops boarded transport ships at 4:30 p.m. for Port of Debarkation, France. Steaming through the night, the Eightieth debarked at Cherbourg, France, at 7 a.m., August 24, and marched four miles up a long, hilly road to British Rest Camp No. 1 near the village of Tourlaville in the northwest part of France. After a day's rest, the Eightieth Brigade left the British Rest Camp on August 25 at 5:30 p.m. to return to Cherbourg and entrain at 8 p.m. for La Guerche, Department of Cher, in central France.[121]

The movement of the Fortieth Division provides an insight into the enormous strain on the French railway system. As the movement of troops and supplies from American harbors increased, the fact became more and more apparent that the French landing ports constituted the neck of the bottle. The great trouble in France lay in their railroads, which were lacking in engines and cars to move the traffic. This situation necessitated transportation of American railroad equipment to France and constituted one of the crucial problems to be solved. The equipment was heavy, bulky and very wasteful of ship space. Prior to this time, the Baldwin Locomotive Works, which was building the locomotives America was sending to France, had assembled and boxed them for shipment at its plant. All were standard size engines but there was great delay in reassembling them on the other side. When the first shipments were made, the average time to get a locomotive

121 *History of the Fortieth (Sunshine) Division; Containing a Brief History of All Units Under the Command of Major General Frederick S. Strong, 1917-1919.* Los Angeles: C.S. Hutson, 1920. September 2, 2008.

in operation, after arrival in France, was thirty-three days and this time was increasing due to the large number of engines being received.

The task of relieving this situation fell upon Mr. S. M. Felton, Director-General of Military Railways, in Washington. Felton combed the tonnage market of the world for single deck steamers with large open holes and at least four hatches of sufficient size to admit locomotives 35 feet 8 inches long and 9 feet wide. He found four such ships that had just been built by the Bethlehem Steel Company. After finding a derrick capable of lifting the locomotives, the first ship, the *Feltore*, was loaded on April 30, 1918. Thirty-three locomotives, and their tenders, practically ready for steam, were placed in the hold of the vessel, between great quantities of tightly compressed bailed hay. The steamer made her voyage from New York to the French port of St. Nazaire without mishap and discharged her valuable cargo. Later an economy of space was affected so it was possible to load thirty-six locomotives, including their water tanks, in the holds of each of these four vessels. Thus the time required in getting an engine in operation after its arrival at St. Nazaire was reduced from thirty-three days to eight hours. Subsequently, Felton was able to obtain twelve other vessels capable of handling locomotives on their wheels. Considering that each locomotive weighed 150,500 pounds, this endeavor was considered one of the great engineering feats of the war.[122]

122 Edward N. Hurley. *The Bridge to France*. Philadelphia: J.B. Lippincott, 1927.

The Journey

Troop trains in France during the period consisted of specially built boxcars called "forty and eight boxcars" that were designed to carry forty men or eight horses although reports indicate many more men were often stuffed in these boxcars. The cars were 20.5 feet long and 8.5 feet wide. With rifles, packs, and other equipment, there was scarcely room to move. Men sat in the open doorway with their legs dangling over the side. At night, conditions were exceptionally bad, for if a few stretched out, the remainder were obliged to either sleep across them or get no sleep at all.[123]

The movement of the Eightieth Brigade alone, with approximately eight thousand men, required somewhere in the range of 160 to 200 boxcars. Add to that the rail cars required for supplies, equipment, food, and the essential materials required for conducting war efforts. Additionally, flatbed cars were provided for moving artillery, tanks, ambulances, and other motor vehicles. An American division like the Fortieth contained around twenty-seven to twenty-eight thousand men. Crunching the numbers, it can be estimated that one thousand rail cars were required just to move the Fortieth Division from the ports to its headquarters in central France. To scope the enormity of the overall task, there were nearly four million Allied troops operating in France in the latter part of 1918. Troop movements alone required a large infrastructure, with tens of thousands of American troops who required transportation to base camps arriving at the ports weekly. From the base camps, replacement troops were transported forward to relieve the embattled divisions while special ambulance trains transported casualties from the battle front.

123 "Forty and Eight Boxcar." Skylighters.

American casualties alone in the Soissons offensive would have required around five hundred ambulance cars to remove the dead and wounded. Further troop movements were required to counter German offensives. Food and supplies were in constant demand at the front. Substantial maintenance crews were required to keep the systems operational. On top of that, the rail system had to accommodate everyday civilian traffic, an enormous task indeed.

After a two-day ride, the Eightieth Infantry Brigade detrained at La Guerche at 10 a.m., August 27, and proceeded by truck to Château Fontenay, Nerondes, Department of Cher, France, where brigade headquarters were established by 6 p.m. Individual units were dispersed and housed in surrounding villages. Dick Bakker would spend the next few weeks in and around the nearby village of Grossouvre, France. On or about the same time, the entire Fortieth Division was arriving at La Guerche by alternate routes. The next day, August 28, the Fortieth Infantry Division was renamed the Sixth Depot Division, much to the disappointment of the officers and men who had trained to engage in battle and strike a direct blow to the enemy. With the mounting casualties occurring within the divisions on the front line, the Allied High Command decided that the Sunshine Division would be stripped to provide replacements for the already proven units. The Fortieth Division, now the Sixth Depot Division, was given orders to train troops for replacements.[124] Dick Bakker was now a member of the American Expeditionary Forces—the United States Armed Forces fighting in Europe.

124 *History of the Fortieth (Sunshine) Division; Containing a Brief History of All Units Under the Command of Major General Frederick S. Strong, 1917-1919.* Los Angeles: C.S. Hutson, 1920. September 2, 2008.

Chapter 12

Behind the Lines, Personal Hygiene

AFTER THREE DAYS IN CAMP, Dick Bakker wrote to the folks at home on Friday, August 30, "In some town in France now. Was in England some time ago. The weather is fine and the country looks fine but it is all so old fashioned. They all have stone houses here. It sure is great to see all of those things." Dick went on to observe, "There are only a few pumps here. They have the old style here yet. They let the bucket down with a roller and a chain and the brooms are made out of little branches tied together with some wire to a long stick. Them are the only kind I have saw here so far."

By this time, Dick and his buddies are enjoying the foreign countryside, "We were picking berries last nite. They are plentiful here and they have more wine than anything else." Two days later, Sunday, September 1: "We have been picking blackberries this forenoon. I got about 2 qts. So I quit. They are so thick here. The people make fences of them all around their land. Everyone, so you can imagine how many there are. Haven't seen a real wire fence since I left U.S. There are some pear trees here but they are not ripe yet and grapes too but not very many. There are oaks and ferns here also and different trees but I don't know the names of the different trees." A week later, he wrote, "We don't realize half the time we are in France but the roads and directions run in seven hundred different ways and all along the roads on both sides there are thick hedges of plum trees and berry bushes. We were out quit a distance yesterday and it is the same all over and lots of berries. I had so many I don't care for them anymore."

Invariably, the farm boy checked out the soil and the crops. "Haven't been any place where there were no sparrows nor crows. The soil is light clay here and is very hard now and lots of timber and flowers too. Threshing is through here for quite a while I think but have seen only one little outfit. There are not very big fields here." By Dick's account, the locals made their living from the farms and orchards in the vicinity using methods handed down from their ancestors. "The people work as hard here on Sundays as other days. They go out at 5:30 in the morning and come in when it is nearly dark. You ought to see the big cows they have here and the big oxen they drive on the wagons. They don't weigh less than a ton apiece the French people say. All they use here mostly is those little mules. They come up as high as a man's hips and they drive one of them in a two wheeled cart. The wheels are higher and heavier than on the old Plymouth." Into this community the Americans brought military vehicles and artillery, not to mention modern rifles and machine guns. It was no doubt an eye-opening experience for these rural folks although the French military had had access to this technology for most of the war.

Grossouvre was a small village of a few hundred citizens at an altitude of two hundred meters. Dick spoke favorably of the area. "We are in about a pretty country as there is in France," He had higher praise for England. "England is prettier than France. England is the prettiest country I have seen so far." The

Americans set up several camps for the troops in the nearby vicinity. In a letter, written September 8, Dick comments, "Am in my sixth camp now." This comment indicates that his troop unit was moved six times in twelve days. While it would be natural that relocations occurred to improve communications and efficiency once the division had settled into the area, the army was also deeply concerned about the enemy learning of troop locations. In his letter from September 1, Dick relates, "This place is in the south eastern part of France very near Italy. So you can imagine where we are." In actuality, Grossouvre is in central France. Was this a misinterpretation on Dick's part, or was the army putting out misleading information?

From Dick's letters, the locals were friendly and tried hard to accommodate the Americans. "The people here are fine but we can't understand them. It sure makes it bad. They want to tell us everything but it is hard to do so." It is likely that every able-bodied young man from these villages was fighting in the French Army. Given the war statistics, it is almost certain that a few parents in these villages had suffered the horrors of war casualties, casualties that would leave their sons debilitated for life—amputations, loss of hearing or eyesight, internal damage, rare diseases, shell shock. And in a parent's worst fears, a son returned in a coffin. In small towns where everyone knows everyone, a death is grieved throughout the village. But now the Americans had arrived; it was time to end the war. While the Americans were welcomed as saviors by most of the population, the influx of a twenty-seven-thousand-man American Division must have been overwhelming to the locals of these small villages. In speculation, if every man in the division picked two quarts of berries like Dick Bakker, the total would amount to over fifty-thousand quarts of berries!

The army was not all work and no play. On Sunday, September 8, Dick wrote, "We are to have a little doings in this town this afternoon—ball games, sack race, and three-legged race. The tallest man tied to the shortest man out of each company and will have a parade. Also tug of war across the canal and a few more things I can't just remember now."

Dick finished his letter Monday forenoon. "Has been raining off and on all the time since yesterday noon. It spoiled some doings mostly yesterday. Had a little ball game and tug of war. F Co. pulled G Co. thru the canal and H Co. pulled F Co. through." The athletic contests undoubtedly provided entertainment for the local citizens while improving troop morale. The sight of the strapping young Americans flexing their muscles must have been uplifting to the locals who were counting on these young men to end the war.

The canal to which Dick referred was the 261-kilometer Canal de Berry which linked the Canal lateral a la Loire at Marseilles-les-Aubigny with the Cher at Noyes rejoining the Loire near Tours. The canal was completed in 1840 with ninety-six locks that were only nine feet wide, which limited barges to sixty tons of freight over the summit. The canal was closed in 1955 with only a twelve-kilometer segment presently in operation.[125] A tug of war across this waterway in 1918 must have been an event that was talked about for years to come.

125 "Canal de Berry." Wikipedia. May 1, 2015.

Undoubtedly, the canal was a factor in the selection of the campsite. The Americans made good use of it. On August 30, shortly after arriving at the camp, Dick wrote, "Done some washing yesterday in the canal and had a bath in it too." After enduring a long arduous journey, a bath was undoubtedly high on the priority list of many of the weary troops. Watching thousands of these young men eagerly jumping into the canal must have been another long-remembered event for these locals.

With the influx of so many soldiers in these rural areas, sanitation required constant vigilance. Overall, sanitation and personal hygiene were issues of great concern to the army in an effort to keep the soldier in peak physical condition. Sanitation, as defined by the army, is the process used to protect the soldier from disease. Sanitation control and training is the responsibility of the Army Medical Services, but sanitation is also the duty of all men in the army. The sanitation process was initiated immediately upon induction, as evidenced by the inoculations administered to Dick Bakker at Camp Lewis and the training he received in personal hygiene. By World War I, the basic rules were well established for personal hygiene and the responsibility for their enforcement. Soldiers were to bathe daily while in camp and weekly when in the field. Teeth were to be brushed at least once a day. Hands were to be washed before meals and after going to the latrine.[126]

While sanitary conditions in the military camps in America could be reasonably controlled with designated resources and facilities, conditions on the Western Front were another matter; there, over a million men and animals were subsisting without

126 "Personal Hygiene." Army of Medical History. June 18, 2009.

the accustomed conveniences of life. Conditions were especially horrific in the trenches. While death was a constant companion to those serving in the front line, disease also wrought a heavy toll. Adverse conditions increased the soldier's vulnerability. Heavy rains created cold, wet, and unsanitary conditions, leading to drainage problems that left the soldiers slogging through muddy, stagnant, unsanitary water. Early on, the soldiers were inflicted with a painful fungal infection labeled "Trench Foot" that caused their feet to numb and swell up to two or three times their normal size. The condition could turn gangrenous and result in amputation. By 1918, procedures had been implemented to prevent the condition, but a few cases were still recorded.

With no field facilities, food and water were brought up in wagons and carried to the front through communications trenches. Not all water in France was potable, and some had to be treated with chlorine before it could be consumed. Nevertheless, thirsty troops sometimes drank polluted water, leading to dysentery and other infectious diseases. Scraps of leftover food thrown on the ground added to the tainted environment. The primitive subsistence led to the need for latrines, which were dug a short distance from the front and were accessible through a connecting trench. A typical latrine during that period was a pit dug to a depth of four to six feet. In some cases, a knee-high log or board was stretched lengthwise along one edge and upheld on each end by two logs fastened together to form an "X" in much the fashion of a sawhorse. One picture taken during the war period shows seven men sitting side by side on a latrine log relieving themselves. Privacy was not an option. Companies typically assigned two men to sanitary duties with the responsibility to keep the latrines in good order. This distasteful assignment was sometimes punishment for breaching the army code. Units were responsible for filling in their own latrines and marking the sites when leaving the area. Near the combat front, latrines were considered a dangerous place to linger. Enemy forces would subject the sites to artillery bombardment or sniper fire when detecting activity in the area. Buckets and even biscuit tins were used in the trenches on many occasions, and they had to be emptied on a daily basis.[127] Toilet paper was any scrap of paper, branch, or leaf that was convenient. A person handing out religious pamphlets on the Western Front would have found many takers, but the pamphlets would have rarely been used for what they were intended.

As a result of the unhygienic environment, the trenches were infested with vermin. Millions of rats, some reportedly as big as cats, infested the trenches, gorging themselves on human remains and grossly disfiguring them by eating their eyes and gnawing on their extremities. In the dark, the rats scampered across the bodies of sleeping or resting soldiers, sometimes even across their faces, creating exasperation and fear. Soldiers tried clubbing the rats and attacking them with their bayonets since firing weapons into one's own trench was looked upon with high disfavor. However, the rats' reproduction capabilities far exceeded these crude extermination methods, and rat infestation remained a problem throughout the war.

Rats were by no means the only source of infection and nuisance. Lice were a never-ending problem, breeding in the

127 Michael Duffy. "Trench Latrines." First World War. 2009.

seams of filthy clothing and causing men to itch unceasingly. Even when clothing was periodically washed and deloused in boiling water, lice eggs invariably remained hidden in the seams; within a few hours of the clothes being re-worn, the body heat generated would cause the eggs to hatch. Lice caused Trench Fever, a particularly painful disease that began suddenly with severe pain followed by high fever. Recovery—away from the trenches—took up to twelve weeks. Lice were not actually identified as the culprit of Trench Fever until 1918. Frogs by the score were found in shell holes covered in water; they were also found in the base of trenches. Slugs and horned beetles crowded the sides of the trenches.[128]

Each American soldier carried his personal items in a roll that was part of his field pack. The roll contained a sewing kit with a needle, thread, and extra buttons; a shaving kit with a razor, a mirror, and extra blades; a soap dish with lid; a condiment can that was used to store salt, sugar, coffee, tobacco and tea bags; a meat can; a mess kit; and a pocket-sized book with information useful to the soldier in the field. Shaving was an important factor at the front as it ensured that the soldier's gas mask fit tightly against his face.[129] Many men also shaved their heads to avoid nits, yet another prevalent scourge.

Existence at the front was psychologically depressing as well as physically debilitating. Soldiers had to endure the appalling odor of numerous conflicting sources: rotting carcasses, overflowing latrines, cordite, poison gas, rotting sandbags, stagnant mud, and

128 Michael Duffy. "Life in the Trenches." First World War. 2009.

129 World War 1 Letters – The Doughboys Uniform and Equipment, 2011

cigarette smoke. Men who had not been afforded the luxury of a bath in weeks or months would emit the pervading odor of dried sweat. The feet were generally accepted to give off the worst odor. Trenches would also smell of creosol or chloride of lime, used to stave off the constant threat of disease and infection.

Trench duty required constant vigilance as the enemy was sometimes only a few hundred feet away. Constant artillery shellfire brought random death. Consequently, trenches were narrow by design to reduce vulnerability to artillery, making it difficult to sleep or even rest with soldiers in close proximity. In addition, many men were killed by a sniper's bullet on their first day in the trench when they succumbed to their natural inclination to peer over the parapet. Many of the men who died were buried where they fell. As there was no time for proper burial, many of these bodies would rise to the surface over time. Under these stressful conditions, the army cycled battalions through trench assignments when possible, spending a week or so at the front followed by a few days in support, then spending a couple weeks in reserve before being allowed a short rest before the cycle was again initiated.[130] Somehow, the men found a way to endure. There was no choice.

While conditions were much better in Dick Bakker's camp, it can be said with near certainty that the local towns of a few hundred people did not have the facilities to accommodate a twenty-seven-thousand-man division. To be clear, the division was spread over a large area that encompassed quite a few villages. Division records indicate that the overall area in which camps were

130 Michael Duffy. "Life in the Trenches." First World War. 2009.

established was twenty-five by forty kilometers in size. That said, a specific unit such as the 160th Infantry entailed around 3,800 men, still a large influx into a few small villages of a few hundred people. A single American company consisting of 250 men would have more than doubled the population of Grossouvre. The three-company tug of war across the canal must have attracted five hundred to a thousand spectators. Perhaps more. Events with large gatherings tend to leave their mark on the local landscape in the form of littering, trampled greenery, etc. These factors soon wear out a visitor's welcome. On the positive side, the Americans provided some stimulus to the local economy. Dick Bakker wrote, "I got my washing done last week. Cost me 40 cents." Was that a bargain?

Campsites were selected for various reasons, and layouts were planned in advance. In that respect, American divisions were set up to provide the necessary support functions and facilities needed by the combat troops. The Fortieth Division contained a quartermaster corps, a regiment of engineers, a sanitary train, an engineer train, a supply train, a dental infirmary, sanitary squads, and a bakery company. The sanitary train was composed of three motorized ambulance companies, one horse-drawn ambulance company, and a field hospital section. La Guerche was a pleasant setting well away from the combat zone. The low-density population allowed room for troop training and drills. Land was available for purchase to establish depot facilities that were used for the transfer of men and supplies both to and from the front.

Upon arrival at La Guerche, the engineer corps designed and constructed an eight-thousand-man classification camp to house casualties returning from combat. Due to the many casualties and a shortage of field surgeons, casualties were classified to establish priorities for surgery. The construction task consisted of the erection of about one hundred frame buildings, principally Bryant barracks about one hundred by twenty feet; the grading of two miles of a sixty-foot road; the construction of three-eighths of a mile of standard-gauge spur track; the erection of two warehouses each 50 by 250 feet; the laying three-fourths of a mile of four-inch water pipe; the installation of pumps, tanks, and other accessories; and the installation of an electric lighting system and various other structures appurtenant to the camp. The work was rushed at all times and undertaken with no skilled labor except that of soldiers. The work crews included three companies of engineers, four companies of supply train, and daily details that encompassed about six hundred men at work at all times. The camp was designed, laid out, and built without engineering instruments other than a hand-level and a tape; rock was quarried without explosives, hauled six miles, crushed, and laid in roads by hand; roofing tacks were driven with awkward French hand axes because there were no hammers available; roads were for the most part rolled with a French road-roller dragged by teams of one hundred soldiers; horses and excavating machinery were not at hand. In conjunction, a 1,500-bed hospital was established at Grossouvre by remodeling a château, and ground was purchased for the establishment of a cemetery near the division hospital where the remains of deceased officers and soldiers were interred. A bakery was also built to feed the troops. During the time the Sunshine Division was camped at La Guerche, the engineers were kept busy building stretchers, roofing, moving shacks, installing electric lights, repairing pumps and boilers, and building latrines and delousing stations.[131] With the troop camps spread over a large area, a multitude of latrines was undoubtedly needed.

While these facilities were being erected, housing for the troops was much more rudimentary. Buster Keaton, assigned to the Eightieth Brigade, 159th Infantry, Company C, wrote of his stay in France. "We slept in circular tents [...], our feet in the center and our heads close to the drafts from the great outdoors. This was the beginning of an experience I have never forgotten. During my seven months as a soldier in France, I slept every night but one on the ground or on the floor of mills, barns, and stables."[132] In his letters home, Dick Bakker never acknowledged meeting Buster although they were both members of the Eightieth Brigade. Apparently, Dick, the farm boy, was more comfortable with the makeshift camps than Buster. In an early letter, Dick wrote, "We have good quarters here."

In a foreign land far from home, letters were the vital link to the soldier's loved ones and the only life they had ever known. Then, as now, support from home was a treasured inspiration to those serving even though the mail took a long time to arrive. Consequently, mail delivery was huge and vitally important in keeping morale high both on the battlefield and at home. Between July 1, 1917,

131 *History of the Fortieth (Sunshine) Division; Containing a Brief History of All Units Under the Command of Major General Frederick S. Strong, 1917-1919.* Los Angeles: C.S. Hutson, 1920. September 2, 2008.

132 Martha R. Jett. "Buster Keaton in World War I." The Doughboy Center. 2000.

and June 30, 1918, the Post Office Department dispatched thirty-five million letters to the American Expeditionary Forces.[133] All mail had to be collected, date-stamped, sorted, dispatched, and delivered. All these functions were performed by hand labor except for the stamping machine. While soldiers were stationed in the continental United States, their mail was handled by the U.S. Postal Service, where the standard method of addressing letters with street or mail box numbers, towns, and states was well understood. However, mail delivery to the American Expeditionary Forces that were constantly relocating was far more complex. Army mail was put in mail sacks and delivered to a pier in New York where they were transported to France onboard ships. From the French ports, the mail sacks were transported by French railway to an American postal center where the letters were again sorted and dispatched to the last-known division headquarters. If and when the mail reached division headquarters, the letters were again sorted and sent to the appropriate camps. Adding to the confusion, the censorship regulations whereby no soldier was allowed to reveal his location often caused letters to become lost. Also adding to the delay was the fact that many well-intentioned relatives and parents jammed the postal service with food, such as bread that was stale by the time it was delivered or jars of canned fruit that were shattered and broken during delivery. Magazines and periodicals printed a message on their cover that stated if a two-cent stamp was placed on the item and dropped in the mail, it would be delivered to a soldier in France. This statement was

133 "Expanded Service 1898-1920s." Postal Museum.

not true and only added more clutter to the already strained postal system.[134] From Dick's letters, it appears that all his mail was delivered albeit four weeks late. Perhaps he was more diligent in providing his company information than others. He always signed his letters with the company letter and the number of the infantry, which was Company F, 160th Infantry while stationed at Grossouvre.

On Sunday, September 1, 1918, Dick was still waiting for letters from home after five days in camp. "Dear folks at home. How is everybody over there? O.K. here. We don't have to drill today so we have a little rest. Drilling is very hard after such a long layoff but that will soon come up to the old swing. After I left the U.S.A., I saw Fred Wilkens at England. He was quite surprised to see me. There were some boys there from Renville that enlisted when Aldig enlisted but I did not see them for it was the last day there when I saw Fred. He told me about it. I don't know where Willys Mc'B. is but I suppose you do. Haven't seen him since we left C. K. Have a few sheets of paper here yet from there. It hasn't rained here for three months. How is it there? Is it very dry or not? I suppose you will be thru plowing when you get this letter."

The letters from America caught up with Dick the next day, Monday, September 2. In response, Dick wrote a long letter the following Sunday, September 8, 1918. "Dear folks at home. How are things over there? I am feeling fine so far. We can write or are allowed rather to write two letters per week. I think that is enough don't you? Had a few letters from the U.S. Monday. Had one from Henry Raske and one from Anna Habben, a card from Abe and

134 R. Staley. "World War I Letters."

a letter from Tetje also. The newest one was from August 2nd. I saw Ike Habben nearly every day since we left C.K. but I have not seen him while in this town. I think he is in a town near here. Say hello to Anna H. and tell her I will try to write her some time.

We have had plenty of rain the last few days. Had quite a hard wind storm here September 6th. I suppose the threshing machines are humming away at it now. Is Will J and Eddie Dikken's machine in use or not? Is nearly eleven o'clock now. You are maybe getting up by this time. Sundays are just like any other days in the Army only we don't work. It is raining a little off and on now.

One thing I would like to say if you are using my harness and saddle it is alright but don't let it go to the dogs. How is Carl Corbul getting along? I bet it takes him a year to do something. Does he handle any flour or not? How is the wheat or how did the wheat crop turn out in Minnesota? We are getting real white bread here. How is Peanuts? I would like to ride him for a change now. Do you use him or not? How are Peter and Fred and Mrs. getting along? Greet them for me. Have Freiborg and Groens heard from the boys lately? How is Peter getting along? I still rather be in my own place than in his on account of his health. Greet Peter special and the folks also.

How are my three hundred dollars coming? Are they getting rusty? If they are, make use of them and my 2nd and 3rd liberty bonds. Turn them over once in a while so they won't get buggy. Did you get my insurance policy or not? We have plenty of flies here too but no mosquitoes. Well it is about 11:30 now and will go for chow and will write this full after dinner."

By Dick's account, the mail was taking one month or longer to reach France when mailed from Minnesota. The letters Dick received from his family, friends, and neighbors shows the close relationships in the small, rural Renville community. Ike Habben's little sister, Annie, was sixteen that summer of 1918 when she wrote to Dick. Annie would go on to marry Dick's younger brother, Bill, and the two continued the Bakker farming tradition in the community. The networking mechanism was in full force through the letters as those serving let the folks back home know that other soldiers from the community were safe. It is interesting to note that Dick instructed his parents to sell his horse, Peanuts, when he was at Camp Lewis, stating that he had no more use for him. Clearly, Dick now has a change of heart. Perhaps one can sense a tinge of homesickness from this comment. Given that Dick was far from home in a foreign land after a month of hard travel, an assumption of homesickness would not be unreasonable. But Dick was not one to complain. All his letters were written with an upbeat tone and an attitude that showed he was proud to serve his country. He would soon get his chance.

Dick finished his letter Monday forenoon, September 9. Apparently, the mail was distributed on Sunday evenings. Dick wrote, "We got mail last nite. Got eight letters and the book from the Presbyterian Church, three letters from home from Geo. R., three from Tetje, one from M. J. B. This is the first time we could not drill on account of rain while in camp. Will close with lots of love and best wishes. This letter leaves me OK and feeling fine. As ever, your son and bro, DWB, Co F., 160th Inf, American Expeditionary Forces, France."

Even though Dick noted in an earlier letter that he had been in six camps, all his letters were addressed from Grossouvre. Dick's letter heads now displayed the YMCA logo on the left side with the following centered heading:

ON ACTIVE SERVICE

WITH

AMERICAN EXPEDITIONARY FORCES

The next weekend, Saturday, September 14, Dick Bakker wrote his weekly letter to the folks at home. His other allotted letter was presumably written to either his sweetheart, Tetje, or other relatives. Dick wrote, "Dear folks at home, how is everybody hitting the trail over there? It is a nice day today and it was a nice day yesterday also. It has rained every day last week but yesterday and today so far. Is about 10 o'clock now. Had pay this forenoon and got 145 franks, 5 franks to a dollar and I have about $30 left beside that so that makes about 295 franks. I am just as handy with French money now as with American money. We get a frank for a 25 cent piece. A frank is 20 cents and a dime is 50 centimes and a nickel is 25 centimes and a penny is worth 2 cents in US money and a half penny is worth 1 cent in US money and a penny is 10 centimes and they have 2 frank pieces too. They are about the size of a half dollar. Have in paper 5 franks, and 1 frank and ½ frank and 10 franks and 20 franks, etc." It is amazing how fast one can learn foreign currency exchange rates. Dick Bakker was no exception. Money talks.

Dick went on to say, "It was quite cold this morning. I haven't been in any camp yet where I could not use two blankets and an overcoat most of the time. That is so different from old Minnesota.

I suppose it is quite hot there now at times. It gets quite warm here at times too. I suppose you will be all through threshing when you get this letter. I think it will take a little longer than a month or about a month. I suppose you will write if John has went in the August draft and where he went. I haven't had mail for a while now. It seems good to get mail from the states. If they are a little old they are new to us.

We have plenty of flies here too. How is the corn crop over there? Ike Habben was here Sunday to see our doings but I did not talk to him. It was raining most of the time. We get up here at 5:30 regular. I bet Drys is in bed most of the time is he not? How did they turn out by going to the cities? I didn't get any of those papers you sent yet but they may come yet. I will quit now and write some more this afternoon." Drys Mulder lived on a farm near the Bakkers. Apparently, he was in ill health. Even in those days, rural folks in Minnesota went to the Twin Cities when special medical treatment was needed. From Renville, the trip was one hundred miles one way, a long trip by horse and buggy. By 1918, quite a few people drove automobiles or took the train.

Dick Bakker continued his letter the next day. "Sunday morning about 9 o'clock now. The sun is very bright and a very nice morning. When it don't rain, we have such splendid mornings. Suppose you are all abed yet while I am writing this letter. We are generally at breakfast when the sun comes up or rather when the sun rises. I received those three papers which you sent last nite. The journal is quite interesting. It is hard to write without a table or desk. Just hold the paper in your hand and write. I saw in the journal that Frank Soderquist was in France. He worked on repairing the elevator when I took the job in the elevator. They sure must start on Class 2 by the way they are taking them out of there.

I think we will go to some other town this afternoon. May go to see Ike Habben. Some of the boys have some acquaintances there too and we have berries all the way. Berries in all directions. We have some big flies here. They look just like tame bees and the same size too. They are lousy here. We call them yellow jackets. They won't leave me alone here for a half a minute, and they sting, too, and they crawl in the horses' nostrils, too. I think I will stop here and write some more tomorrow or tonight as they don't censor today. Just in the afternoons, excluding Sundays."

The "flies" that Dick describes are most likely wasps. It is interesting that Dick did not recognize them. Wasps, and specifically yellow jackets, are present in Minnesota although data on the Minnesota wasp population in 1918 was not found. However, there are tens of thousands of wasp varieties. Obviously, Dick did not recognize this European variety of wasp.

Dick's letters from this time on were censored. The censorship task was assigned to unit officers. Sometimes the chaplain or a medical officer would be assigned the job. The objective was to delete information that would be of value to the enemy. Forbidden information included references to locations, numbers and strength of troops, and even the weather.[135] The censors were also concerned with troop morale and signs of discontent such as criticism of superiors that would lower a soldier's commitment

135 Anthony Richards. "Letter Censorship on the Front Line." *The Daily Telegraph*, May 30, 2014.

to battle. Depending upon the amount of information to be deleted, censors would either confiscate the letter, cut out the information, or obliterate it with ink. In extreme cases when a spy was suspected, special chemicals were used to check for invisible writing.[136] In this letter, Grossouvre was blotted out in the address so as to not reveal Dick's location. Loose lips sink ships.

Dick finished his letter Sunday evening. "Here I am again. Had a good supper and am feeling fine. We were not out this afternoon. Nearly everybody was gone and so we did not go. It was a very nice day today. Was chatting with some French girls all afternoon. It sure takes books and dictionaries with French and English. We have quite a few of them. It takes quite a long time to talk a few words. Still we can understand each other pretty good but those this afternoon didn't talk much American so it took more time and books. Even the English were hard to understand in England. Well I think I will close as I do not know much more news just now. I think we will have some more mail soon. Will write later. Greet the neighbors and friends for me as I can write only 2 letters a week. This leaves me in the very best of health and hope the same over there. As ever, your son and bro, DWBakker, Co F., 160th Inf, American Expeditionary Forces, France."

Given the fact that Dick stated that he was "not out," then it would be reasonable to assume that he stayed in camp. From that standpoint, then, the French girls must have been allowed to enter the campsite. Since they chatted "all afternoon," one would have to assume the girls were there for a social call as opposed to being there as part of a work unit providing services such as cleaning or food preparation. Apparently, visitors were allowed in

136 "American Experience." PBS.

some areas of the camp, at least on Sundays, although it is highly unlikely that any of the American troops had friends or relatives in the area. With the paranoia riding high concerning spies obtaining information on troop strength and locations, one has to wonder why the French girls were allowed into the camp. On the one hand, contact with the opposite sex was a morale booster for the young men far from their loved ones in a foreign land. On the other hand, perhaps the guard was just a sucker for a pretty face.

On Thursday, September 19, Dick wrote a letter to his cousin, Ruth Sikkink. By this time, the two letter per week restriction had been lifted. Dick wrote, "Dearest Cousin Ruth, received you and your mother's and Harold's letters last nite. So I thought I would answer today as it is raining this afternoon. I sure was glad to get those letters. I received 21 letters and 3 papers after I landed in France. So you see it is not so bad but they don't come regular. Received them in 3 times. Well I am feeling OK and I wish the same to you over there. We miss the YMCA considerable which we have not here but we may soon be where they have. Writing paper is scarce here and we were allowed only two letters a week for a while but now we may write a few more if we wish. So maybe you would be a long time waiting if we could not have done so. It is quite hard to write on a little paper box which I have on my lap. I miss the Y tables to write on. We still get letters from Camp Kearny. They get pretty old sometimes before they get here but they are brand new for us.

I am in the same company as Peter Mathews. He knows Uncle Edd Sikkink real well. He worked for him when he got his fingers cut off in the sawmill. There are quite a few here yet from Fillmore County from the May draft. There is one in the same billet as I am from Harmony. I knew him ever since we left Camp Lewis and is an extra chum of mine and everybody thinks we are brothers. Even the corporals and sergeants can't get our names apart yet. We sure must look alike for we are together most of the time and we heard it hundreds of times. Are you brothers? We are the same height and both slim. His name is Reuben Brokken, the name nearly alike too.

"Well Ruth I think I will close as in can't think of much news just now so I will close and hope to hear from you soon and write often and greet the folks for me. This letter will have to do for Aunt Senia and Harold this time if it is possible. Wish you good luck in every way, so goodbye. DWBakker."

In this letter, Dick Bakker exemplifies the strong bond that develops between fellow soldiers isolated in a foreign land and anticipating the danger of battle lurking on the horizon. Dick's grandparents on his mother's side emigrated from Holland and eventually homesteaded a farm near Harmony, Minnesota, which most likely provided a common thread for the friendship with Reuben Brokken. But they would soon part. The orders came down on September 20 to transfer to the Seventy-Seventh Division.[137]

It took Dick Bakker and his buddies four days to reach the Seventy-Seventh Division's camp. On September 21, he wrote, "Somewhere in France now. Dear folks at home. How is everybody over there. Recd Helmer's letter a few days ago & recd the one from ma & Josie last nite. Recd 25 letters after I landed

---

137 *History of the Fortieth (Sunshine) Division; Containing a Brief History of All Units Under the Command of Major General Frederick S. Strong, 1917-1919.* Los Angeles: C.S. Hutson, 1920. September 2, 2008.

overseas. You wrote that you did not get a card from me that I arrived overseas. I don't think you will get any either as I forgot to mail it on the boat the day we went aboard it was so crowded & in such a hurry that half forgot to mail them. I sailed on the same boat Ike did. If you did not get a card from me I am here just the same. Well we are not working this afternoon so I have a little time to write. I wrote to Ruth & Tootsie too & H & Reka also. So Elsie had a close call. I suppose John is in some camp by this time. That will make Bill & Helmer get their hind leg ahead won't it. Well there are many that are worse off than that. This is not so bad yet but will be if it keeps on too long but I think we will be back pretty soon. It is real nice weather today. Some of the boys are picking berries but I am not going at least I have not planned on going. Well we are getting so far we can understand the French people a little better. It sure was disagreeable at first but isn't half bad now. A French man snapped a picture of about 7 of us. It is real good but I cannot send it home now. I wish I would have a box of candy like ma sent me for a change. We can't buy any candy here at all. Only about once a week we can get a taste that is about all. How is Nello hitting the road with my old Ford. I bet it has not got over its habit yet of turning the wrong corner. Well I don't know much news to write just now. We can write as many letters as we wish as long as it lasts. I suppose you will tell me all about who went in the Sept. draft so I will not ask. This leaves me in the best of health & hope to hear from you before long. Greet Geo & Lizzie & how is P.B.F. Greet him for me & tell him we will see him before long. Your son & Bro, DWB."

By September 24, Dick had arrived at the Seventy-Seventh Division campsite. Before he went, Dick sent home an embroidered silk handkerchief to his little sister, Toots. The handkerchief displayed a woman waving an American flag on top of an eagle with spread wings clutching arrows in its claws. The eagle stood on three crossed American flags with "U.S.A" inscribed below in a wreath. The handkerchief carried the inscription:

Just Hello
I'd like to be with you a while and hear about the folks,
I'd like to sit and see you smile at the same old jokes,
But since you are so far away, I cannot hope to go,
I'll send along this little token, just to say HELLO.

It was a touching missive to a dear sister as Dick Bakker set out for combat duties. Toots kept the handkerchief in a special place till her dying day.

World War 1 Embroidered Silk Handkerchief

Chapter 13

Shell Shock

I am sick and tired of war. Its glory is all moonshine. It is only those who have neither fired a shot nor heard the shrieks and groans of the wounded who cry aloud for blood, for vengeance, for desolation. War is hell.
William Tecumseh Sherman

DICK BAKKER WAS ABOUT TO enter the combat zone. He had no idea of the perils that awaited. The colossal destructive firepower of the new military technologies employed by both sides in World War I created a level of psychological trauma never before encountered during wartime. This acute psychological trauma was given the title of "shell shock." These conditions are known today as post-traumatic stress disorder (PTSD), which is defined as a type of anxiety disorder that can occur after one has experienced or witnessed a terrifying event that involves the threat of injury or death.

These new weapons fired high-explosive shells that detonated with such a powerful force that just the sound of an incoming round created terror and disorientation. The reverberation was likened to the roar of an express train, growing louder as it neared with tremendous speed, coming and coming until it burst with a shattering crash. The ensuing blast was like being struck by a huge ocean wave—a concussive blow in the face, the stomach, all over. So devastating was the psychological effect, it was rumored the shells emanated dark, invisible forces that destroyed men's brains.[138]

The Germans had developed long-range heavy-artillery weapons with calibers ranging from 7.7 centimeters to 42 centimeters. One of the more powerful weapons was the twenty-one-centimeter Morser 16, a heavy howitzer that could fire either a 249-pound high-explosive shell or a 268-pound concrete-piercing shell over a range of nearly seven miles at a rate of one to two rounds per minute. Another devastating weapon, the forty-two-centimeter M-great, commonly known as Big Bertha, was a super-heavy mortar that could deliver an 1,807-pound high-explosive semi-armor-piercing shell at a distance of 7.8 miles. The mortar was a road-mobile weapon mounted on a two-wheeled massive carriage towed by a specially designed tractor. The gun was highly effective in destroying Belgium forts during the opening days of the war. Fourteen M-Gerats were built, twelve of which were used during the war. Two Big Berthas were captured by the U.S. Army at the end of the war, and one was taken to the United States and evaluated at Aberdeen Proving Grounds.

The Germans also built a long-range siege gun known as the Paris Gun, several of which were used to bombard Paris from seventy-five miles away during March 1918. The Paris Gun fired 234-pound shells with fifteen pounds of TNT, which resulted in a small explosive effect. An eyewitness described a crater produced

138 Reprinted with permission from the author, Caroline Alexander. "The Shock of War." Smithsonian Magazine, September 2010.

by the shells as ten to twelve feet in diameter and four feet deep. A total of around 320 to 367 shells were fired on Paris at a maximum rate of around twenty per day. The shells killed 250 people and wounded 620 and caused considerable damage to property. As a military weapon, the Paris Gun was not a great success; the payload was miniscule, the barrel required frequent replacement, and its accuracy was only good enough for city-sized targets. The German objective was to create a psychological weapon to attack the morale of the Parisians, not to destroy the city itself. The gun was never captured by the allies and is believed to have been destroyed by the Germans. The Paris Gun shells were the first to reach the stratosphere. These pieces of technology were the roots that led to the V-2 rocket that was used in World War II.[139]

Various accounts credit the artillery with sustaining the majority of casualties during the war. In certain engagements, the accumulated massive artillery fired a hundred thousand shells in a single day. A rolling barrage could sweep ten acres of terrain, 435 yards deep, in less than fifty seconds.[140] For major offensives, the attacks lasted for days, inflicting horrific, and often fatal, wounds—disintegrated bodies, severed limbs, disfigured faces, collapsed lungs, deep burns. The explosions plowed craters several meters deep, exposing mass graves of battlefield dead who had been buried where they fell while at the same time collapsing trenches that buried men alive.

139 "List of German Weapons in World War I." Wikipedia. June 2, 2016.

140 Reprinted with permission from the author, Caroline Alexander. "The Shock of War." *Smithsonian Magazine*, September 2010.

Men cope with stress in different ways. During periods of inactivity, a soldier could rationalize that, in all probability, a bombshell would not find its way to him. This process of denial allowed the soldier to go about his duties for the day without excessive fear. In some cases, a soldier has the option to retreat when under attack. Other times, a unit will be angered to the point it will counterattack. During a long-range artillery barrage, however, there were few options to charge or retreat for the trench soldier. Once the options to take action were eliminated, the feeling of helplessness had devastating traumatic effects as the soldier was forced to endure the barrage for long periods of time.

In actuality, there were other factors besides artillery fire that caused psychological trauma. Soldiers who had bayoneted men in the face developed hysterical tics of their own facial muscles. Snipers lost their sight. Stomach cramps seized men who knifed their foes in the abdomen. Terrifying nightmares of being unable to withdraw bayonets from the enemies' bodies persisted long after the slaughter. The experience of "going over the top" was often a horrifying event. A British soldier, Arthur Hubbard, wrote to his mother why he was no longer in France: "We had strict orders not to take prisoners, no matter if wounded. My first job when I had finished cutting some of their wire away was to empty my magazine on three Germans that came out of one of their deep dugouts, bleeding badly, and put them out of misery. They cried for mercy, but I had my orders. They had no feeling whatever for us poor chaps... It makes my head jump to think about it." Hubbard had managed to fight as far as the fourth line of trenches. With his entire battalion practically wiped out, he was buried by German artillery fire, dug himself out, and during the subsequent retreat was almost killed my machine-gun fire. Within this landscape of horror, he collapsed.[141]

In another documented case, a shell explosion flung a young officer face first into a bloated German corpse, rupturing the swollen abdomen. The impact filled the officer's mouth with the decomposed entrails of the enemy. When the officer regained consciousness, he was traumatized for several days, vomiting frequently, haunted by the lingering aura of the horrifying taste and smell.[142]

From the military standpoint, shell shock was simply cowardice or malingering, and there were those who reasoned the condition would be better addressed by military discipline. This viewpoint was apparent throughout the Allied Command. There was great urgency to maintain as many men on active duty as possible to fend against the massive German legions, and there was no sympathy for emotional weakness. While there were those who were officially diagnosed with shell shock, a larger number of British soldiers with similar symptoms were classified as malingerers and sent back to the front line. Under the extreme pressure, some men committed suicide, some broke down and refused to obey orders, and others just up and deserted.

Military punishment for this behavior was severe as there was concern among the higher command that others might follow

141 Reprinted with permission from the author, Joanna Bourke. "Shell Shock during World War One." BBC. March 10, 2011. Further discussion can be found in Joanna Bourke, An Intimate History of Killing: Face-to-Face Killing in Twentieth Century Warfare (New York: Basic Books, 1999)

142 W.H. Rivers. "The Repression of War Experience." First World War. August 22, 2009.

suit. Discontinuity within a fighting unit greatly weakens its effectiveness and endangers those who continue to battle. Sufferers were made to hang their heads in shame as their reputation as a soldier and a man had been dealt a severe blow in the minds of their peers. Sometimes soldiers in the British ranks who disobeyed orders were shot on the spot by their own officer. Others were court-martialed. Official figures state that over three hundred British soldiers were court-martialed and executed.[143] A common punishment for disobeying orders was Field Punishment Number One. This involved the offender being attached to a fixed object for up to two hours a day and for a period up to three months. These men were often put in a place within range of enemy shellfire. In one instance, a soldier who accidentally fired off a round during inspection was tied up against a wagon by ankles and wrists for two hours a day, one hour in the morning and one in the afternoon, in the middle of winter and under shellfire. Public exposure was part of the punishment. In another instance, military policemen lashed a British Tommy to the wheel of a wagon in full view of a crowd of villagers. After a dramatic silence, the villagers began jeering and ridiculing the man.[144]

Doctors struggled to find a cure for this newfound affliction. Adding to the confusion was the lack of documentation accompanying the soldier returning from the front. Overworked field medics and nurses had no time to interview officers and fill out paperwork. Consequently, it was seldom clear whether the affliction was due to a blast force or a psychological trauma. As a result, a wide variety of treatments were applied to the

143 "Shellshock." Spartacus Educational.

144 "Field Punishment Number One." Spartacus Educational.

battle-strained soldier depending on the primitive theories of the clinical doctors. The most notorious treatment was the electric shock therapy used by Dr. Lewis Yealland at the National Hospital for Paralyses and Epileptic at Queen Square, London. Yealland asserted that his treatment cured all the most common "hysterical disorders of warfare" after application to some 250 cases. According to Yealland, these disorders included shaking and trembling as well as the paralysis and disorders of speech. The electric stimulus was applied to the part of the body that was demonstrating the disorder, such as a shaking hand or leg. The electric shock was applied to the face or sometimes even in the mouth of soldiers demonstrating speech disorders—remedies that are now considered cruel, barbaric, and even criminal.

Other strategies included electric heat baths, milk diets, hypnotism, clamps, and machines that mechanically forced stubborn limbs out of their frozen position. As the war continued and shell shock became better understood, the afflicted soldier was placed under the care of neurology specialists where treatments progressed to rest, peace and quiet, and modest rehabilitative activities sometimes accompanied by psychotherapy sessions.[145] One of the interesting statistics that came out of this era was that officers incurred shell shock at a higher percentage rate than the common soldier. Doctors went on to conclude that every soldier has a breaking point, no matter how well trained. While the objective was to rehabilitate the soldier so that he could return to battle, the vast majority were not cured of their affliction to the degree that they could be returned to their military units. One

145 Reprinted with permission from the author, Caroline Alexander. "The Shock of War." *Smithsonian Magazine*, September 2010.

account asserts that only one-fifth of the men treated in the British hospitals for shell shock ever returned to military duty.[146]

While the emphasis was on curing the soldier, women were also afflicted with PTSD during the war period. There were some noted cases of neurosis in London as a result of the German air raids. On the war front, hundreds of women worked in France and Belgium as nurses and ambulance drivers, right alongside the male soldiers. Their experiences included tremendous violence and physical suffering. Their diaries and letters home include descriptions of being fired on by enemy forces, who used the ambulances to gauge distance to the trenches; spending long nights trapped in No Man's Land; suffering amputations and broken bones from crashes and falling shells; and even getting hit with "secondary gas," as acrid fumes still present around victims they were helping burnt their eyes.

They also wrote of mental anxieties and traumas that bore striking resemblance to the era's understanding of shell shock— but they largely suffered them without diagnosis or treatment. If a female ambulance driver or nurse could not stand the strain of war, she was simply sent home. Unlike the male soldiers, women were expected to be mentally incapable of handling the trauma of war, and high female attrition was hardly a concern. The tremendous effort put into "curing" men with shell shock was due to the army's need for combat-ready men. The supply of women was not rapidly diminishing.[147]

146 "This Day in History: December 4, 1917." History.com.

147 Hannah Grouch-Begley. "The Forgotten Female Shell-Shock Victims of World War I." The Atlantic. September 8, 2014.

Shell shock, or PTSD, was an issue of equal, if not greater, magnitude for the French Army as well as the Germans. Each country dealt with PTSD in its own way. In general, the attitudes, treatments and results were the same as those experienced in England as everyone was struggling to cope with the affliction. By the time the United States entered the war in 1917, shell shock was a recognized psychological disorder, at least in some segments of the medical profession, if not the military. By this time, the medical community had suggested more appropriate names such as "war neurosis," but "shell shock" had already caught on with the public. Records indicate that the American military command in Europe was conferring with consultants in neuropsychiatry. However, with the mad rush to deploy troops into Europe and build an American army, there is little evidence that the military ever attempted to evaluate a soldier's ability to cope with the psychological trauma of combat. On the contrary, Pershing, the Iron Commander, had demonstrated more than once that any soldier who did not obey orders would be court-martialed. The mindset of the American officer was presented by Hanson Ely who later wrote, "Men must be trained that when they have been in battle for days and nights, when perhaps they have been badly handled by the enemy and have had heavy casualties, yet when the signal comes to go they will go again to *the limit of their endurance.*"[148] To be sure, there were those who did go again when the signal came—and again and again. They paid the price. And into this arena stepped the young farm boy, Dick Bakker.

148 Douglas V. Johnson II and Rolfe L. Hillman, Jr., Soissons 1918, Chapter 8, Texas A&M University Press, Kindle, 1999

Chapter 14

Meuse-Argonne

THE HINDENBURG LINE WAS THE last and strongest of the German Army's defense networks. With four years to prepare defenses, the Germans had gone at it with Teutonic thoroughness. The First Position was mainly barbed wire and sacrificial machine-gun units. Three miles behind it was the Intermediate Position, cannoned and fortified in depth from the Aisne River in the west to the fort on the heights of the Meuse.

Behind this outlying complex was the first of the three main Hindenburg barriers—the Giselher Stellung, with the hill of Montfaucon at the grim center of a promontory from which the Hohenzollern Crown Prince, in the safety of a bombproof, had watched the agony of one million men at Verdun in 1916, over half of them killed or wounded. Behind Montfaucon, five miles to the rear, was the Kriemhilde Stellung, strongest natural line in France. Five miles back of those heights were the bristling eminences around Buzancy, the last-ditch barrier, the Freya Stellung. The Germans had named their three strong barriers after Wagnerian witches. "What bitches they were," the Doughboys said later.

"Every goddam German there who didn't have a machine gun had a cannon."[149]

Pershing chose to attack the Hindenburg fortifications on the front between the Argonne Forest on the left and the Meuse River on the right. Looking north from the center of Pershing's line, woods and farmland gently rise over a progression of east-west ridges to the Barricourt Heights, some twelve miles away. On the left, running all the way to these heights, is the fordable Aire River and beyond it the Argonne Forest, an ancient broadleaf forest growing on ridges that rise three hundred feet or so above the surrounding land. On the right of the sector is the Meuse River. Beyond the river, running parallel to the Argonne, are the Meuse Heights, a range of hills rising on occasion to six hundred feet above the battlefield. Montfaucon, the hill standing in the center of the battlefield, rises to 1,250 feet.

The effect of the high ground to the left and right was to turn the sector into a long, shallow channel. This configuration, with the ridges running across the sector and Montfaucon in the center, gave the Germans good observation over eighty percent of the battlefield, with the remaining visible from balloons or aircraft. Montfaucon had twenty-three artillery observation posts on it because the lie of the land gave it panoramic views as far south as Verdun. In 1918, with artillery at a peak of accuracy, the sector was effectively a shooting gallery, with the attacking troops

149 Laurence Stallings. *The Doughboys: The Story of the AEF, 1917-1918*. New York: Harper and Row, 1963, 225.

and rear areas exposed to shell fire at all times—an ideal defensive terrain.[150]

Pershing's nine divisions were aligned against the scarce defenders as follows: One would advance through the Argonne Forest, and eight would attack from the eastern edge of the forest across the eighteen-odd miles to the Meuse River. Hunter Liggett's I Corps, consisting of the Seventy-Seventh, Twenty-Eighth, and Thirty-Fifth Divisions, was situated on the left. The Seventy-Seventh would advance through the Argonne Forest, while the Twenty-Eighth and Thirty-Fifth would drive north along the Aire Valley. George Cameron's V Corps, consisting of the Ninety-First, Thirty-Seventh, and Seventy-Ninth Divisions, had the unenviable task of advancing in the center through Montfaucon. On the right, Robert Bullard's III Corps, consisting of the Fourth, Eightieth, and Thirty-Third Divisions, would advance along the Meuse, peeling back to secure the flank. In addition, the African-American Ninety-Second Division was placed on the left of the Seventy-Seventh under the direction of the French.

Pershing intended that his army should reach the approaches to the Kriemhilde Position by the end of the first day and go through on the second. He was giving the First Army less than two days to advance over heavily fortified and difficult terrain for a distance of ten miles—which would mean advancing at twice the speed achieved at Saint-Mihiel, where the Germans had been in full retreat.

150 Meirion Harries and Susie Harries. *The Last Days of Innocence: America at War, 1917-1918.* New York: Vintage Books, 1997, 349-350.

On the face of it, it was an ambitious plan. Pershing's army was brand-new and unbloodied. None of his best divisions were available; four of the divisions chosen for the attack in the Meuse-Argonne had no experience of the front even in quiet sectors, and for many of the men, as Private Vernon Nicholls recalled with grim humor, "going over the top" was "still a figure of speech." They had neither the training nor the discipline for complex maneuvering. Patton's tanks and Billy Mitchell's squadron were tasked to support the advance; the infantry would carry with them Stokes mortars, two-man operated 35-millimeter guns, and rifle grenades, and each battalion was supposed to be accompanied by two 75-millimeter guns. By the evening of September 25, the attack formations were in place, such as they were. In the two-week time span, the First Army staff had miraculously assembled a platform of guns, tanks, aircraft, material, and men from which to launch this historical offensive. They crossed their fingers that the parts could combine with a destructive power sufficient to rip through some of the most powerful defenses ever devised.[151]

The big guns opened with a harassing bombardment at 11 p.m. on September 25. Three hours later, every battery let loose, filling the sky with blinding, deafening sheets of flame. Nothing their instructors had told them in camp, no newspaper reports or veterans' memoirs, nothing they had heard in France had prepared the green troops for this mind-numbing noise and terror. After a week in the woods in wet clothes and wet feet topped off with a long march without any sleep the night before, the troops' nerves were already raw. Now they cowered in awe in the mire of the

151 Ibid., 353-355.

forward trenches as the ground shook beneath them.[152] In a trench in the Argonne, Dick Bakker was taking it all in.

One of the officers directing artillery batteries that morning for the Thirty-Fifth was Captain Harry S. Truman. Sergeant Paul Shaffer, blacksmith for the Signal Corp, remembered Captain Truman, a banty officer in spectacles, directing salvos into a spot to the northeast, all the while running and cussing at the same time, shouting back ranges and giving bearings. Standing in the drenching rain with shell casings flipping back, Shaffer had never heard a man cuss so well or so intelligently. Shaffer never saw Captain Truman after that day until he voted for him in 1948.[153]

"Fix bayonets!" The order passed along the line from man to man. At 5:30 a.m., the whistles blew, and young officers led their men up the ladders and over the top. For fifteen miles from the Argonne to the Meuse, Americans were advancing virtually shoulder to shoulder. Fog laced with acrid powder fumes stung their eyes and burned their throats as they roared and cheered. For the moment, the whole line was shrouded in thick fog and untroubled by the Germans. With visibility down to barely forty feet, the men stuck close to their platoon commanders, each of whom had a luminous compass and orders "to follow the azimuth 330 degrees to the corps objective regardless of obstacles, machine-gun nests, etc." Unfortunately, no one had realized that the weight of steel embedded in this old Verdun battlefield had its own magnetic polarity that distorted compass bearings.

152 Ibid., 356.

153 Laurence Stallings. *The Doughboys: The Story of the AEF, 1917-1918*. New York: Harper and Row, 1963, 239-240.

In the center, facing Montfaucon, the Seventy-Ninth encountered difficulty hacking through the barbed wire, causing disorganized units to lose formation as well as contact with the rolling barrage. Confused, deafened by the noise, and blinded by the fog, the men formed their own ad hoc units and pushed on across the German front line into the first outpost zone. Shell fire had plowed up the earth all around them. "Debris of every kind strews the ground," reported twenty-two-year-old Leroy Y. Haile. "Many dead are lying around, and many who have been buried are tossed out of their graves. The stench is terrible." Germans in the front line caught by American shells were the first victims of war that many of the doughboys had ever seen. One private remembered, "Some of them were terribly wounded. A slight feeling of sickness came over me as I looked at them, but I fought it off. I must get used to this." PFC Casper Swartz, Company C, 314th Regiment, encountered another astonishing sight: "We came across two men and a boy about fourteen or fifteen years old chained to a heavy machine gun. They were left there to hold the American troops back and kill all they could."

The troops raced forward until mid-morning when the fog lifted. Then at once they found themselves under fire from the crests of the Argonne to their left and Montfaucon to their front and right. Colonel Howland, commanding the 138th Regiment, Thirty-Fifth Division, remembered, "The shelling was so heavy that more than a score of my men were instantly killed, several blown into shapeless masses of blood, flesh, and clothes. Simultaneously, enemy machine guns opened a terrific fire from both flanks and front." The survivors took cover in a ditch while a

French officer, with great bravery, went to call some nearby tanks to the rescue. For three hours, Howland and his men lay under intense shelling and machine gun fire. When the tanks arrived, the little band of raw recruits launched their charge, and the machine-gun nests were wiped out, the crews killed or captured. This kind of piecemeal engagement was repeated up and down the front as the fog lifted and the German gunners gained sight of their enemy. But the Americans had gained the surprise they needed, and the Germans mounted no counterattacks. Traversing the first outpost zone, the First Army crossed the first real line of resistance on schedule.

By 11 a.m., the Twenty-Eighth and Thirty-Fifth Divisions on the far left, astride the Aire River, had reached the objective set for Liggett's I Corps. Now, as ordered, they halted, waiting for Cameron's V Corps to come up in the center. On the right of the attack, on the Meuse side, the three divisions of Bullard's III Corps also advanced steadily. While Liggett and Bullard drove forward to their flanking positions, in the very center of the attack Major General Joseph E. Kuhn's Seventy-Ninth Division approached Montfaucon. These men from Pennsylvania, Maryland, and the District of Columbia were almost the newest to combat of any in the First Army, and their training had been among the worst. More than half the division's personnel had been assigned to it since May 1918, from camps all over the United States. The last units had reached France on August 3. Then, just as the division had begun training in France, its senior officers had been transferred and replacements appointed. The division was in no sense an organic entity; its artillery brigade had remained behind in training, and new gunners were assigned, arriving just as the infantry took up position in the front line.

Now, as soon as the Seventy-Ninth was put to the test, its attack formation was ruined by the fog and the wire. The 314th Regiment lost entire sections and gained two companies of the 325th that was supposed to be in support. When the fog lifted, the lead units found that they had stumbled into a thicket of German machine-gun nests with bullets streaming at them from all points of the compass. The Fourth Division to the right had neglected to mop up the extreme edge of its sector, leaving a line of enemy machine guns entrenched on a ridge on Kuhn's flank. Kuhn had no means of communicating with his artillery to have them take out these guns. As darkness fell, the Seventy-Ninth had not taken Montfaucon, and panic was beginning to set in. Their advance had been slowed as the regimental machine guns and 37-millimeter guns had been unable to keep up with the advance, forcing riflemen to take on machine-gun nests. The support tanks had been of little use that first day of battle. After fourteen hours of combat, the men were badly in need of food and rest, but there could be no respite. The Seventy-Ninth Division, spearhead of the First Army's attack was already lagging badly; the divisions to the right and left had all pushed well past Montfaucon, and Kun ordered Colonel Claude Sweezey, 313th Regiment Commander, to take the stronghold that night.

V Corps artillery pounded the hill, and two tanks arrived to help the infantry cross the open ground into the lashing machine guns. The tanks went forward about two hundred yards in the twilight, stopped, turned around, and withdrew from the field of action, leaving the unsupported infantry to be cut down mercilessly and forced to retreat. Kuhn summoned Brigadier General Robert Noble who was commanding the support brigade and gave him the appalling order to attack at once with the 314th and 315th Regiments. The division had been in combat for nearly twenty hours with heavy casualties and was disorganized; its telephone communications were out, it was pitch dark, and now it was raining.

At 2:15 a.m., Noble tried to establish contact with his regimental commanders, but the road forward was so congested with traffic that he had to walk and did not reach rendezvous until after 5 a.m. A major crisis was now building in the dawn of September 27. Pershing's strategy of rapid penetration before the Germans could reinforce was falling apart due to the failure of the Seventy-Ninth Division to take Montfaucon. Per the plan, the division should have been some six miles forward at that time, confronting the Kriemhilde Position.

Colonel Oury, Commander of the 314th Regiment, was promoted to brigade commander. Oury established liaison with the artillery and at last the 37-millimeter guns arrived. With Pershing frantic to get the advance moving, every available gun fired at Montfaucon, deluging the hill with gas and high-explosives, while all four regiments tried to envelop the defenders in a coordinated attack. By 7:30 a.m., the Germans had beaten the Americans back in savage fighting, and frantic demands came for more artillery support. With the aid of a barrage that turned the hill into "one great belching spout of dirt and dust," Seezey pressed home his attack. Finally, the message came back: "Montfaucon captured 11H45."[154]

With Montfaucon taken, the First Army entered the combat zone, covering the approaches to the Kriemhilde Position. By the second day of the attack, the element of surprise had gone. The Germans were fully alert, their guns more numerous and effective, and reserves were desperately rushing to shore up the defenses. Three new German divisions appeared on Ligget's I Corps front alone. At this crucial time, when the First Army needed to maintain all its destructive power and momentum if the strategy of rapid penetration were to succeed, the attack faltered.

After twenty-four hours of combat, many of the units were disorganized and disoriented. The men were tired after a night spent in cold, muddy holes under the noise and sudden glare of star shells, artillery bursts, and machine-gun bullets. Vernon Nicholls, with the Ninety-First Division, woke up on the second morning in the drizzle, stiff, cold, and thirsty. He drank from a nearby stream and then sat watching "infantry and artillery tanks and supply wagons moving around in the mud and rain, most of them trying to locate their respective outfits. [...] The carcasses of four horses were lying a few yards away, and not far from where we sat were four Yanks, killed by one shell as they slept together in a shell hole." Eventually he and his buddies were gathered up by an officer they had never seen before, who tried to push them on.

But the situation in the rear was even worse. Since midmorning the previous day, guns, artillery trains, food and water supplies,

154 Meirion Harries and Susie Harries. *The Last Days of Innocence: America at War, 1917-1918*. New York: Vintage Books, 1997, 356-361.

ammunition trucks, and divisional staff had been trying to move forward. As they tried to cross the no man's land, trucks and horses alike slipped and sank and bogged down in shell holes, wire, and collapsed trenches. This three-mile band of murderous man-made swamp running across the entire front proved virtually impassable. As fast as roadbeds were laid down, the press of traffic caused them to collapse. Nothing could get forward. The burden of the advance rested squarely on the shoulders of the infantry which was advancing without artillery coordination and support.

Throughout the second day and the next, the Thirty-Fifth Division labored painfully up the valley of the Aire, harassed by enemy planes above and machine guns and artillery below. The forward elements of the Thirty-Fifth spent the third night concealed in Montrebeau Wood about six miles north of the jump-off line in the shadow of the Argonne Heights. In the early dawn of September 29, the 137th Regiment prepared to attack Exermont, a strongly held village in a ravine just ahead. Jump-off was set for 5:30 a.m., and the men were promised a squadron from the Second Cavalry to reconnoiter the flanks, with a rolling barrage and tanks to lead their advance. None materialized. After three days of attrition in the open—mired in mud, tormented by incessant machine-gun fire, high explosives, shrapnel and gas, and strafed and bombed from enemy aircraft—the vaunted "staying power" of the double-sized American divisions had vanished. Influenza was spreading rapidly, and while the food supply was adequate, the men had been driven to drink water from shell holes and were now ravaged by dysentery.

Major Kalloch, 137th Regiment Commander, himself a replacement officer sent forward, now discovered on the brink of attack just how many of the other officers and NCOs were already dead or wounded. As a functioning organization, the Thirty-Fifth Division was all but extinct. Nevertheless, at 5:34 a.m., Kalloch led his men out without protection, obeying the orders to move forward. They got within one hundred yards of the German lines before they were encircled by a murderous fire from flanking machine guns and artillery firing from the Argonne and Exermont. They had been caught in a carefully prepared death trap. Without support, Kalloch ordered the survivors of his group to withdraw at 8 a.m. They made every effort to bring in all the wounded, but there were several who were left behind.

The Thirty-Fifth's other regiments suffered equally. By late morning on September 29, the Thirty-Fifth Division was in serious trouble. It was deep within the German killing grounds, without an effective organization to repel a determined counterattack. With casualties totaling around seven thousand, Division Commander Traub had no option but to withdraw his shattered columns to an entrenched position on a ridge behind Mantrebeau Wood, well short of the line they had reached on the second day.

Traub's division was not the only one to have been broken by the fourth day. That Sunday, Major General C.S. Farnsworth, commander of the Thirty-Seventh, watched his men attack Cierges-sous-Montfaucon to the east of Exermont and then falter and stall under intense shelling. Their failure exposed the flank of the Ninety-First Division, but Farnsworth could not move his left flank up because "the physical condition of his men on account of exposure and fatigue was such that it would be impractical to advance."

On Farnsworth's right, Kuhn's Seventy-Ninth, having taken Montfaucon at immense cost, had found themselves virtually cut off by the stream of shells pouring onto them from the reinforced German defenses. They could not push on, nor could they bring up supplies or even set up dressing stations that were at all safe. The troops were practically without food for three days, and their only water was scooped, foul and lethal, from shell holes.

From the second day on, the worsening chaos in the rear not only denied units the support they needed in order to push forward, but it also began to function actively as a brake on their progress. Even after four days of struggle, none of the hideous problems of crossing no man's land had been resolved. In places, vehicles stood stationary for anything between sixteen and thirty hours; elsewhere the average speed was just over one mile per hour.

The men were becoming so desperate for food that the divisional rolling kitchens and food trucks, stalled in the traffic snarl, were being looted by men of other divisions forced to drop back. Heavy artillery was immobilized for seven days. Even command decisions could not get through. On September 27, Pershing had sent orders at 11:30 p.m. for V Corps to attack at seven the next morning. The orders did not arrive until four hours after the appointed jump-off time.

This monstrous traffic snarl, which was an anxiety and a frustration for the commanders, spelled torture for the sick and wounded. If a wounded man were lucky, he would be collected by a stretcher party and carried to a first-aid station. From there he would be taken through the traffic jams into the back areas, a journey that could take twenty-four hours, with a further forty-eight hours in transit back to the nearest field hospital if major surgery were called for. If he were unlucky, he would lie on the battlefield for days.

The First Army had taken forty-five thousand casualties in four days, and its attack had at best been slowed, at worst stalled. Frontline troops were in retreat in places, and several of the divisions were incapable of even defending the line against German counterattack. The rear areas were gripped by chaos. The difficult terrain and foul weather, the haste with which the offensive had been thrown together, the inexperience of so many of the divisions involved... All had played a part in the breakdown. The First Army's difficulties were caused not by lack of will or courage but by the failure of its staff to overcome the fearsome logistical problems of this stretch of the Western Front. But no rationalizations, no excuses, could soften the fact that there had been no breakthrough. On the eve of September 29, Pershing accepted the inevitable and suspended the offensive. He had lost his gamble, and his men had paid the price.[155] But there would be more to pay.

155 Ibid., 362-367.

Chapter 15

Trapped

IN THE DEPTHS OF THE Argonne Forest, New York's so-called "ghetto" troops of the Seventy-Seventh "Liberty" Division, now mixed with Fortieth Division replacement troops from the western states, were fighting their own war. The Seventy-Seventh, commanded by General Robert Alexander, attacked across a five-mile front. Alexander, the son of a circuit court justice from Baltimore, Maryland, studied law for two years before enlisting as a private in the army in 1886. From there, he rose through the ranks to command the Seventy-Seventh during the final battles of World War I. Alexander was another commander who made personal visits to the front line, encouraging men verbally as well as with his presence. He was awarded the Distinguished Service Cross for his efforts.[156] The 308th Infantry was on the far left under the command of Colonel Austin F. Prescott. Prescott reported to the 154th Brigade Commander, Brigadier General Evan Johnson. Immediately to the right of the 308th was the 307th, the other regiment of the 154th Brigade commanded by Colonel Eugene Houghton. Then came the 306th and 305th regiments of the 153rd Brigade in that order from left to right. The Ninety-Sec-

156 "Robert Alexander (United States Army Officer)." Wikipedia. September 20, 2016.

ond Negro Division under French command was immediately to the left of the 308th. The 308th Regiment's First Battalion was the attack battalion commanded by Major Charles W. Whittlesey, a thirty-four-year-old, tall, gawky, spectacled, serious Harvard Law School graduate who practiced his profession in New York City. The Second and Third Battalions were assigned the support and reserve roles, respectively. The Second Battalion, commanded by Major Kenneth P. Budd, was lined up five hundred meters behind Whittlesey's attack battalion. Budd placed Companies H and E in the lead, followed by Companies G and F respectively. Dick Bakker, now under Major Budd's command as a member of Company E in the support battalion, was about to experience his first combat action. The Seventy-Seventh's first objective was a four-kilometer advance from the point of departure.[157]

At precisely 5:55 a.m. in the thick, foggy morning darkness of September 26, the First Battalion, 308th, surged up and over the top into no man's land behind a rolling artillery barrage. Major Whittlesey himself blew the whistle, then leaped forward with a pistol in one hand and a massive pair of wire-cutters in the other. It was an ominous start. The men quickly lost formation in the frosty blanket of darkness, falling into unseen shell holes and deep trenches. The dense fog obscured the open lanes that the artillery barrage was supposed to have created. As a result, troops became entangled in rusted, hidden barriers of barbed wire and hard wire cables with protruding knife blades. With the advance

157 Robert J. Laplander. *Finding the Lost Battalion: Beyond the Rumors, Myths, and Legends of America's Famous WWI Epic.* Waterford: Lulu Press, 2006, 82-83.

held up, engineers came forward to carve a way through the wire or to throw rolls of two-ply chicken wire thirty feet long and eight feet wide over the dense wire fields. The engineers also carried twenty-foot sections of light footbridge for crossing wire barriers as well as shell holes and trenches. At one deep trench, the only way across was a single wooden log that an entire company had to cross one-by-one. To add to the misery, the odor of stagnant, muddy pools emanated through the dank, cold forest air. The delays caused the infantry to lose the cover of the artillery barrage which had advanced a thousand meters ahead. German machine guns that had survived the rolling barrage began firing blindly into the fog while German artillery began to lob gas as well as high-explosive and shrapnel shells into the oncoming wave.

Five hundred meters back, the Second Battalion, with Dick Bakker in Company E, did not get off until ten minutes after six. Once under way, the Second Battalion took the brunt of the German shellfire as the Boche tried to find the range of the Allied attack units. In the dense fog, the battalion dispersed into small units, with the Westerners tending to band together while the New Yorkers formed their own groups. Adding to the misdirection were the metal shell fragments in the ground from former battles that warped the compasses of the company commanders.

The dispersion of units resulting from the difficulties of terrain and weather continued throughout the morning as the attack advanced. Communications between companies as well as between companies and Regimental PC bogged down as runners got lost in the fog and couldn't find their designated message recipients. By early morning, Second Battalion units were intermingling with First Battalion units, despite orders to avoid doing so. Around 9 a.m., the fog began to lift, and the First Battalion reached the first of the major German trench lines, the Ludwig Stellung, where a firefight ensued, resulting in four German prisoners.

With the fog lifting, commanders gathered the troops into platoon-size units, and the First Battalion advanced to within six hundred meters of the corps objective by 10:30 that morning. German reconnaissance planes were beginning to fly overhead, spotting for artillery fire. At this time, Whittlesey brought the advance to a temporary halt to regroup and organize a line of defense. Whittlesey then sent word for Major Budd to bring the Second Battalion up adjacent on the left, which Budd did over the midday, although with some difficulty. Here, the two battalions accepted a shared responsibility for portions of the front line for the time being while they continued to gather stragglers and discuss the morning's events.

At 11:20 a.m., Whittlesey and Budd received orders from Colonel Prescott that an advancing artillery barrage would begin at half past noon. Whittlesey's First Battalion was to follow the barrage at 1 p.m. followed by Budd's Second Battalion in support, again with orders not to intermingle. Reorganization of the units continued until slightly after 1 p.m., when the First Battalion stepped off for the second time that day with orders to plow ahead as fast as possible toward the Combined Army Objective: the Giselher Stellung some seven to ten kilometers from the original jump-off line.

The afternoon advance failed to gain any real ground, with the First Battalion attack breaking down into poorly coordinated local actions and the Second Battalion doing a lot of Indian fighting. The rest break had helped the Germans as well, and the First Battalion took their first serious casualties of the day. In the fading light with the clouds rolling in, Whittlesey called a halt to operations and set up a Battalion PC in the Karlplatz trench system, a complex of several nicely built and furnished concrete and log huts combined with interlocking well-constructed trenches. As night fell, so did the temperatures, but no fires were allowed as a hard rain set in. No food had come up all day. Hungry and shivering, men began to suffer without blankets, overcoats, or shelter halves. Funk holes filled with muddy water, forcing men to crawl out and try to sleep exposed on the open ground. The shelling that had started in the afternoon continued throughout the night along with sporadic machine-gun and rifle fire. In the heat of battle, it was far too cold and wet to get much sleep. Out on the line, men stared out into the rainy darkness, hopeful that tomorrow would be easier but probably knowing in their hearts that it would not. Somewhere in the trenches, Dick Bakker was pondering his first day of combat.[158]

Orders for September 27 directed the attack to jump-start at 6 a.m. after a half-hour artillery barrage. The orders specifically stated that each unit should push forward without regard to troops on the left or right, an order that would lead to dire consequences in the days ahead. It had rained hard all night through the early morning hours. All the while, German shellfire continued to harass the troops. The 308th commanders got little sleep working

158 Ibid., 92-107.

to reorganize their fractured, scattered companies and trying to scare up some rations. But there had been no ration details nor rolling kitchens brought forward, so the troops remained hungry as they prepared for battle. Despite the efforts of Whittelsey and Budd, many men had moved into the jump-off line on the twenty-fifth with no rations. These same men went into battle on the twenty-seventh hungry again. Likewise, no clean water made it up to the lines, forcing canteens to be filled with rain water caught overnight or water from shell or funk holes, which was muddy at best and gas-contaminated at worst.

The morning dawned murky and dirty, with a blanket of fog rolled over the muddy, shivering Doughboys as they huddled in their funk holes. The artillery barrage flew overhead right on time at 5:30 a.m., and the troops of the 308th prepared to move forward. But the final orders authorizing the advance had yet to come down from Colonel Prescott. For reasons still unknown, perhaps due to communications difficulties, Prescott never sent out the final orders that morning. When the news reached division headquarters, Prescott was immediately relieved of his command, put under arrest, and replaced with Colonel Cromwell Stacey. It was just after 1:30 p.m. when the First and Second Battalions of the 308th climbed out of their muddy funk holes in a drizzling rain and began to advance into the heavy woodland before them.[159]

Up and down the line, the New Yorkers soon learned that the "streets," the network of trails through the forest, were dangerous killing grounds covered by machine guns emplaced every fifteen yards along one overgrown ridge. Time and again, they would be

159 Ibid., 111-118.

caught by hidden machine-gun snipers buried in the undergrowth, muzzle flashes invisible behind their screens. They had to learn wood lore: how to advance through the undergrowth in single file, stealthily following officers who were themselves navigating by compass.[160]

Sometimes there was a lull as the men lay on the ground, and absolute quiet reigned. A snapping of twigs in the bushes, the noise of a stealthy approach brushing aside the branches, would fall on the ear. Not a sound from the American line. Suddenly, the air would be torn to shreds by the racket of a hundred rifles and Chauchats going off at once. A dozen men would shout, "I got him," and someone would run out and drag in a limp form of a Bache machine gunner, caught in the attempt to steal forward under cover and get the Doughboys by surprise. Often, there were at least fifty bullet holes in the body. Everybody's eye had been on him. The East-siders and West-siders of New York, the soldiers from Third Avenue and from Central Park West, were becoming adept woodsmen and learning the craft of the forest hunter.[161]

The Germans used every trick in the book in close-quarter, savage fighting. Company K of the 306th Regiment came across a group of Germans who held up their hands and said, "Kamarad." Thinking they had surrendered, the Americans moved forward only to have the Boche produce hand grenades and cause

160 Meirion Harries and Susie Harries. *The Last Days of Innocence: America at War, 1917-1918.* New York: Vintage Books, 1997, 371.

161 United States Army Infantry Division, 77th, *History of the Seventy Seventh Division, August 25th, 1917, November 11th, 1918,* New York City, W.H. Crawford Company, 1919, 69

considerable casualties. On the face of it, a polyglot of Poles, Jews, Italians, Greeks, Irish, Armenians, and now farm boys from the west might not have been expected to cohere. But the heat of battle warmed the melting pot, and men who could communicate only in broken English phrases risked their lives for one another. The New Yorkers gained a new respect for the Fortieth Division "hayseeds" and "appleknockers" who were more at home in the forest while the Westerners found themselves admiring the sheer tenacity of the New Yorkers in battle.

With the four regiments thinly spread across the forest among the trees and crags, split up by gullies and ravines, there was no weight to its advance, no chance of punching through the enemy lines in the initial attack. In the tangled undergrowth, it was difficult to maintain contact at all, and the fighting evolved into a recurring pattern of small units pushing forward stealthily, with the Germans, equally furtive, infiltrating behind to cut them off. Units trapped like this were under orders not to surrender; they were the forward base on which the advance could build. "Any ground gained must be held," Brigadier General Johnson told his officers. "The troops holding it must be supported. If I find anybody ordering a withdrawal from ground once held, I will see that he leaves the Service."[162]

In the 308th sector, Whittlesey called for Budd's Second Battalion to come forward after advancing 150 hard-fought meters against interlocking fields of machine-gun fire. Budd quickly moved his men up to the left on an even line with Whittlesey's

162 Meirion Harries and Susie Harries. *The Last Days of Innocence: America at War, 1917-1918*. New York: Vintage Books, 1997, 371.

troops. Budd, a Harvard graduate, was the most experienced battalion commander in the 308th. The two units inched forward through the underbrush in clusters of small troops, cutting through barbed wire while cleaning out machine-gun nests. At 4:30 p.m., Whittlesey received orders from headquarters to dig in, reorganize, and wait for the units on his flanks to catch up. Overall, the 308th advanced four hundred meters that afternoon, still outdistancing the 307th on its right flank, and the 368th Negro Unit on its left was nowhere in sight. As the men dug in, the chilly, misty rain continued into the night. No one had been dry for two days. No food was brought up, and the men were forced to scavenge for water from puddles or the falling rain. Carrying parties went out to fetch more ammo and grenades from nearby dumps. As a result of the little sleep from the night before, brutal exhaustion came creeping in with the evening shadows. And once again, it would be a long and nerve-wracking night with artillery from both sides continuing overhead and machine guns popping off at the slightest sound in the darkness.

In the early morning of September 28, the third day of the advance, Major Whittlesey and Major Budd met with their new Regimental Commander, Colonel Stacey, to review the orders for the day. That same morning, General Order No. 27 came down from Major General Alexander, reinforcing the position that no ground taken could be given up without a direct order from headquarters. Earlier, Whittlesey had sent a request to Brigade Headquarters for stretchers and litter bearers to attend to their heavy casualties. The rain and mist had stopped just before dawn, but clouds and fog shrouded the battlefield. Some rations had been brought up, but hunger was still an emphatic problem. Yet by 6 a.m., most of the two battalions got off behind the usual half-hour artillery barrage. Initially, resistance was unusually light as forward scouts passed by craters with bloody remains.[163]

By 8:30 a.m., Whittlesey's and Budd's men had progressed forward nearly a kilometer through a rain of enemy shells. Here they met their first serious resistance from well-placed machine-gun nests in a gentle valley with a narrow-gauge railroad track running north and south across their attack path. A kilometer or so ahead was the Moulin de l'Homme Mort (Dead Man's Mill), a complex of concrete huts and machine-gun posts that was the day's objective. The mill itself was situated in a deep, wide ravine running north and south.

Facing stiff resistance, Whittlesey sent a message back through the runner chain to Colonel Stacey stating their situation and requesting food and water. Stacey then requested an artillery barrage from General Johnson at Brigade Headquarters. Johnson scheduled the barrage from 11:30 a.m. to 12 p.m. Receiving news of the barrage, Majors Whittlesey and Budd pulled their men back several hundred meters and began planning for the upcoming attack as shells started flying overhead. The plan entailed splitting the two battalions to attack on each side of the ravine, keeping to the high ground. Charging directly down the ravine would have made them easy targets for German snipers from the heights above. The First Battalion was to attack on the west, and the

---

163 Robert J. Laplander. *Finding the Lost Battalion: Beyond the Rumors, Myths, and Legends of America's Famous WWI Epic*. Waterford: Lulu Press, 2006, 120-127.

Second Battalion was to attack on the east. The Second Battalion attacked with Company B in assault and Companies E and H in support. The battalions would reunite at the mill complex and take it in a combined effort. Single runners were to provide liaison between the two forces. Commanding Company E that day was probably the best-liked and most respected company commander in the whole of the 308th, Captain George G. McMurtry, a cheery, short, nimble, ruddy-faced Harvard man and ex-Rough rider from New York.

But shortly before the barrage was scheduled to begin, ration and water carrying parties finally arrived, as Major Whittlesey had requested. For many, it was the first meal since the initial jump-off, and for some, it would be their last. For the moment, though, they got some relief and were able to forget about the dangers ahead. Yet, there were still those in the outposts who missed out. Unfortunately, for those men, it would be some time before rations appeared again.

The artillery barrage went off on schedule, and the two battalions jumped off in their separate directions shortly after noon. But the advance of the Second Battalion quickly stalled, and Major Budd called a halt around 1:30. He then called Captain McMurtry and Company E, left behind where the two companies had split, to come forward. Company E, with Dick Bakker somewhere in its midst, arrived at 2 p.m., when Major Budd put them in the rear of the advance zone. Budd then resumed the advance forward with Company B as the assault battalion and Company E following behind. The Second Battalion was now connected to the 307th Regiment on their right flank, which was fighting its way through terrible entanglements of barbed wire overgrown with weeds. Shortly, enemy machine guns opened up at the juncture with the 307th, and Captain McMurtry sent out a Chauchat team to silence them. All the while, long-range Hotchkiss fire continued to skim over the heads of the Doughboys.

Out ahead, the two platoons of Company B ran into fire from directly in front and hunkered down to deal with it. Not realizing they had halted, Captain McMurtry kept E moving and soon had them running up into B from the rear. McMurtry called a halt, but it took some time to straighten out the situation. Meanwhile, the enemy shellfire started coming in heavier, and the men caught the heavy scent of mustard gas mixed with it. Masks on, they continued to try to work their way around the nests. It was almost 2:30 p.m.

About this time, Major Budd crossed the ravine to combine his PC with that of Major Whittlesey. This seemed like a good idea at the time, but the move left the Second Battalion leaderless as the afternoon wore on. Meanwhile, the First Battalion was advancing up the gentle slope of l'Homme Mort with Company A out in front, slugging it out with determined German machine-gun crews. Pushing ahead, they came upon an unpretentious German cemetery surrounded by a low wooden fence, all the while taking machine-gun fire. The battalion passed the cemetery and over the crest of l'Homme Mort. As evening set in, they had made it to a small clearing at the north foot of l'Homme Mort, where they set up camp. There was a fine concrete bunker tucked in a wash nearby where Whittlesey set up the combined Battalion

PC. They moved the wounded into some huts and light buildings in the vicinity.

Coming up to the crest and over the top, there had been a fierce fight of grenades, machine-gun fire, and stiff resistance of every kind. Still there had been few casualties. Scouts reported that they were within 150 to 200 meters of the mill, the day's objective. Dark was falling rapidly along with a steady light rain. As they had not heard from the Second Battalion in some time and the 368th was still nowhere to be found, Whittlesey and Budd started to feel uneasy that the battalion could be cut off from the rear and surrounded. They dug in for the night, dispositioned in a narrow hollow square. Whittlesey sent a message down the runner chain and also flew a message out by pigeon. Unfortunately, the pigeon's message would not be found until noon of the thirtieth. As thunder echoed across the hillside, the men shook their head and swore. As the night set in, so did a heavy cold rain. No food had been brought up, and those who tried to get water from a nearby stream found themselves under sniper fire.

By about 3:30 p.m., the Second Battalion had run into serious trouble. Combat teams from Company E reported back to Captain McMurtry that Germans were all over the place on their left flank. McMurtry was still back with the majority of Company E, to the rear of Company B, when a German machine gun opened up from their right flank and tore into the right rear of Company E. Men began to drop, and American rifles poured general fire toward the right and rear, trying to keep the enemy at bay. A wedge of Germans had pushed its way between the 307th and 308th and was attempting to surround the Second Battalion. There seemed little choice but to pull back, which was a violation of General Order No. 27 without orders from headquarters. However, there was no time to wait for such an order to be approved. It has never been confirmed as to who made the decision to retreat, although it was most likely McMurty. Nevertheless, the Second Battalion retreated back to a line along a railroad track around 4:30 p.m., leaving Whittlesey and the First Battalion some four hundred meters ahead of the main body of the 308th with no flank support and only a thin runner line connecting them to the rear as the night set in.

In the pre-dawn hours of September 29, Whittlesey's designated runner, Sergeant Hitlin, had finally worked his way through the drizzling rain and the German encampments to arrive at Regimental PC. Around that time, Captain McMurtry also arrived. The two confirmed that Major Whittlesey was indeed cut off. Stacey began laying out plans for an attack that would bring the main line up to Whittlesey's position. The First Corps orders for September 29 were to begin an advance following the usual artillery barrage at 5:30 a.m. The orders also reiterated that the attack would again be pushed forward "without reference to troops to the right or left" and had unchanged objectives.[164]

The hard rain continued through the night and tapered to a steady, irritating drizzle in the pre-dawn that would continue sporadically throughout the day. Chilled to the bone in soaked-through uniforms, the men shivered almost uncontrollably without overcoats or blankets as they stood in slimy, water-filled

164 Ibid., 134-149.

funk holes, peering through the icy ground fog around them, teeth chattering, watching for signs of enemy movement.

Just before 4 a.m., Lieutenant Arthur McKeogh, the battalion adjutant, sent another messenger back with a request for food and supplies. A short time later, muffled machine-gun fire ripped the air from the hill above. Before long, the runner came crashing back down the hill and reported to the company commanders that he had been challenged in German and fired upon. As they spoke, more machine-gun fire, distinctly German, came from beyond the hill. Quickly, Major Whittlesey had Lt. McKeogh assemble a three-man scout patrol and sent them out to find out what was going on with the line of communications. It was now 4:45 a.m.

The two battalion commanders started making rounds at daybreak, getting reports from overnight patrols. The news was disturbing—suspicious movements in the woods all about and gunfire in the rear. Hold in the patrols. Do not engage if it can be avoided. Sit tight and keep quiet. Then sporadic German machine-gun fire erupted again in the woods. Two men appeared out of the woods, one with a bandage around his leg. They were from runner post eleven. The third man had been killed. They reported that runner post ten had also been attacked. The runner chain was broken.

Off in the distance, the morning U.S. artillery barrage started, and the sound of cannon fire rolled over the hill and echoed down the ravine. Whittlesey decided it was time to find out what was going on. Shortly after 6:30 a.m., he sent Lieutenant Keogh to the rear with a small combat force to check out the runner line, repair it if needed, and report back his finding. He then sent another strong scouting party into the wet brush of the dank morning under Battalion Sergeant Major Benjamin F. Gaedeke, a dependable New York boy, to reconnoiter the immediate vicinity. After that, he sent a strong patrol of Company F scouts to the east to liaison with the Second Battalion if indeed they were forward again. After the patrols disappeared into the woods, Whittlesey sent another message by pigeon back to Regimental PC advising them of his situation.

By the time the bird landed in the loft around 7:20 a.m., an attempt had already been made to break through to Major Whittlesey. At the first peak of dawn, Colonel Stacey ordered Lieutenant Colonel Fred Smith to assemble a team of ten combat men from Company B, fifteen runners, and two officers and set out for the First Battalion position. The team moved rapidly through the tangle in the pre-dawn darkness but soon ran into stiff resistance after taking the wrong branch of a fork in the trail near the cemetery. Lieutenant Colonel Smith was killed, and the rest of the rescue party was forced to return to Regimental PC.

Back in the forest, Lieutenant Keogh and his small band were working their way through the cold drizzle in an attempt to repair the line of communications, establishing runner posts every 150 meters or so. At about 7:30 a.m., they encountered their first skirmish with German patrols, killing a German non-commissioned officer while capturing a private and his machine gun. Sergeant Major Gaedeke came along with his patrol and took the two Germans back to the First Battalion PC along with a wounded Doughboy. With the sounds of machine guns waking up and chattering all around them, it became apparent that they were in German-held territory. Lieutenant Keogh then decided to disperse his men in a combat formation near runner post twelve rather than in a column down the trail. Shortly, a German officer brandishing a long barreled pistol in his hand along with a sergeant walked right through their position. All rifles went off together, and down flopped the two Germans. The wounded officer informed them that he had seventy men up ahead to oppose their advance. Lieutenant Keogh sent the officer back to Whittlesey along with his maps and papers. Keogh then turned his men down the hill and continued south on his mission to re-establish the line of communications.

Back at the First Battalion bivouac position, Whittlesey released another carrier pigeon to the regimental command post informing headquarters that the runner communications links were broken and requesting that a unit come forward from the rear to help re-establish the link so that the First Battalion could continue their advance. When the patrol brought the German officer's maps to Whittlesey and Budd, the maps revealed many important details of the German positions ahead—a magnificent find! As daylight set in, the men were working at improving their mud-filled funk holes. The quiet of the morning began to break as the Germans tested the Doughboy force from all directions with rifle and machine-gun fire along with potato-masher grenades. Intense sniper fire raked the open edges of the clearing and cut down any Doughboy who tried to get water from the nearby stream. Through it all, Whittlesey and Budd stalked all over the bivouac, going from funk hole to funk hole lending moral support and encouragement and assisting company commanders in directing return fire. Whittlesey's ability to keep the troops calm and under control during this peril provides an insight into his leadership qualities.

Whittlesey sent out two more patrols during the morning that both came back with the news that the battalion was surrounded by Germans. With casualties mounting and no apparent help from either flank, Whittlesey sent off another message by pigeon around 1 p.m. requesting help from the rear. Throughout the afternoon, Whittlesey could hear attempts from the rear to break through, but the Germans had placed a great many machine guns in the intervening space. Patrols that were sent out to link up with the main force were either scattered, killed, or captured. At mid-afternoon, Lieutenant Keogh was still pinned down in skirmishes at the cemetery. Things were not looking up. Only a lucky few had food to eat. Sniper fire prevented getting water from the stream. The Germans had launched squad-sized attacks all day long. The order went out to conserve ammunition and grenades as both were running low. At 4 p.m., Whittlesey called for another bird and scrawled out another message that merely reiterated the other three with some added details.

The 308th Second Battalion had gone into battle behind the morning barrage in good order, but they soon ran into stiff machine-gun fire. By noon, the Second Battalion was in liaison with the 307th on their right but were getting their teeth kicked under heavy artillery and machine-gun fire. By 7:30 p.m. on September 29, the 154th Brigade attacks were all but over. The 307th and 308th regiments had been driven away from the slopes of the Depot ravine and were again held up on a general line three hundred meters or so south, almost where they had started. There had been virtually no gain at all for much blood spilled.

In the First Battalion bivouac, the men only knew that they were cold, wet, hungry, and surrounded as the sun went down. The day had been a bad one, and tomorrow could prove to be worse. Troops were almost completely out of food and water and almost out of ammunition. Tensions were high as rumors spread of an early morning attack. On the positive side, there had been few casualties and even fewer killed. Then it started to rain...again.

As the light faded, Lieutenant Keogh and his two men were painfully crawling through the brush again. Coming upon two Germans, Keogh took a bullet in the right hand in a skirmish that killed the Germans. Shivering in the wet brush, they decided to wait until full darkness before setting out again. Around 8 p.m., they skirmished again with another German patrol but were able to escape and hide in the brush. At this time, the three runners broke up on the premise that one of them would get through to deliver Whittlesey's message. Around 2 a.m., a driving rain pelted the countryside, and at about 4 a.m., Keogh set off again. As dawn broke, Keogh was staggering down a road in an exhausted state when a patrol from Company I of the 307th found him and took him back to the Regimental PC to deliver his message. Shortly thereafter, the other two runners were brought into the Regimental PC. All three men received the Distinguished Service Cross.[165]

With General Pershing calling a halt to the assault on the evening of September 29, no line of attack occurred on the morning of the September 30. Positions were to be consolidated

165 Ibid., 154-175.

and reorganized in depth with strong reconnaissance patrols sent out to the front to maintain contact with the enemy. This included cleaning up back areas of stray enemy troops and substantiating supply lines. Throughout the morning, carrying parties were sent back to supply dumps to return with huge quantities of rifle, machine-gun, and Stokes ammunition. Some food and water was brought up, and the rolling kitchens came as far as the captured and repaired roads would take them.

Major Whittlesey's men awoke, stiff and sore, as the dim, gray morning found them strained and with little sleep. Nerves already shaken by hunger and cold were stretched further as the usual Argonne morning fog rolled in and once again blanketed everything. Most of the men had not been out of their funk holes for two days except to relieve themselves. The effects were beginning to show in the form of cramped muscles, swollen feet, and painful rheumatoid joints. Sickness, too, was setting in. As a result of their existing in nothing but continuously wet wool uniforms for five days, exposure was beginning to grip many. Colds and deep rattling coughs that presaged pneumonia, the flu, and diarrhea were all present. Men were filthy and unshaven, having been unable to wash or clean their teeth in almost a week. Many were infested with body lice and suffering from gas poisoning. The deep, raw hunger pain emanating from low in the stomach had to be the worst of all. A few had not eaten since the start of the offensive five days before. Getting water from the stream was next to impossible, and the last packages of smokes had long been emptied.

Whittlesey was making his rounds well before dawn, gathering information and encouraging the men. Yet, with ammunition and supplies nearly gone, their position seemed precarious at best. No patrols sent out during the night had made contact with anyone friendly. But just after 6:30 a.m., everything was still surprisingly quiet—no allied artillery barrage, no Boche counter-attack. It came as a great surprise, then, when a small stray patrol of four men in khaki snaked up the hill from the south, dragging with them two German prisoners. Upon Lieutenant Keogh's arrival, Colonel Stacey had decided to send out three small patrols to blaze a path through to Major Whittlesey. The first patrol that had left at 4:30 a.m. armed mainly with grenades and led by an acting Sergeant Legers had now made its way through to Whittlesey's bivouac. Standing on the edge of the clearing with the incredulous Majors Whittlesey and Budd, the patrol related that they had seen relatively few German troops on the hillside.

Whittlesey then sent out some patrols that came back around 7 a.m. with reports that it indeed appeared that most of the Germans had pulled out overnight. There were still machine-gun nests and snipers to deal with, and the artillery was again starting to fall in heavy behind them. With that information, Whittlesey sent Sgt. Legers and his scout patrol back the way they had come with the German prisoners and a message for Colonel Stacey. Meanwhile, two other separate sixteen-man patrols that had been sent out by Colonel Stacey to break through to Major Whittlesey were spotted by the Germans and driven back without success. All morning, other strong probing patrols were sent out to test the German line, but none were able to break through.

Sergeant Legers came back to Regimental PC around 8:45 a.m. with the message from Whittlesey. Breathing a sigh of relief, Colonel Stacey started sending small parties carrying food, water, and ammunition back through the established runner chain with orders to attract as little attention as possible. Throughout the day, small relief parties of men continued moving up and down the thin runner line to the First Battalion's position, carrying supplies to the beleaguered men. The sick and the wounded were also sent back down the line, a few at a time. There was some enemy shellfire to the rear and toward the head of the ravine to the right of the position, but none on the First Battalion's bivouac. Sniper fire was the worst threat, yet men still crawled out aboveground to work the kinks out of bodies that had been folded into narrow, muddy holes for two days and nights. Private Nell later recalled how his hands had cramped up so bad he could not grip his rifle.

Around noon, General Alexander felt that his division was reorganized to the point that he could resume the attack. Therefore, at about 3:30 p.m., Division PC sent orders to General Johnson for the afternoon attack to get under way. A little after 4 p.m., the thirty-minute artillery barrage in the 308th Second Battalion's zone erupted.[166]

It was on this day, September 30, that Dick Bakker wrote his last letter to the folks at home. While there is no time stamp on the letter, it most likely was written during the morning hours when the reorganization was taking place. Clearly, it had to be written before the afternoon attack. The paper was lined with a small American flag in the upper left-hand corner. The handwriting

166 Ibid., 179-184.

was jagged and irregular, indicating that it was most likely written in haste at his position in a vermin-infested trench using whatever flat surface he could find for support. By this time, Dick had endured four days in a cold, rain-soaked uniform, watching his fellow soldiers getting shot up in the mayhem of machine-gun and artillery fire. Thrust into combat with no end in sight, facing a dense forest where snipers and machine gunners lay waiting for one false move, any illusions of grandeur had long left the farm boy's mind. No doubt hungry and thirsty, the basic instincts of survival had set in with understandable concerns for safety in his first battle, a battle of enormous magnitude.

The letter read, "Somewhere in France. Just a few lines to let you know how I am getting along. Suppose you recd my last letter maybe about a week ago or so & told where I was going. I left next day. Have been over the top already. That is going pretty fast is it not? We are having lots of rain here & quite cold too. I think I will close as I have not much time & news to write & may be a long long time before I get a letter from home. So I will close & greet all the folks at home for me & say hello to Tetje too as I have not time now for a while. Hope it may be over soon. This leaves me feeling okay so far & hope to hear from you soon, As ever, your Son & Bro. DW Bakker Co E, 308 Inf, Am EF."

It is somewhat amazing that trench letters found their way home in the utter chaos of battle. The army allowed soldiers to carry paper, pencil, and even fountain pens in their packs. Many a soldier took a moment to write a note home in the midst of combat on the premonition that it might be his last chance to send a message to his loved ones. Dick Bakker was one who took that moment. With army restrictions on divulging troop locations and other strategic information, there was not a lot that Dick could say other than to let the folks at home know that he was okay. The one sentence, "Hope it is over soon," says quite a bit as to his state of mind. Nonetheless, Dick was now engaged in hand-to-hand combat in the Argonne Forest. And the situation was about to get worse.

Once the artillery barrage lifted, the waterlogged Doughboys slowly rose from their muddy funk holes and plodded forward. Captain McMurty now had temporary command of the Second Battalion with Company B out front as assault unit under orders to get through to Major Whittlesey and the First Battalion. Company E with Dick Bakker, now led by Lieutenant Karl Wilhelm, attacked on the right. Shelling from the Germans increased in tempo and intensity. Machine-gun fire sang out, light but accurate. The Second Battalion slowly pushed the line as the afternoon light dissolved, clearing machine-gun nests as they advanced with caution.

Around 5:30 p.m., the men of the First Battalion heard the rest of the regiment coming on in considerable force, but a storm of artillery shells drove the Second Battalion back. Finally, at 6:30 p.m., Captain McMurtry slammed the Second Battalion forward again and broke through the line with the Germans high-tailing it northwestward. At about the same time, Lieutenant Taylor was leading Company K down the north slope of l'Homme Mort hill and into the open area next to Major Whittlesey's PC, heavily loaded with much more food, water, and ammunition. By 7 p.m. or so, the line back down the hillside was pronounced safe and secure, and the 307th had drawn up on an even line farther to the east and made liaison with the 308th's advanced line. Up and down the line, there was a huge sigh of relief.

Lieutenant Taylor brought with him orders to send Major Budd back to Brigade. Captain McMurtry was to take command of the Second Battalion. Lieutenant Wilhelm was to command Company E. Colonel Stacey also wanted to talk to Major Whittlesey in person. Leaving Captain McMurtry in command, Whittlesey was led back to Regimental Advance Headquarters by guides in the dark of night. After briefing Colonel Stacey, Whittlesey returned to his battalion through the darkness in the same manner. Orders were to advance at daybreak.[167]

167 Ibid., 184-195.

Chapter 16

The Lost Battalion

FOR ONCE, THERE WAS FOOD for breakfast on the morning of October 1 as the carrying parties worked all night bringing up hard tack and canned corn beef as well as hot stuff from the rolling kitchens. The wounded were carried back to an ambulance station as sporadic German shellfire continued through the night. Stray snipers created some intense moments in the dark of the forest. Well before dawn, after a good night's rest, the First Battalion commanders had the men situated in the jump-off positions. It was yet another frosty, damp morning, but there was no rain.

The First Battalion was again to lead the attack with the Second Battalion in support some three hundred meters behind. Major Whittlesey's orders were to advance straight north up the Ravin d'Argonne to a point where it terminated at the east-west-running Ravin d'Charlevaux. Once at the junction, the regiment was to move across the Charlevaux brook, take the Charlevaux Mill beyond, and then extend a general line eastward along the Binarville-La Biergette road. The advance would cover slightly over two kilometers of machine-gun infested Argonne woods.

The First Battalion jumped off at 7 a.m., a little behind the usual half-hour artillery barrage. The troops pushed slowly and carefully along the heavily wooded ravine with Company A on the left ridge and Company C on the right, encountering only occasional sniper fire. At about 10 a.m., after advancing about a half-kilometer, the First Battalion encountered stiff German resistance, and a battle broke out all over the ravine. There seemed to be machine guns everywhere, and enemy trench mortar shells were coming into the Doughboy positions with relative precision, along with regular shellfire and gas. They were coming up on more barbed wire as well, weed-grown and well camouflaged. Though they kept the pressure on all morning, the Doughboy advance had ground to a halt by 11 a.m.

Around 1:15 p.m., with the First Battalion taking a serious beating, Whittlesey sent a message to Captain McMurtry to bring the Second Battalion forward. It took until 3 p.m. to get everyone in position, and, once again, the two battalions were close up and acting as one unit. The Major then sent out the order to try another advance down the ravine. Just after 5 p.m., the 308th's attack ground to a halt after having advanced about three-quarters of a kilometer. They set up a shaky perimeter across it. A flatcar clattered up the narrow gauge line at the bottom of the ravine, pushed by hand, carrying lots of rations, water, ammunition, and grenades—still no overcoats, blankets, or shelter halves. Enemy artillery and trench mortars continued dropping into the ravine sporadically along with gas shells. The men dug funk holes wearing gas masks and slipped off to nibble on hardtack or corn willy. As the night set in, German flares revealed the limp, wet American corpses hanging from the thick belt of rusty wire that lay between the opposing forces. It had been a rough day, by far the roughest day they had yet seen since the twenty-sixth. Rain threatened again.

Around 10 p.m. that night, Colonel Stacey's adjutant, Captain Francis Weld, came up the runner line with orders for the next morning's attack. He found Major Whittlesey, Captain McMurtry, Lieutenant William Cullen of H, Captain Stromee of C, and a couple of new lieutenants huddled in a bunker around a small coke stove. In the shadowy light of the oil lanterns, Weld read the order, "The advance will be resumed on October 2 at 6 a.m. Your objective is the line 294.5-276.6. You will take your objective and hold it at any cost until support arrives." The officers sat in strained silence. The order represented nothing less than operational suicide. The position described was nigh on untenable with the known German placements, and the position would most likely leave them again with no flank support. Lieutenant Cullen broke the silence, "Then it will be the same thing. We will be cut off again." Captain Weld replied to no one in particular, "That possibility has been considered, but the attack has been ordered nevertheless."

It was inconceivable to the officers that they were to repeat the same bloodbath that had failed that day. Around 10:30 p.m., Major Whittlesey made the trek down the runner line in a chilly night fog, hanging on to the cartridge belt of the runner leading him through the dark. Once at Regimental PC, Whittlesey wasted no time in telling Colonel Stacey that he thought the order was definitely a bad idea. Stacey agreed that the orders were difficult, but the attack plan had come down from General Liggett at First Corps headquarters. The orders would stand.[168]

Just before 7 a.m. on the morning of October 2, the 308th Regiment surged into the ravine following the half-hour barrage. The objective per the coordinates was the Binarville-La Viergette road. It had been a cold night, with temperatures dropping into the mid-forties Fahrenheit as shivering sergeants reported their status to Whittlesey. Cold rations, water, ammunition, and grenades had been brought up overnight, and the men were glad to have eaten breakfast for the second day in a row. Companies D and F attacked along the west ridge under command of Lieutenants Knight and Kiefer. The rest of the two battalions started a flanking movement over Hill 198. Beyond Hill 198 was the Charlevaux Ravine, a narrow slit between two steep slopes: Hill 198 to the south and Mont d'Charlevaux to the north. Companies A and G advanced down the center of the ravine. On the right ridge, Company C took the lead with B in support and E with Dick Bakker right behind them. Whittlesey kept the Battalion PC with the flanking units.

The assault units were quickly met with rifle volleys followed by machine-gun fire and trench mortars. Companies D and F drew heavy fire on the west ridge from the La Palette Pavilion on Hill 205. Lieutenant Kiefer was wounded and was replaced by Lieutenant Turner. As the minutes ticked by, the Germans continued a steady rain of rifle and machine-gun fire on the

168 Robert J. Laplander. *Finding the Lost Battalion: Beyond the Rumors, Myths, and Legends of America's Famous WWI Epic.* Waterford: Lulu Press, 2006, 199-220.

attack companies, and German artillery began hitting the support companies. Shortly after 10 a.m., the advance up the ravine had hit an impasse. Unknown to Whittlesey, Lieutenant Turner with a platoon of fourteen men had been cut off by the Germans that morning on the west ridge.

At this time, Whittlesey sent a message down the runner chain to notify Colonel Stacey, who, in turn, passed it on up to General Johnson at Brigade PC. Johnson was packing to move his Brigade PC forward when he received Stacey's call with the bad news. Furthermore, a runner from Colonel Houghton, 307th Commander, had arrived with similar news. With neither regiment moving, Johnson called General Alexander, who received the message around 10:30 a.m. and, by all accounts, promptly hit the roof. Alexander had just received a similar message from General Whittenmeyer, that the 153rd Brigade was stalled as well. From Alexander's standpoint, things could not have been worse.[169]

By this time, all four regiments of the Seventy-Seventh were heavily engaged in hand-to-hand dogfights in the deep pockets of the forest, most of them experiencing situations similar to that of Whittlesey. As the infantry plunged farther into the forest, it was only with the utmost difficulty that food and ammunition could be supplied to them. A great part of these supplies had to be carried in on the backs of men. At all times, rations were short, and hunger was an ever-present companion. Battling an invisible enemy fighting from concealed positions with the deadliest weapons of modern warfare, the rain-soaked troops dug in at the end of each day in the damp and dripping woods and shivered through the

169 Ibid., 229-239.

cold night in funk holes half-full of water, bereft of overcoats and blankets that had been discarded at the beginning so as not to impede progress. Rest was seldom undisturbed as the Germans had exceptional knowledge of the terrain. Searching batteries of German artillery were constantly seeking the Americans throughout the night with high explosives and trench mortar shells. The machine gunners from the regimental companies and brigade battalions attached to the infantry were obliged to carry their heavy guns, tripods, ammunition boxes, and equipment by hand as they struggled through dripping bushes in the wake of the infantry line. At night, the Hotchkiss gunners, exhausted as they were, posted their guns on the flanks of the bivouacked infantry and guarded the lines against counterattack.

On the other side, the German soldiers were enduring the same environments. However, prior to the American assault, not every German soldier was "roughing it" in the depths of the Argonne jungle. On September 28, the 307th Battalion had advanced three kilometers ahead as far as the heights bordering the Abri du Crochet, its line running west about a half-kilometer along the east and west trail leading to Bagatelle Pavilion. Along the slopes and heights of Abri du Crochet and Champ Mahaut to the southeast, the advancing troops uncovered a German paradise. Here was located one of the famous rest areas of the German armies, where battle-worn and weary Boches were taken to fatten up and recover morale amidst amazing comforts and luxuries.

On the reverse slopes of these hills, huge, deep dugouts had been constructed, each capable of housing fifty men or more in perfect safety from hostile shelling. On the heights above these dugouts, more pretentious abodes had been constructed for officers and non-commissioned officers. These were built of concrete, with logs and concrete roofing, twenty feet in depth, and were ornamented to resemble Swiss chalets and Black Forest hunting lodges with peaked roofs and exterior fresco work of burnt oak. Within were oak wainscoted chambers, fitted with electric lights and running water, supplied from the power house in the valley below. Benches and tables, in rustic solid oak, were supplemented by plush arm chairs and hair mattresses to cater to the comforts of weary warriors, and outside the doors, rose-gardens and favorite flowers from the Fatherland were cheerfully blooming. "Waldhaus Martha," "Waldhaus Albertin," and "Unter den Linden," as they were variously named, vied with each other in coziness.

Adjoining "Waldhaus Martha," was a bowling alley, with an open-air restaurant and beer garden built above it, where sat the onlookers on a sunny afternoon, quaffing their beer and cheering on the bowlers. Down in the ravine below, where the brook ran, was a great concrete swimming pool, a close rival to the one in the Columbia College gymnasium, and here also were found spacious shower baths supplied with hot water by modern boilers and concrete furnaces.

Within the complex, the men found a chapel; a library teeming with the best works of German science and literature including, even from hated England, the tales of Rider Haggard and Conan Doyle; an officers' club with its attractive bar; and a big theater fitted for moving-picture exhibitions—all assembled to create an ideal spot for quiet life and recreation. In the photographer's shop, the men found hundreds of plates showing Germans, short and tall, fat and thin, single and in hilarious groups, having all kinds of good times with hunting parties, beer parties, singing parties, and Christmas parties—high festivities generally in their valley paradise. The Germans had rested securely in these comfortable facilities for over four years.

But on that day of September 28, the rude hands of war were dealt so suddenly, the recreational German soldiers barely had time to get out before the American infantry was upon them. Upon entering the complex, the Americans discovered evidence of hasty flight. Uniforms were still hanging in the closets; cigars, wines, and other food luxuries were undisturbed in the storerooms; and meals were laid on the tables, ready to be eaten.[170]

Nevertheless, General Alexander found himself with his back to the wall on the morning of October 2, 1918, with the advance of the Seventy-Seventh Division grinding to a standstill and General Pershing livid over it. Fuming, Alexander left a telephone message at the 154th Brigade command post, "You tell General Johnson that the 154th Brigade is holding back the French on the left and is holding back everything on the right and that the 154th Brigade must push forward to their objective today. By must I mean must, and by today I mean today, not next week. You report heavy machine-gun fire, but the casualty lists do not substantiate this." Yet the attack was stalled, and around 11 a.m. Johnson called Alexander and reported the details of the situation, some good and

170 United States Army Infantry Division, 77th, *History of the Seventy Seventh Division, August 25th, 1917, November 11th, 1918*, New York City, W.H. Crawford Company, 1919, 69-70

some bad. Johnson then received a blistering diatribe in which he was told that the attack was to go on regardless of flanks and losses, and if he could not do it, then Alexander would get someone who could. General Alexander then ordered a twenty-minute artillery barrage for 12:20 p.m., after which the Seventy-Seventh was to move forward at 12:50 p.m. at the rate of one hundred yards every five minutes.

No doubt seething inside, General Johnson relayed the orders to Colonel Stacey and Colonel Houghton. Seeing no point in arguing further, Stacey accepted the orders with little comment. Houghton, on the other hand, replied in no uncertain terms that the German line ahead was so heavily wired in and so accurately defended with intense trench mortar, machine-gun, and artillery fire that he seriously doubted his regiment's ability to drive through it in their present undermanned and exhausted state. Houghton was perhaps the most experienced battalion commander in the division. Nevertheless, General Johnson explained, those were the orders, and he expected them to be carried out. Both Stacey and Houghton expressed disbelief when Johnson told them their flanks would be supported. Because of the dense forest combined with clouds and rain, support from the air had been largely ineffective. When Stacey telephoned the orders down to Major Whittlesey, the exasperated major pronounced, "It will only lead to the same thing again. We will be cut off!" To which Colonel Stacey replied irritably, "You are just getting panicky. Proceed with the attack as ordered, Major."[171]

171 Robert J. Laplander. *Finding the Lost Battalion: Beyond the Rumors, Myths, and Legends of America's Famous WWI Epic.* Waterford: Lulu Press, 2006, 240-247.

At almost exactly 12:50 p.m., with a slight mist falling, the barrage rolled forward, and the tired Doughboys rose from the mud of the Ravin d'Argonne once again to push against the Giselher Stellung line. On the right, Company B, supported by Company H, slowly carved lanes through the dense twenty-meter rusted wire belt up on Hill 198 as occasional machine-gun bursts and mortar shells slashed the forest around them. To their left, Company C, supported by Company E with Dick Bakker, drove carefully up the marshy ravine bottom and along the eastern slope through the dropping shells. On the far left, the remains of Companies D and F soon encountered murderous rifle fire and grenade activity as they attempted to rescue Lieutenant Turner and his men.

By 1:25 p.m., the flanking movement had advanced three hundred meters and some fifty to sixty men had fallen due to the machine-gun and sniper fire. Shortly after 2 p.m., Companies C and E had found the breaks in the wire and the paths across the marshy part of the ravine. About that time, a detail headed by Sergeant Thomas Owens of Company B took out a German machine-gun nest, capturing a lieutenant, four NCOs, and twenty-three privates to be taken to the prisoner pens. The Germans gave up readily and were glad to be out of the war.

The enemy fire slowly decreased as the 308th pressed forward, taking out machine-gun nests as they advanced. Around 3:30 p.m., a runner came down to the Battalion PC with news that Company C scouts had crossed a major trench line atop Hill 198 and were on a narrow road behind it with nary a German in sight. Climbing to the top of the hill, Whittlesey and McMurtry could see the Binarville-La Viergette road in the distance across the Charleveaux Ravine. They had come to the Giselher line! The objective was in sight. The flanking movement had worked. Whittlesey's orders were clear; he had to continue on into the Charleveaux Ravine through the break they had found. But he had a bad feeling. It was all too easy. On the west ridge of the Ravin d'Argonne, Companies D and F had been beaten back to the position they had held at noon without rescuing Lieutenant Turner's men and were in the process of setting up for the night. Companies D and F were now separated from the rest of the 308th.

About 4:30 p.m., Captain McMurtry and Major Whittlesey began planning dispositions as they stood atop Hill 198 along a path of brambles, brush, and trees that led into the Charleveaux Ravine. The path continued to a flat spot near the meandering Charleveaux Brook with a rustic footbridge crossing it. A clearing of trampled grass, barely a dozen meters to the left of the footbridge, appeared to be a German drill field of sorts, flanked on all sides by tall rush grass but few trees. Beyond the brook, the path went left of a marshy strip and terminated into a wagon road running east and west at the foot of the slope. They picked a spot to set up camp north of the brook at the foot of Mont d'Charlevaux facing a high, steep slope covered by trees and thick brush. The camp would provide access to water and protection from German artillery attacks from the reverse side of Mont d'Charlevaux due to the steep slopes.

At about a quarter to five, after dashing off a note to Colonel Stacey, Whittlesey led the combined Battalion PC down the path toward the small clearing in front of the footbridge. Halfway down the slope, they spotted two men in coal shuttle helmets watching them from a distance. Private Rainwater, a First Battalion replacement scout of Indian heritage from Montana, fired off two shots but missed as the two Germans disappeared into the brush. At the bottom of the hill, Whittlesey sent out shallow patrols to the east and west again. He sent Captain McMurtry over the bridge first with his Second Battalion PC and a small group of scouts to coordinate things. With the light fading fast, the other officers started their men across the foot bridge in twos and threes at a dead run for safety. Then a machine-gun on the eastern side of La Palette hill along with another near Charlevaux Mill began to pepper the area with sprays of long-range lead. The Germans had them in their sights. Bullets splashed the water around their feet as the men rambled through the tall grass and across the narrow plank bridge. A few went down and had to be snatched up by the next men coming across. Last over the bridge and into the area that would become world-famous as "the Pocket" was Major Whittlesey himself and his First Battalion PC. It was 6:30 p.m.

Dispositions were quickly straightened out, and men rapidly began to dig in. On the far left, wrapping its way east around an outward bulge in the hill near the footbridge was Company H under First Lieutenant Maurice V. Griffin and First Lieutenant William Cullen, one of the Second Battalion's most experienced leaders. Protecting the important left flank was a line of six tripod-mounted Hotchkiss guns from Company D/306th Machine-Gun Battalion under Second Lieutenants Marshall G. Peabody and Maurice P. Revnes. The left flank was exposed to the concentration of enemy troops on La Palette Hill as well as Charlevaux Mill, now only seven hundred meters west of the position. The French were still nowhere to be found.

To the right of Company H Whittlesey placed Company B, top-heavy with replacements after suffering heavy casualties, led by Lieutenant Harry Rogers. The First Battalion's strong Company C, under Captain Leo Stromee, Second Lieutenant Gordon Schenck, and Second Lieutenant Leo W. Trainor, was placed to the right of Company B. Whittlesey located the Battalion PC just to the right of Company C, which he shared with Captain McMurtry. To the right of the PC position came the weaker Company G, being commanded by Second Lieutenant Frederick Buhler and the brand new Lieutenant Eager. Augmenting Company G, was Company A, now a mere eighteen men strong, commanded by Second Lieutenant Williamson. Finally, on the far right was Company E, second strongest of the Second Battalion, led by the highly experienced First Lieutenant Karl Wilhelm, First Lieutenant James V. Leak, and the brand new Second Lieutenant Victor A. Harrington. Three Hotchkiss guns were placed to the right of Company E to protect that flank. At that time, Whittlesey was expecting the 307th to soon close on his right flank. Whittlesey spaced out the few auto rifles they had left below the lip of the road to fire forward in case of attack.

A check of company commanders revealed that they had incurred eighty-seven casualties coming over the hill. The combined force now totaled slightly under five hundred effective troops instead of the 1,800 rifles that two full-strength battalions would have at their disposal. Well after 6:30 p.m., Whittlesey sent his last message for the night to Colonel Stacey giving his status and position. Whittlesey was now some seven hundred meters ahead of Companies D and F that were digging in along the main attack line leaving his left flank exposed. On the right, the 307th was some five hundred meters to the rear, having taken heavy enemy fire during the afternoon.

Sniper and machine-gun fire from Hill 205 and the Charlevaux Mill continued to rain down on the campsite through the evening, and even potato-masher grenades came sailing down from the hill above. But Whittlesey and McMurtry had set up a good defensive position with plenty of natural cover from brush and heavy woods. Whittlesey sent out basic scout patrols and liaison parties to the flanks. McMurtry assigned Newcom and Hutt of G to push out on the left and look for the French, who were supposed to be covering the flanks of the Seventy-Seventh. Neither Whittlesey nor McMurtry were surprised that the patrols found no one friendly on the flanks. With full darkness, the enemy fire subsided and the Pocket became eerily quiet.

Headquarters received the good news of Whittlesey's advance around eight that evening and immediately began worrying about the flanks. Under pressure from General Alexander, General Johnson ordered the 308th Third Reserve Battalion to move forward and connect with Companies D and F and then spread west to connect with the French just outside of Binarville on Whittlesey's left. However, Johnson did not see the need for the Third Reserve Battalion to move forward until the next morning, a command that would later be heavily criticized. Johnson then ordered Houghton of the 307th to send up his Third Battalion in support of Whittlesey at once. Johnson sent the 307th First Reserve Battalion forward to replace the Third Battalion.

Houghton's battalion, composed of four companies, K, I, M, and F, all pretty strong and in good condition, moved out around midnight led by Second Lieutenant Bernard Currier from Regimental PC along with a small squad of three or four enlisted runners. Company K followed directly behind Lieutenant Currier and the guides led by Lieutenant Tom Pool and Captain Nelson Holderman. Holderman, a hearty young man from California, liked soldiering so much, he even liked its discomforts, the whole business a perpetual party to him and the best war he was ever in. Each man crept forward in the muddy, pitch-black ravine with a finger hooked into the back of the cartridge belt of the man in front of him. Following K was I, now augmented by the wrecked F. The column picked up Company M, commanded by First Lieutenant Andrew F. Shelata, and slipped them in line between Companies K and I/F before continuing on their way. Progress was slow and slower as deceptive chimneys and cuts ruffled the slope by which they were steering. Frequently, men stumbled and fell, causing halts so as not to break the chain.[172]

Around 2 a.m., there was an extended halt as the lead guide had gotten out too far ahead. Exhausted and grumbling, with a light rain tapping soothingly on their helmets, the men began to fall out and flop down on either side of the trail. Around 2:30 a.m., the guide found them, and the battalion again moved forward. Captain Holderman had kept Company K on their feet, but an exhausted Lieutenant Shelata of Company M, had dropped to

172 Ibid., 249-275.

one knee and soon fell asleep. When he awoke, the man whose belt he had been holding was long gone, and Company M took a wrong trail and became hopelessly lost. Too weary to care what happened next, Shelata posted guards and had the men dig in to wait for daylight. Company I/F broke loose when M did and strayed into some old German dugouts where they bedded down for the night, planning to cross the crest of the hill and link up with Whittlesey in the morning. It was around this time on the west ridge of Ravin d'Argonne that three mud-covered men dragging a wounded comrade came sliding through the weeds toward the Company D positions. They were the only survivors of Lieutenant Turner's platoon; the rest had been killed down to a man.

Holderman's K alone held the true line. They were now barely over one hundred men, having sent a ration detail back earlier. About 3:30 a.m., they found a runner post that gave them directions to the crest of Hill 198. Holderman dismissed Lieutenant Currier and his guides. The runner led the company to the top of the hill where they received more instructions. With great difficulty, Company K moved forward down the steep slope in complete darkness. With no one to point them in the right direction, they were unable to find the bridge or the open field. One runner post was unmanned. It was coming up on 4 a.m. when Holderman set outposts and gave the men a little shut-eye for the few remaining hours of the night. Holderman sent out a nine-man reconnaissance patrol to make sure the surrounding area was secure. They never returned. Meanwhile, Captain Holderman's ration party had met resistance from the Germans and had to return to Depot, where they reported the situation. In the morning hours, reports began to filter into headquarters that communication with Whittlesey's position had been cut off.

Just before dawn the next day, October 3, a German officer was captured by Whittlesey's men near the leftmost outpost. Upon interrogation, the officer revealed that his regiment was nearby with more to come. His statements were backed up by a morning patrol which reported seeing numbers of Germans beyond the road. When one American got a shot at one, light machine-gun fire was returned. These events convinced Whittlesey that the rear elements had not closed up to him, or that the French had not made any advances. He immediately became concerned about protecting his left rear, through which some German elements had evidently already filtered.

Shortly thereafter, around 6:30 a.m., Captain Holderman came across the brook, and the two officers compared their orders. At that time, Holderman still believed that the three lost companies in his battalion were close behind Company K. It was decided to send Lieutenant Wilhelm and Company down the west ravine to connect with Companies D and F and close the left flank. Wilhelm gathered his troops, including Dick Bakker, and Company E trotted across the bridge, turned slightly right, and disappeared into the early autumn foliage. As Company E left, Company K, 307, began to filter across the bridge and file into position to cover the flank E had vacated. All the while, a machine gunner up on La Palette hill was dropping shots on the men coming and going. Major Whittlesey then sat down and scrawled his first message of the day to Colonel Stacey and handed it off to a runner. It was 6:50 a.m.

Around 7:30 a.m., an enemy plane wheeled overhead and disappeared. Shortly thereafter, a few artillery shells started to come in from the north, sending up tremendous geysers of dirty water and mud. But the artillery had little impact on the protected positions against the foot of the steep slope of Mont d'Charlevaux other than a psychological effect. At about this time, a message came down the chain of runner posts that was timed at 7 p.m. the previous evening, which meant that his runner chain was working so badly that it had taken all night to get a message through.

An officer reported that some men had no reserve rations. Captain McMurtry quickly assembled a carrying party of fifteen men and a medic to bring up rations and medical supplies. Captain Holderman then came up with a report that a runner had been unable to get through due to Germans roaming all around Hill 198, and he had found a complete absence of manned runner posts. With the situation looking bleak, Whittlesey sent a message back through the runner chain stating their position including coordinates. It then occurred to Captain McMurtry that Major Whittlesey had not included Headquarters PC or machine gunners in the ration request, so he sent out a runner with a message to catch up to the rations party. This message was written at 8:42 a.m.

By now, the shelling into the Pocket was increasing, and the Doughboys were picking up a few shrapnel wounds. Whittlesey called up Omar Richards, the York State French-Canadian who was the number one pigeon man, and sent a faster message by one of his birds requesting artillery support. Lieutenant Teichmoeller of the 305th Field Artillery was present when the messages were discussed and offered to get in touch with his own organization. Teichmoeller sent off a message with a second pigeon requesting artillery support and providing headquarters with what he believed to be their exact coordinates. Unfortunately, Teichmoeller gave a vertical coordinate that was eight hundred meters south of his true line. Coordinates were defined by a detailed set of French Army maps carried by all officers. Both birds landed at divisional mobile loft number nine, near the town of Forent, where the messages were logged into the message center at 10:55 a.m. but were not immediately acted upon.

With the gunfire getting heavier, Major Whittlesey sent out a patrol from Company H on the left flank to size up the situation. Captain Holderman sent out a squad on a similar mission on the right flank. Within half an hour, the flank patrols were back and reporting both directions blocked by small parties of heavily armed Germans operating not far off in the brush. Liaison was impossible without actually fighting a way through. Then just before 10 a.m., Leak and Harrington of E came staggering into the position. Of the fifty-one men who had gone out with Wilhelm a few hours before, there were only eighteen left, most of them wounded.

Leak reported the encounter. They had crossed the Charlevaux and started to climb the slope of Hill 198 at an oblique angle around the end of the hill, rather than directly over the ridge and down the runner line on the assumption that this was a more direct line over to Companies D and F. When they were about thirty meters from the crest, a voice called down from above. "Americans?"

There was no Teutonic accent; it could hardly be a trap. The Doughboys froze, and then a little Greek answered, "Yes."

"What company?"

"E Company, 308th," three or four men answered back.

There was silence. Then a voice snapped something in German.

"He's giving them our range!" shouted Louis Probst, who had a brother in the German Army.

Lieutenant Wilhelm was just giving the order to move out when all hell broke loose. From above, rifle and machine-gun fire tore down into the under-strength company, potato-masher grenades sailed through the air, and men ducked into whatever cover was at hand. Another machine gun opened up from across the slope. A squad tried to flank it, but then another opened up, and then another. Men retraced their steps but were cut off when another gun, below them on the slope, opened up. Company E now had from five to seven machine guns ripping into their tanks from three sides, while from across the ravine snipers picked off the wounded trying to crawl to cover. Leak was hit, and so was Harrington. Private Henry Miller snaked through the underbrush to drill a sniper with a rifle bullet. "I got him," Miller cried turning his head, but just at that moment a machine gun got Miller in turn. His Distinguished Service Cross was posthumous. With his company half-gone and both the other officers hit, Wilhelm finally ordered the others back. He himself with ten men tried to push on through, and he finally made it through American lines at 3 a.m.

on October 4, though with a wound and only four men left when he got to regimental headquarters.[173]

By all accounts, Dick Bakker was brutally slain that morning of October 3, 1918, on Hill 198 after enduring a week of merciless combat in bone-chilling rain in the Argonne Forest. One burial document noted a shattered skull indicating a round or more to the head that put an abrupt gruesome end to his young life. Official military records list his death as October 8, 1918. In the "war to end all wars," his bullet-riddled body lay in the mud and grime of the rain-soaked battlefield for several days until the burial parties arrived, motionless in the still of the forest among countless unheralded brave, young soldiers who gave their lives so that "liberty shall not perish from the earth."

Dick was initially buried in Grave Number 9 in Temporary Cemetery #745 at the bottom of the ravine with the other men from the ambushed patrol. The recorded date of this first burial was October 11, 1918. He was wrapped in a burlap blanket and buried in his uniform in a wooden box. The sole means of recognition were his army identification tags. A cross was planted to mark the grave. Embalming was not administered leaving the body to decompose rapidly. Dick's body would be exhumed and buried two more times in the coming years. Sad indeed.

Unknown to Whittlesey's men, the Germans had infiltrated a large number of troops through one or other of the flanks, and set up numerous machine-gun nests and much new wire between the Pocket and the main American line during the night. Further attempts to send runners back to the main forces was met with

173 Ibid., 279-295.

a blaze of deadly fire. By 1:30 p.m. that first day, every man in the Pocket knew they were cut off and that they must hold the position and await relief. Their only hope of communication was the carrier pigeons they had brought with them.[174]

Whittlesey's men would be pinned down in the Pocket under brutal enemy fire for another five days. The Germans launched daily attacks, both morning and afternoon, raining pure hell for hours at a time with rifles, machine guns, grenades, and trench mortar bombs. As battles raged, Doughboys began falling, and hunks of German bodies and blood rained down disgustingly from the cliffs above. In the wounded area, sterile bandages and field dressing packs ran out as well as the Dakin-Carrell solution used to clean out wounds. Medics scavenged the dead for unused bandages and shoelaces to tie up wounds. They had nothing for pain, not even cigarettes.[175] Men relieved themselves wherever they could as the Germans were watching the latrines, and getting to them was difficult. Most of the men were forced to drink muddy water from the shell craters. If they tried to get to the spring or brook, they were met with enemy fire.

The burial parties tiredly scraped open graves in the rocky, root-filled earth of the hillside. Many were buried in shallow excavations with just enough shovelfuls of dirt to cover them from sight. There were bodies and body parts everywhere. The worst spot was where the medics worked, tying torn flesh together using everything from rifle slings and bits of underwear to spiral puttee

174 Ibid., 309-311.

175 Ibid., 318.

leggings and leaving any maggots found on the wounds there to eat out the rot and infection.[176]

The sky in the west was beginning to look like rain around 2:30 on October 4 when the telltale screech of artillery fire coming from the south alerted the troops that these were American guns! The intense barrage first burst up on the opposite ridge along Hill 198. For a few minutes, every heart lifted, and then the line of fire moved forward as precisely as a line of advancing troops. It came to a halt square on the hillside where the battalion lay and stayed there, a terrible, relentless barrage of whizzing steel and ear-popping explosions. Trees crashed down; brush flew into the air, stripping the cover from the 308th. Surrounded in the Pocket, the men had no escape. They had no choice but to hunker down and take it. The Germans gleefully joined in, throwing trench mortar shells, hand grenades, and machine-gun fire into the fray, adding to the Doughboys' misery. Men were buried alive as the shells dug deep craters in the position. A fortunate few were able to dig themselves out.

The artillery shelling continued until 4 p.m., but it was not until 6 p.m. that the Germans abandoned their machine-gun barrage, and a profound silence filled the air except for the ringing in men's ears and the shrieks and wails of the wounded and dying. Much cover had been stripped from the hillside, and a wide swath across the position was studded with smoking, shallow shell craters and blackened stumps. Pieces of cadaver littered the scene, along with bloody heaps of rag that had once been uniforms, or bandages, or part of a man. Entrails were scattered everywhere.

176 Ibid., 335.

Men peered over the top of funk holes with terrified tears coursing down their dirty cheeks. Some breathed a silent prayer of thanks while others prayed aloud. Down at the wounded area, the medics sorted the living from the dead as the sky opened up with a slow, cold rainfall. Adding to the grisly scene was a low wall of dead bodies that had been set up to protect the wounded from machine-gun fire only. Major Whittlesey quickly set men to cover those corpses with the muddy, churned-up earth and some fallen brush. Web belt tourniquets and shirt strip bandages were now all that the medics had left to offer, as well as used bandages now being scavenged from the many bodies already littering the scene.[177]

The Americans continued to repulse brutal German attacks for another three days with no food and little water. Attempts to airlift food to the Pocket resulted in the planes dropping the bundles into German territory, a situation that only increased the angst of the starving Doughboys. On the afternoon of October 6, from the wagon road, toward the right flank, plumes of oily black smoke drifted skyward—foreboding. Long, glowing pennons of living flame blasted through what remained of the trees. A strange, bone-chilling hissing sound froze the Doughboys in their tracks. German flame throwers! The Doughboys sat spellbound, watching the unearthly spectacle advancing slowly toward them. Then Captain Holderman rose from his hole, two broken rifles supporting his terribly hurt frame, shouting commands, his automatic blazing away in his outstretched right hand—a moment in history. The spell was broken. The hillside burst again with rifle fire. As abruptly as it had begun, the most ferocious attack to

177 Ibid., 348-363.

that point ended at around 4 p.m., leaving behind in the silence only the groans and wails of the wounded. The reckless action of the men, ferociously inhuman in nature, spoke volumes to the extent of their extreme duress. In stark reality, some of the men had convinced themselves that they were never getting out alive, and they had nothing left to lose. The position was on the verge of imploding, one way or another.[178]

The next afternoon, October 7, the Germans sent Private Lowell Hollingshead, previously captured at the brook, back to Whittlesey with a message to wave a white flag and surrender in an appeal to human sentiments. After reading the message, all three officers looked at each other and began to grin—a grin of sarcasm at an appeal to "human sentiments" from the man who had been sending grenades, trench mortar bombs, and flame-thrower attacks at them for a week now. McMurtry pulled himself upright. "We've got them licked!" he cried. "Or they wouldn't have sent this!"

As the word of the letter flew around the Pocket, a queer sort of tenacity of spirit combined with rage seemed to emanate from the very ground. Men who had been on the verge of despair minutes before, convinced that their deaths would be for naught, now became grimly determined to make those deaths stand for something. A desire for vengeance swept across the hillside. No American command had ever surrendered all at once, as far as anyone could remember just then. Nearly to a man they became determined not to be the first, if just on principle. If those Hienie

178 Ibid., 429-430.

bastards wanted that useless hillside, they were going to have to come down and get it by force.

The German attack hit hard at the perimeter line about 5 p.m., a hurricane from all four points of the compass at once, their last chance at Whittlesey. Heavy machine-gun fire and round after round of grenades spearheaded the assault. Waves of field gray followed, firing as they came—the most ferocious attack yet. The Doughboys answered with the same ferocity, ignited by the rage brought on by the surrender letter. New Yorkers and Westerners stood side by side in a controlled and coordinated effort, depending on each other—no distinction between the two. It was the hard, rock-bottom, born-again moment of their young lives, a phoenix rising from the ashes. A grim, single-minded determination set in, intensified by a peculiar, low, almost animal-like growling mixed in among the many barked orders and shouts of encouragement. All across the Pocket, a unity of thought and deed prevailed in the mayhem. No matter what, the Germans would not take the hillside from them. Not *this* time.[179]

As darkness descended, the German attack broke apart. It was about ten minutes before 6 p.m. Their assault had failed. The *Americanernest* still stood. Miraculously, the Doughboys suffered few casualties. Nevertheless, the afternoon defense marked the absolute end to the Doughboys' abilities to hold the position. Ammunition was virtually gone, strength all but played out, resolve all but faded. Doughboys slept where the end of the attack found them, too tired and used up to crawl back into a hole. Others sat with vacant stares, seeing nothing, feeling nothing. For

179 Ibid., 468-479.

good or bad, it was over. In the evening drizzle, no word needed to be spoken. Everyone knew the next morning's attack would likely be the last.

But unknown to Major Whittlesey and his men, Lieutenant Fredrick Tillman and Company B/307th had broken through a gap in the wire, slid down Hill 198, and were carefully and deliberately pushing forward in the Charlevaux Ravine. Lieutenant Tillman, at the head of Company B's advance, moved stealthily through the brush along the side of the wagon road with his forty-five in hand and the hillside on his right. The putrid smell of decay was getting stronger the farther up the ravine they went, and he had to fight to keep from putting on his gas mask. Then the lieutenant stumbled in the dark, tripping through a hole from which a sharp yelp of pain emitted. A bayonet flashed into the dirt at his side. Behind the lethal weapon, Lieutenant Tillman could make out an American helmet rising from the hole to make another attempt. The helmet belonged to Private Robert Pou of Company E who was protecting his wounded buddy at their outpost station. Quickly, the confrontation was diffused, and at long last, Whittlesey's men were relieved. Private Pou was rewarded with a cigarette.[180]

The rescue party, appalled at the sights they found, still made their way through the bivouac, handing out what food, tobacco, and drink they had, trying hard not to break down in front of the wreckage of humanity they found in the holes around them and not in any hurry to eat again any too soon for it. It was hardest for the relieving force at the wounded area, where they found

180 Ibid., 483-484.

the dead laying thick, every imaginable kind of horrible wound, many blackened, rotting, and oozing puss, and where the rain had washed the mud from the corpse wall to expose the horror that lay beneath. Many relieving men, though long hardened to the horrors of combat, turned away and vomited. Yet the men were met at every corner by a dazed smile and sometimes tear tracks coursing down the dirt-stained face attached to the smile. The handwriting was on the wall. It was now only a matter of days. Armistice negotiations were already under way.[181]

By the best count available, 687 men went into the pocket that October, including those brought in by Captain Holderman. Only 194 men were able to walk out of the ravine under their own power. The rest were either dead, missing, or wounded. Of the nineteen officers who had commanded in the ravine, only three, Major Whittlesey, Lieutenant Eager, and Lieutenant Cullen, stood untouched. The achievement, the collective courage and endurance of the command during its siege, under both friendly and hostile fire, beating off daily attacks, had been one of the finest in American history. The ordeal, known as the Lost Battalion, would become legend as the years passed.[182]

Dick Bakker is now a legend, a war hero, in the eyes of his family—the handsome soldier they never got to know. Having met his death on the second day of the saga of the Lost Battalion, we will never know how the haunting horrors of the Pocket may have affected his personality. Tragic as it was, perhaps his passing was a blessing, given the ordeal endured by the others, but perhaps not.

181 Ibid., 488-489.

182 Ibid., 527.

The Journey

For the Bakker family, life would never be the same. The family would soon ache for a son and brother who would never come home. Like the other families who lost a son, they would never recover from this dreadful war.

Chapter 17

Armistice, Dealing With War Dead

ON THE EAST COAST OF America, it was 6 a.m., November 11, 1918. The first news flashes had reached New York three hours before, and sleep had been shattered by the hoots of tugs in the harbor, automobile horns, sirens, factory whistles, and church bells. The Armistice had been signed. Fighting had ceased. The Statue of Liberty prickled with lights in the darkness, and bonfires burned on street corners. As dawn came, Fifth Avenue was already thronged, and by noon the city was one seething celebration—bands competing shrilly, parades emerging from every corner to collide with one another. Veterans were carried shoulder high for blocks, mobbed, kissed, and pelted with flowers. The Kaiser was hanged, burned, blinded, castrated, and dismembered repeatedly throughout the day.[183]

The message flashed down the wire to Renville at 2:30 a.m. on Monday, November 11. The small community awoke to bells ringing, dynamite exploding, gunshots filling the air. The town's only fire bell rang all day. When a ringer tired, another was waiting to take his place. As people filed into the post office for the

183 Meirion Harries and Susie Harries. *The Last Days of Innocence: America at War, 1917-1918*. New York: Vintage Books, 1997, 421-422.

morning mail, they danced about and hugged each other for joy. In the forenoon, the school was let out, and children carrying flags assembled and marched around the streets carrying a large service flag. In the afternoon, the town band came out and enlivened the scene with music. Inspired by the band, the sidewalks leading to the schoolhouse were lined in the evening to watch the Kaiser hanged in effigy and then burned. There had never been so much rejoicing.[184] It was a day long remembered. Yet for some, a long day it was—a long day for the wounded lying in military hospitals longing to be home, a long day for those families trying to understand why God chose their sons to die for democracy, a long day for those mothers waiting to hear that their son was still alive.

For the Bakker family, the news must have been a bittersweet event. While the town and the rest of the world celebrated, the Bakkers were among those who waited for the confirmation that their son was safe, thankful, no doubt, that the fighting had ended. At this time, the Bakkers had not received Dick's last two letters revealing that he had gone to the front and was in combat. Son John had departed to Olivia the day before to be sworn in and leave for military training camp—yet another worry. As the local people were celebrating Armistice Day, John was sitting on a train waiting to depart. It was then that an officer boarded the train and dismissed the recruits. They were no longer needed. John

184 Adrian Bottge and Dan Licklider. *Adrian Looks Back: An Historic Account Gleaned from Early Newspapers of Renville, Minnesota.* Renville: Historic Renville Preservation Committee and the *Renville Star Farmer,* 1988, 184-185.

returned home, giving the Bakkers at least one measure of relief on a day rife with emotions.

Based on Grace's letter of December 11 below, the family received Dick's last two letters together sometime between the middle and latter part of November, a good two to three weeks after Armistice Day. In these letters, Dick revealed that he had been "over the top" and he stated that he was not afraid to die. These messages put the family in a high state of distress, especially mother Grace. They tried frantically to contact Washington through the town bank to obtain information on his status, but the lines were congested as there were many who were trying to get answers. There was nothing much more that they could do except anxiously wait and worry while trying to focus on the daily farm chores. The crops were mostly harvested by now. Perhaps there was a field of corn still standing that needed to be shucked, but mostly it was feed the animals, milk cows, gather eggs, wash clothes, clean, clean again. Keep busy. Don't think about this dreadful war.

After two almost unbearable weeks, the message from the war department was delivered on Wednesday, December 4 at 8 p.m. in the harsh cold of the Minnesota winter. It came in the form of a Western Union telegram. The telegram arrived at the Western Union terminal in the town bank. The bank operator telephoned the Bakker family. Fifteen-year-old Josie answered the party line phone which she handed to her father. Josie never forgot the gut-wrenching feeling when she realized the significance of the call.

The war department messages were brief and to the point. Addressed to Walter Bakker, this one would have read something like, "WE REGRET TO INFORM YOU THAT PRIVATE FIRST CLASS DICK W. BAKKER IS OFFICIALLY REPORTED AS KILLED IN ACTION OCTOBER EIGHTH. ADJUTANT GENERAL. 800PM." And there it was—no accolades, no details, no thanks, no further instructions. Your son is dead. One can only imagine the thoughts racing through the despondent minds of the family upon receiving the devastating news. How can this be? Where? When? Did he suffer? Where is the body? How do we bring it home?

In later years, Josie remembered that her mother went outside into the cold Minnesota winter and wailed upon receiving the fateful news. There was little sleep in the Bakker home that night. A devastated mother Grace pulled herself together the next morning and notified her sister, Senia in a brief letter:

Dear Sister,

Got your letter yesterday. I am broken-hearted as all our family is. We received the message last night at 8 o'clock that our dear son and brother was killed in action in France some time ago. Let the other relatives know as I can't write.

Your sister,

Grace

D. Kent Decker

The relatives responded quickly with letters of condolence and support. Six days later, December 11, Grace was able to write a more detailed letter to her brothers and sisters:

Renville, Minnesota
December 11, 1918
Dear Sister, Brother and all,
I will answer your letter we received Monday. Hope you are feeling better—that is, I mean Nettie. Well, I was glad to get your letter, as all of the sisters and brother Garrett wrote, which made me feel good. But you can imagine how hard a shock it was for us to bear. Almost more than we can bear. But, as you say, bear it with a Christian-like submission. Yes, we were so anxious the last couple of weeks. I hardly knew what I was doing half the time. I hardly expected he would go to the front so soon. But when we got his last two letters dated September 24 and September 30, when he said, "I have been on the front five days and over the top already," you know how we felt. I did not sleep much nights. Before his last letter was sent from France, he was dead nearly two weeks, as it was stamped on the envelope October 17. It was a trench envelope. Little did we think of his being killed then. He never told us he was near the front till September 24. He told us he would go in a few days, and we got the last letter dated September 30, the same time saying he was there five days. He was killed October 6, so was on the front eleven days. We can hardly believe it, but such is life. He wrote last and said, "It may not sound good to you that I am going there, but I have no fears to meet death any time." We are so glad to get those words from him, a comfort in

these trying times. Hope he is rejoicing in heaven and need not to see any more of this terrible, wicked world. Nothing but sorrow nearly everywhere you go. But I feel that God is giving us strength to bear this.

Monday was the funeral of Mrs. George Bakker. We got the message Wednesday evening (about Dick), and Thursday morning he got the message from St. Peter that she died that morning of typhoid fever. He was down every week after she had typhoid fever, the last time he could not see her as it was all quarantined of the flu. But she did tell him too, that the sooner she could die the better she would like it. She wanted to die a year ago. She told me she wished she was in her mother's place, who is nearly 84 years now. Then she knew she would not have to live long. We hope and trust she rests in peace. She left home a little before our dear one, both have had something this summer no tongue will ever tell. We sometimes imagined he would soon be home singing for us the songs he learned there. He wrote and said, "When I get home, I will sing those beautiful songs for you." Our hearts ache, but what does it matter to the world It moves on. His girl is broken-hearted, too. She was so patient. She got only three letters from him since he was in France. He told us to tell her he could not write to her, the last two we got. She kept writing to him just the same, nearly every day. He told us, "I have four letters from my honey last week and I know she won't get four from me in a month." One week he could write as many as he wished, then he wrote to quite a number—that was around September 15 or 20. He never told us he got a letter from you over there, but he got some in camp here. He said he had 25 letters over there and four or five papers I sent him. I wrote to him two times a week over there. Sometimes three times besides the rest of the family. I sent my last one a week ago Saturday and that day we got the message. We went to town to get word to Washington to find out about him. We were so uneasy. Then the banker told us we had better wait that week yet, as all the lines and cables were so congested. But my fears were not made known to my family – I think each one had their own.

Walter had been to Minneapolis with cattle and he said there were quite a few on the train that had gotten message like it from their boys, and he could hardly stay on the train anymore. Sunday we will have a memorial service, if our township board does not close the church.

The flu has broken out anew—so many cases now in town and all over the country, too. A number of schools are closed again. We had service in church Monday as the weather was not fit to be outside. It rained and snowed all day. On funerals we are not allowed to group together. One of our neighbor's daughters lives in Iowa. She lost her husband at twelve o'clock, the oldest boy, 16, at two o'clock and a girl, 13, at four o'clock in one day. She had twelve children and two nurses. The nurses took sick, went to the hospital and then her sister went to help her, who also took sick and died Saturday. Her father went down when the man was so bad, but has not been inside unless he did now when his girl died. Such a thing is awful. Don't know how she will stand it. Besides, she has nothing to live on, he worked by the day.

Well, this is all for this time. Tell the other folks about Dick as I can't write anymore.

Sister Grace

The flu of which Grace writes was known as the 1918 flu pandemic or the Spanish flu that hit with a vengeance in the winter of 1918/1919 piling even more grief on families trying to cope with their war losses. The disease killed tens of millions of people worldwide according to current estimates. After the holidays, a more composed Grace Bakker wrote a letter to the War Department:

Renville, Minnesota
January 1st, 1919
War department

Dear Sirs,

I would like to know more about my Son who was killed in France Oct. 6. We rec'd the message Dec.5 two months later. Now can you give me any information how he was killed, whether he was killed outright, or lingered along. On Sept. 18 he told us in a letter, he had pay day, got 145 franks, had $30.00 U.S. money besides. Sept. 30th he wrote his last letter saying he had been on the front 5 days and had been over the top already. Now what had become of that money and his valuables. He had a ring and a good fountain pen he wrote his last letter with. He also told us he had a picture of himself with 6 others in a group and would like to send it if he only could. Have they our boys not a place where they can leave their belongings over there when they are on the front lines. I would like to hear more about this as I think I am entitled to his money and his belongings. Hope you will answer my letter before long. This is his last address.

Pvt. Dick W. Bakker

Co. E. 308 infantry
American E. F.
Army no. 3129880

How about the bodies of our boys to be shipped to U.S.A. do they put anything on them at time of death to preserve them, is one allowed to see them here, and what are the expenses? Will you kindly let me know as soon as you possibly can and be sure of my gratitude to you.

Mrs. Bakker

The letter was stamped as received on January 7, 1919. The War Department responded to Grace Bakker in a letter dated January 22, 1919.

Mrs. W. J. Bakker
R 1, Box 35
Renville, Minnesota

Dear Madam:

Referring to your letter of recent date, relative to the death of your son, Dick W. Bakker, late Private, Company E, 308th Infantry, I beg leave to inform you that this office is not advised as to the particulars surrounding the death of your son, and for such information it is suggested that you communicate with the following:

Commanding Officer,
Company E, 308th Infantry,
American Expeditionary Forces.

With respect to the personal effects of you son, kindly communicate with the Effects Bureau, Port of Embarkation, Hoboken, New Jersey.

Your attention is invited to the enclosed Memorandum of Information, which outlines the policy of the War Department relative to the disposition of the remains of our soldiers who died abroad.

Permit me to express to you the deep sympathy of the Department, on account of the loss of your son, and to commend you for the great sacrifice which you have made to the cause for which your boy gave his life.

Very sincerely yours,

J. C. Ashburn

Adjutant General

"J. C. Ashburn" was stamped as opposed to a signature. As the death toll mounted, the War Department was inundated with letters similar to the one received from Grace Bakker from parents wanting to know the details of their son's death, the provisions for bringing the body home, and the procedure for preserving the body for viewing. Mothers wanted to know if their son suffered and if there were any last words. The American government's lack of war preparations manifested itself in delays and lack of information with no clear plan for dealing with the remains of the war dead. With thousands of American families demanding that their sons be brought home, the government was faced with an enormous and expensive undertaking. An initial tally estimated that over 70,000 men were buried in temporary battlefield graves.[185] Most of the battlefield dead were initially buried where they fell, hastily covered with earth by their comrades. Shell holes became mass graves, topped by rough crosses or cairns of rubble, marked with indications of the units involved to attract the attention of the burial parties coming up behind. Amid the chaos, danger, and misery, the soldiers performed this service for their buddies as carefully as they could. Miraculously, perhaps by the grace of God, less than two percent of the recovered bodies remain unidentified.[186]

In an effort to reduce costs, government and military leaders attempted to sell the idea that the greatest glory would come to those buried on the battlefield with their fallen comrades. With dissention and outrage mounting, the War Department finally agreed to give families the option of bringing the remains home or leaving them buried in American military cemeteries in France. Eight permanent military cemeteries were set up in Britain, Belgium, and France, where recovered bodies from the battlefield graves were reinterred. These cemeteries include the Aisne-Marne American Cemetery located at the foot of Belleau Wood (2,289 burials); Brookwood American Cemetery in Brookwood, Surrey, England (468 burials); Flanders Field American Cemetery in Waregem, Belgium (368 burials); Meuse-Argonne American Cemetery near Romagne-sous-Montfaucon, France (14,246 burials), Oise-Aisne American Cemetery in Serignes-et-

185 Drew Lindsay, "Rest in Peace? Bringing Home U.S. Dead," History Net, 9/18/2012

186 Meirion Harries and Susie Harries. *The Last Days of Innocence: America at War, 1917-1918.* New York: Vintage Books, 1997, 451-452.

Nesles, France (6,012 burials); Somme American Cemetery near Bony, France (1,844 burials); St. Mihiel American Cemetery in Thiaucourt, France (4,153 burials); and Suresnes American Cemetery in Suresnes, France (1,565 burials). These cemeteries are currently maintained by the American Battle Monuments Committee and are among the most beautiful and meticulously maintained in the world.[187]

Unfortunately, the burial process would take years to complete. America's Allies were vehemently opposed to the specter of the Americans exhuming their dead and shipping them home. French leaders, wanting to restore their country and put the horrors of war behind them, balked at the specter of Americans filling their trains with caskets of war dead. Consequently, the French put a ban on removal of bodies which was not lifted until late in 1920. England was reeling from a costly war. With over 700,000 bodies still in France, British leaders did not want the Americans to set a precedence in the disposition of war remains.[188] Nevertheless, the American War Department set about the ghoulish task of giving their war dead a proper final resting place. By the close of 1921, the gruesome burial work was nearly complete after the American military had shipped close to 46,000 dead to the United States and 764 to European places of birth.[189] Based on the cemetery count, a total of 30,945 World War I soldiers were buried in Europe.

187 "Cemeteries and Memorials." American Battle Monuments Commission.

188 Drew Lindsay, "Rest in Peace? Bringing Home U.S. Dead," History Net, 9/18/2012

189 Ibid.

Dick Bakker was one of those soldiers. On March 26, 1919, Dick's body was disinterred and reburied in Grave #13, Section 5, Plot 1, in Meuse Argonne Cemetery #1232. The condition of the body upon disinterment was reported as: "Burial good. Buried in blanket. Body slightly decomposed." Identification tags were found on the body. No other means of identification were found. A cross was placed on the grave that showed the grave number thirteen and identified the body as Dick W. Bakker, PVT, U.S.A.

Dick Bakker Grave Marker,
Meuse-Argonne Cemetery #1232

After the response to mother Grace's letter, there was no further correspondence between the family and the War Department until early in 1921. At that time, the War Department contacted the Bakker family by letter to offer them the option to bring Dick's remains back to Minnesota or to have the body moved to a permanent burial site in France. A pre-printed card, to be returned with the family's reply, was enclosed with the letter. Walter took the responsibility for filling out the card. The soldier's name, rank, serial, number, and organization were typed at the top. In this case it read: Bakker Dick W; army serial number 3,129,880; Pvt Co E 308 Inf. The first line read: State your relationship to the deceased. Walter entered: father. The traumatic question on the card was next: Do you desire the remains brought to the United States? Walter replied with a single word: no. Walter then signed the card as W. J. Bakker, Rural Route 1, Renville, Minnesota. No further explanation was provided as to the reason for this decision. One can only speculate that the thought of bringing home decomposed, unidentifiable remains after three years of waiting was just too repugnant for the family to endure.

War Department Burial Card

The card was received by the War Department on March 18, 1921, and forwarded to the quartermaster corps in France. Almost one year later, March 9, 1922, Dick Bakker's remains were again disinterred and reburied in Grave 5, Row 16, Block B, in the Meuse-Argonne American cemetery in Romagne-sous-Montfaucon, Department of Meuse, France. These burial records state that the body was badly decomposed, skull shattered, features unrecognizable.

Another year would pass before the Bakker family was notified of Dick's final resting place. A letter to Walter Bakker, dated March 14, 1923, read:

Dear Sir,

The Quartermaster General desires that you be informed that the permanent grave of the late Private Dick W. Bakker, Company E, 308th Infantry, is Grave 5, Row 16, Block B, Meuse-Argonne American cemetery, Romagne-sous-Montfaucon, Department of Meuse, France.

This is one of the permanent American military cemeteries to be maintained by the Government in Europe. Each grave will be marked by a headstone of white marble, of suitable design, with name, rank, organization, date of soldier's death and State from which he came. The headstone will be placed at all graves in connection with the improvement work now in progress, as soon as possible and without waiting for special action or request on the part of relatives.

In effecting removal, the utmost care and reverence were exacted and were more than willingly accorded by those performing this sacred duty. The grave of the deceased will be perpetually maintained by this Government in a manner befitting the last resting place of a soldier.

Very truly yours,

H. J. Conner,

Assistant

Dick Bakker Permanent Grave Marker

The typing clearly indicated that this letter was a government form letter with the designated soldier's details typed into the first paragraph. While this notification undoubtedly provided a measure of comfort to the Bakker family after five years, there would be yet another stressful decision ahead. In March 1929, eleven years after the Armistice, Congress passed a law authorizing the use of government funds to pay for mothers and widows of fallen veterans to visit the graves of their loved ones buried in the American cemeteries in Europe. The program, known as the Gold Star Mothers Pilgrimages, was carried out from 1930 through 1933. Grace Bakker received a letter from the War Department every year from 1929 to 1932 inquiring if she would like to make the pilgrimage to France to visit her son's grave. Each year, Grace declined. The Great Depression had set in, and times were hard. In 1929, Grace attached a note informing the War Department that Dick was not married at the time of his death. In 1930, Grace replied, "No, my health will not permit." In 1931, at age sixty, Grace replied, "No, I never intend to. I could use the money better, that the trip would amount to." The Great Depression had hit.

Dick's $10,000 life insurance policy was paid out to Walter, the beneficiary, in monthly stipends of $57.50 over twenty years commencing October 8, 1918. For a long time, Walter, a proud man, would not touch the money they were receiving for the death of his son. Walter retired from farming in 1931, and he and Grace moved to Renville. Their son, Helmer, took over the farm site with his new bride, Jennie. At that time, Walter had to swallow a bit of his pride and use Dick's insurance money to build a house in town as the Great Depression had reduced their income. It was a lovely retirement home, but Grace was never happy there. Apparently, she could never get past the fact that the house was built with the money received from the loss of her cherished son. She was quoted as saying once in German, "I wish this house was on a boat in the middle of the ocean." Walter passed away in 1935. Grace was forced to petition for the remainder of Dick's insurance money—yet one more indignity heaped upon a grieving Gold Star mother.

In memory, Grace Bakker cut Dick's three suits into squares and made them into a quilt. The quilt is kept in good condition by the family today. Relatives remember that Grace was never the same person after Dick's death. She carried her grief till she passed away in 1943, never fully getting closure for the son who she could never bring home. Grace was again filled with dread when World War II broke out, and they listened to the news broadcasting troubles in Europe once again. Walter and Grace are buried side by side in the Ebenezer Presbyterian Church cemetery north of Renville. The family keeps their graves in fine order in fond memory. Tetje Sietsema never married. She kept a picture of her honey on her dresser until her days on earth came to an end.

Sister Josie was the last of her generation to pass away. Before she went in 1993, Josie placed a grave marker between the grave markers of Walter and Grace, a final tribute to honor the memory of a son and brother. The marker reads: DICK W. BAKKER, CO E 308TH INFANTRY, ARGONNE FOREST, WW I, JULY 3, 1893, OCT 6, 1918, BURIED IN FRANCE.

Dick Bakker Grave Marker, Presbyterian Cemetery, Renville, Minnesota

Kentt Habben, grandson of Christine, along with his new wife, Emily, was the first Bakker family member to visit the World War I grave in France on their honeymoon in 1994. Previously, a cousin had attempted to visit the grave but was unsuccessful in finding its location. Kimberly Decker, granddaughter of Christine, visited Dick's grave in 2013 with her then-husband, Matt. No other relative has been able to visit the last burial site of this brave soldier.

As we commemorate the one hundredth anniversary of America's entry into World War I, we shall always remember the heroic deeds of the brave, for bravery teemed in every battle. We shall always be indebted to those who fought with honor, for honor was the fuel that propelled the war machine to victory. But we must also waken to the deep penetration of war's wounds, wounds that never heal. Will we ever learn?

Epilogue

Chapter 18

A New World Order

IN ITS AFTERMATH, WORLD WAR I changed the face of the earth with the collapse of the German, Austro-Hungarian, Ottoman, and Russian empires. The Hohenzollern, Habsburg, and Romanov dynasties disappeared as well, leaving communist and socialistic movements in their place as a ravaged and traumatized Europe struggled to rebuild. It was the beginning of a new world order. New national states appeared out of the wreckage of these empires. Poland reemerged as an independent country after more than a century. The Kingdom of Serbia and its dynasty, as a "minor Entente nation" and the country with the most casualties per capita, became the backbone of a new multinational state, the Kingdom of Serbs, Croats, and Slovenes, later renamed Yugoslavia. Czechoslovakia, combining the Kingdom of Bohemia with parts of the Kingdom of Hungary, became a new nation. Russia became the Soviet Union and lost Finland, Estonia, Lithuania, and Latvia, which became independent countries. The Ottoman Empire was soon replaced by Turkey and several other countries in the Middle East.[190]

The cost of the war was immense in the outflow of money and resources and, most painfully, in the expenditure of human lives.

190 "World War I." Wikipedia. October 1, 2016.

The exact accounting of war casualties is still in dispute, especially civilian casualties, because of different definitions used in each category, the questionable accuracy of the recording system used, and the loss or destruction of a number of official records. The rough numbers below give one a sense of the violence and slaughter that occurred in the Great War. The total number of casualties in World War I, both military and civilian, is estimated at about thirty-seven million: seventeen million deaths and twenty million wounded. The total number of deaths includes ten million military personnel and about seven million civilians. The Allies lost six million soldiers and the Central Powers about four million. At least two million died from accidents and diseases, and six million went missing, presumed dead.[191,192] Germany lost 15.1 percent of its active male population, Austria-Hungary lost 17.1 percent, and France lost 10.5 percent. The United States, in little over a year of combat, incurred over 116,000 military deaths, 1,100 civilian deaths, and over 205,000 wounded.

The statistics include men killed in action before receiving medical attention as well as those that died of their wounds after receiving medical aid. There were a little over four million recorded as prisoners or missing who were assumed to be dead. The majority of disease-related deaths were from the influenza although there were recorded cases of typhus carried by lice. A minority of cases were recorded from suicide, murder, or accident. United States death statistics include the Army, Navy, and Marine Corps. The figures include 279 deaths during the

191 "World War I Casualties." Wikipedia. September 27, 2016.

192 "World War I Casualties." Military Wiki.

Allied intervention in the Russian Civil War from 1918–1920. The U.S. Coast Guard lost 192 dead (111 deaths in action and 81 from other causes). United States civilian losses include those killed in the sinking of the RMS *Lusitania*, Merchant Mariners killed in enemy submarine attacks on their merchant ships, and nurses serving overseas.[193]

Victors and losers alike suffered from the ravages of a long, ruinous war that ended in a manner that left both sides wallowing in hatred, outrage, distrust, and a thirst for revenge once the dust had settled and the peace terms were finalized. The countries of Western Europe viewed the war as a senseless tragedy of waste and destruction. On the other hand, the masses of Central and Eastern Europe, finally freed from centuries of autocratic rule, saw the opportunity for self-determination and national independence as articulated by Woodrow Wilson. However, Eastern Europe was in a chaotic state of transition, with various political factions vying for control of governments that had collapsed in a matter of a few days, leaving ineffective provisional administrations in charge.

The centerpiece of the post-war negotiations known as the Paris Settlement was the Versailles Treaty, which was carved out with many compromises between the Allied negotiators themselves. The end result produced a great deal of dissatisfaction among all parties involved. The treaty included a total of 440 articles. The major terms dictated that Germany was to lose all of its colonies and about thirteen percent of its prewar territory in Europe, involving about ten percent of its population. This included Alsace and Lorraine, the provinces that had been taken

193 "World War I." Wikipedia. October 1, 2016.

from France in 1871. It also included disputed territories that were to fall to Belgium and to Denmark. Large provinces in the East, which were comprised of mixed German-Polish populations, now became part of a new, resurrected Poland.

The German army was limited to a very small volunteer force of one hundred thousand men, drastically reduced from the proud millions that had been fielded in war. No conscription was allowed—no draft. Germany was to divest itself of the destructive new technologies that had played a role in World War I. Germany was to have no air force and no submarines. Gas weapons were emphatically banned.

Territorially, the Rhineland on Germany's western front was to be demilitarized with a buffer zone on a belt of thirty miles wide, to be left bare of German military forces. The west bank of the Rhine was to be occupied by the Allies for about fifteen years. Germany would also have to pay an unspecified amount in war reparations which was later set at $32 billion in 1921. Limitations were also placed on German industry and commerce in an effort to shackle the German revival that many felt was sure to come. The agreement forbade the Germans to use famous French brand names in the marketing of their products. For example, Germans, henceforth, could not market their brandy as cognac or their sparkling wines as champagne. Of all the articles, the psychological bombshell was Article 231, which was unofficially called the "War Guilt Clause." Article 231 aimed to establish a legal foundation for the claims to reparations defined in the treaty. Germany was made to accept the blame for starting the war.

D. Kent Decker

When the terms of the treaty were announced, the German public was thunderstruck to the point that outrage spread on a gigantic scale. Across nearly every political spectrum, the rejection of the Versailles Treaty terms by German public opinion was unanimous. In protest, German naval officers scuttled and sank the entire German fleet so that it would not fall into enemy hands. German nationalists denounced this *Diktat*, the German phrase for a dictated peace. Nevertheless, the Allies were adamant. The terms were to be accepted, or the blockade would continue and the war would recommence. In spite of the outrage and protest, the German delegation, ultimately, had no choice. It signed the Versailles Treaty on June 28, 1919, in a famous and significant historical location, the Hall of Mirrors in Versailles. The site was important because back in 1871, the Hall of Mirrors was where the German Empire had been officially declared victor over a defeated France, humiliating the French additionally.

And so it was that five years to the day from the assassination in Sarajevo that had sparked the First World War, the Versailles Treaty was signed.[194] In the end, the results of the horse trading was that Britain got its reparations, France got control of the Saar and other security guarantees, and Woodrow Wilson got his League of Nations. However, when Wilson presented the terms of the Versailles Treaty to Congress, it was rejected, and America remained technically at war. The Europeans, America's allies in

194 *World War I: The "Great War"*, Part 3 of 3, The Teaching Company LLC, ©2006, 137-141, Reproduced with permission from the Teaching Company, LLC. www.thegreatcouses.com

war, were left to administer the League of Nations and enforce the treaty.

After all was said and done, there many who were dissatisfied with the controversial Paris Settlement that left many issues on the table. Around the world, Britain and France kept their colonial possessions, thus disappointing representatives of those peoples under their colonial rule who had hoped for self-determination as an outcome of the war. The European victors, it seemed, were more interested in preserving, and even extending, their empire than creating Wilson's idealistic world of self-determined nations. One observer mused, "After a war to end all wars, this might very well end up to be a peace to end all peace."[195]

Indeed, after all the treaties were signed, battles continued to rage across much of Central and Eastern Europe. National self-determination proved to be problematic as various ethnic groups and political factions battled for their own turf. A violently brutal civil war surged across Russia as revolutionary "Red" Bolshevik forces battled counter-revolutionary "Whites." In the new Baltic Republics, German mercenaries and the invading Red Army clashed with the forces of the independent states. Radical socialist revolts in Hungary, Finland, and Germany erupted before being repressed. Soviet Russia and independent Poland clashed. As new nation-states were formed, they battled repeatedly over where borders were to be drawn.

These conflicts and civil strife that followed in the wake of the Great War pointed to a new level of ideological violence that had been reached after the war's end. These struggles pitted

195 Ibid., 145

revolutionaries against counter-revolutionaries, and nationalists of different ethnic groups against one another, in multifaceted, complex shifting battles with shifting fronts. As the Western Front closed, the world opened out to a new level of conflict and violence.[196]

The new political factions that arose from the battle for self-determination initially seemed to fill the hopes of Woodrow Wilson for a new democratic world order. However, these were soon replaced by a wave of dictatorships that were totalitarian in their aspirations. In essence, these dictatorships sought to capture and mobilize all of the individuals under their control, not merely wanting passive acquiescence, but something far larger, enthusiastic participation—heart, mind, body, and soul. These totalitarian movements included Benito Mussolini's Fascism in Italy, Adolf Hitler's Nazism in Germany, and the Communism of Lenin and Stalin in the Soviet Union. The dictatorships aimed to control the masses by a combination of fear administered through terror, ideological faith, and true belief.

While these totalitarian regimes carried different ideological messages, they shared similarities that included a strong cult leader with whom the movement itself was identified, and dynamic claims of ideological infallibility that spurred them to constant action to make their claims come true. The ideologies of these movements made their goals universal and drove them toward their final goal of world domination. A logical conclusion is that the roots of these movements arose from the World War 1

196 Ibid., 154-155

experience where the mobilization for total war resulted in the overthrow of four empires.[197]

On an interesting note, a twenty-five-year-old Vietnamese named Nguyen Ai Quoc tried to submit a paper to Woodrow Wilson to obtain the right of self-determination for the Vietnamese people. His request was refused. Forty years later, under the name of Ho Chi Minh, he emerged as a Communist leader, determined to drive France out of Vietnam. He would soon engage the military might of the United States Armed Forces.[198] Similarly, representatives of a Pan-African Congress lobbied in vain for independence for African countries. Proposals for racial equality, put forth by the Japanese, were also ignored.[199]

The League of Nations was officially established in Geneva in January 1920, without the United States or the Soviet Union. Unfortunately, the League could never muster the influence to force governments or other political factions to adhere to a universal set of rules and come to the negotiating table to settle their differences.[200] So the struggles continued, eventually leading to World War II, an even more devastating conflict. World War II

197 Ibid., 190-192

198 Martin Gilbert. *The First World War: A Complete History*. 2nd ed. New York: Holt Paperbacks, 1994., 509-510

199 *World War I: The "Great War"*, Part 3 of 3, The Teaching Company LLC, ©2006, 144, Reproduced with permission from the Teaching Company, LLC. www.thegreatcouses.com

200 Ibid., 143

brought on the United Nations with the United States and Russia participating, but the ideological violence continued in Korea and Vietnam, and is evident today in organizations such as Al Qaeda and ISIS as regimes such as that of Saddam Hussein are toppled, with different factions competing for power. In its aftermath, "the war to end all wars" never ended.

Chapter 19

Post-War America

ONCE THE ARMISTICE WAS SIGNED, the United States incurred the problem of shutting down its massive war industry without collapsing the economy. The two million healthy and wounded troops stationed in Europe had to be transported home along with the associated civilian support personnel. An additional 1.7 million troops stationed in the American camps were to be discharged.[201] In addition to giving those killed in action a proper burial, there was somewhere around 190,000 in the hospitals that had to be moved home. They arrived at Brest in American boxcars laden with tiers of stretchers three-deep on either side of the aisle, case histories recorded in swatches on cords around their necks. Surgeons worked in a half-finished hospital on the heights above Brest as the troops waited to be assigned to a boat for the voyage back to America. Their injuries and maladies were countless: broken and missing extremities, broken jaws, gunshot and shrapnel wounds, internal bleeding, gangrene, gas sickness, shell shock, influenza. The suffering was monumental, but the Yankee spirit was, and still is, hard to break. At night the wards were alive with dice games and fifths of Martinique rum. After the horrors of the

201 Meirion Harries and Susie Harries. *The Last Days of Innocence: America at War, 1917-1918*. New York: Vintage Books, 1997, 455.

Western Front, the nurses working round the clock looked quite pretty to these Doughboys. One nurse was heard to whisper to a girl with a basin, gauzes, and Dakin solution, "Watch out when you change Captain Reddison's bandages. He's a garter-popper. I'm black and blue."[202]

Now free of U-boat attacks, ships from various countries carried the Americans home. Troops lined up to take the next boat arriving in port. Getting home was the foremost thing on their minds. Lawrence Stallings told of the experience, "The next boat was the old French liner *France*. We boarded it at midnight. Topsides were jammed with home-going troops, and the passageways in steerage were too narrow for any but ambulatory immigrants the *France* had once shoveled ashore at Ellis Island like scoops of coal. French seamen placed us rump-side on tarpaulins and dragged us along the steel plates to portless iron cells in the bowels of the ship, many of us with no immediate foreign-born background marveling at the guts it must have taken for the backwash of Europe's slums to have made such a seemingly forlorn voyage. We were eight to a cell, and the ambulatory brought news to the stretcher-ridden of topside doings, as well as rationing us and helping the few sleepless nurses change bandages. It was a timeless voyage; no day or night, just the single light bulb and the roar of the overhead blower. Messengers eventually brought word that the decks were filled with cheering men as we passed

202 Laurence Stallings. *The Doughboys: The Story of the AEF, 1917-1918*. New York: Harper and Row, 1963, 369-370.

the Statue of Liberty." The men below were just glad that the old girl was still there.[203]

As the boatloads poured into the American ports, the medical community struggled with mending the wounds so specific to the Western Front. To deal with the numerous injuries to the face, typical of trench warfare, American dentists developed a new expertise, and American physicians gave medical science the team approach to reconstructive facial surgery. Many soldiers with wounds afflicted with dirt-contaminated shrapnel developed gangrene and often needed amputation. More left arms were lost than right, as the left arm lay generally unprotected while the soldier lay in positions for shooting. America led the world in the manufacture of artificial limbs. There was even experimentation in artificial eyes and artificial ears.

The Americans also had to deal with their share of soldiers temporarily or permanently afflicted with battle shock. Their treatment methods were at the same rudimentary level as their European counterparts'. To try to understand the nature and effects of the war, Eleanor Roosevelt made herself visit the mental ward of Saint Elizabeth's Hospital in Washington, D.C. To be allowed to talk to the men, she had to be locked into the ward, and she never forgot the time she spent with battle-shocked sailors, "some chained to their beds, others unable to stop shouting of the horrors they had seen."[204]

203 Ibid., 372-373.

204 Meirion Harries and Susie Harries. *The Last Days of Innocence: America at War, 1917-1918*. New York: Vintage Books, 1997, 452-454.

Those soldiers who came home healthy were processed and discharged through the military camps. After the Armistice was signed, Camp Lewis became a separation center where soldiers returned from overseas and were discharged. The separation activities were discontinued in 1920 with the camp in a deteriorated state due to a lean military budget. After the whirlwind activities of 1918, the camp was a virtual ghost town, with buildings abandoned or destroyed by fire and a population of a little over a thousand soldiers. The camp remained in disrepair until 1926 when Congress passed a bill for base reconstruction. In 1927, the camp was renamed Fort Lewis, and it became a permanent army base, with the construction effort lasting until 1939. The base functioned as a training and preparedness post during World War II. Colonel Dwight D. Eisenhower (1890-1969), the future general and president, served at Fort Lewis from 1940 to 1941. The post would go on to train soldiers for Korea, Vietnam, and the War on Terror. In 2010, the post was designated Joint Base Lewis McChord as the result of a merger of Fort Lewis and the United States Air Force's McChord Air Force Base and is presently operating under the jurisdiction of the United States Army Joint Base Garrison.[205]

After the war, Camp Kearny was used as a demobilization and convalescent center, and in 1920, it ceased to function as a military base. The camp was unused until 1927 when Charles Lindbergh, whose Spirit of St. Louis was built by Ryan Airlines Corp. in nearby San Diego, used the abandoned parade field to

205 Duane Colt Denfeld. "Fort Lewis, Part 1, 1917-1927." HistoryLink. January 16, 2008.

practice tricky landings and take-offs with the new plane, which had no forward-looking windshield. From San Diego, he took off for New York, Paris, and international fame.

In the 1930s, the U.S. Navy launched dirigibles out of Camp Kearny. These large, helium-filled airships were used to patrol long distances along the coasts. Two 785-foot-long airships, *USS Akron* and *USS Macon*, could launch and retrieve five Curtiss F9C-2 Sparrowhawk pursuit aircraft in mid-air, like flying aircraft carriers. In 1932, a mooring mast and hangar were built at the camp for the dirigibles. (It was claimed that the hangar was so huge that it had its own weather system!) When the navy gave up the airship program, Kearny was quiet once again. Camp Kearny lay dormant for a few more years until the clouds of war again appeared on the U.S. horizon in the form of World War II. Since that time, the camp has been occupied by either the navy or Marines and is now known as Marine Corps Air Station Miramar.[206]

From the separation and demobilization centers, the veterans returned to their hometowns to reunite with their families and resume their lives. Many received welcoming parades and other fanfare. Many found their jobs were gone. They stood in unemployment lines facing astonishing price increases. The war had changed the composition of the work force. With immigration halted, the void left by the abrupt removal of five million men from industry and agriculture opened a broad spectrum of jobs to women. Women had begun to move up the proverbial "food chain" in a wide variety of industries from services to finance, advertising, communications, and even heavy industries such

206 "Miramar History." Miramar Air Show.

as chemicals, iron, and steel. As white female clerks and factory girls moved into men's jobs, black women moved into the white women's jobs left vacant. The jobs were the least desirable, but they represented a shift away from the traditional occupations of black women that would never be completely reversed. With both white and black women gaining confidence, militant women camped before the gates of the White House and embarrassed the President and Congress into passing the Nineteenth Amendment, which made suffrage every citizen's right. The Amendment was passed by the House of Representatives on January 10, 1918, and the Senate in June 1919.

When the soldiers returned home and began filling up the labor pool, horizons for women contracted once again. Women held onto their gains in non-war related areas. On the other hand, where jobs had opened purely because of the war, women were promptly evicted. They found no support from labor unions who wanted to keep the labor pool low in order to leverage up wages.

The war economy had been volatile in its almost instantaneous ramp-up, with its expending huge government dollars for war-needed resources; driving already thriving industries toward integration, standardization, and greater time efficiency; enforcing government controls and rationing; demanding sacrifice; inviting suspicion, mistrust, and hatred; and tugging at the souls of almost every facet of the diverse American society. Now, in less than two years, it was unraveling in varied and unpredictable ways that were both damaging and beneficial. America would never quite be the same.

Inevitably, it was the African Americans who suffered worst. Blacks' cooperation in the war effort was barely recognized, let alone rewarded with reforms. The black community had been encouraged by the government propaganda machine to think of themselves as partners in the service of the nation. They had begun to hope for the vote, the right to serve on juries, better education, an end to the "Jim Crow" laws, justice in the courts, and access to jobs in the civil service. Instead, they were seeing an escalation in racial violence: thirty-eight lynchings in 1917, fifty-eight in 1918, seventy in 1919. Black protests grew louder when returning veterans reported on their treatment in the American Army.[207]

There are those who assert that America was the biggest winner coming out of the Great War. Before the war, America had been a debtor nation, her extraordinary growth fueled by foreign investment and loans. By 1916, the debt was gone, and virtually all foreign-held securities had been returned to American hands. Now America held most of the world's gold, and Secretary of the Treasury McAdoo saw the time approaching when Wall Street would displace the City of London as the leading financial center, and the dollar would become the currency of international trade.[208]

The wartime economy had been driven by Allied spending and the huge federal budget. The waging of economic warfare abroad offered extraordinary insights into the workings of the

207 Meirion Harries and Susie Harries. *The Last Days of Innocence: America at War, 1917-1918*. New York: Vintage Books, 1997, 435-439.

208 Ibid., 28.

world trading systems, which America's new wealth had the power to dominate. At home, the drive for integration, standardization, and time efficiency revolutionized business methods. The massive wartime investment, both public and private, in research and development in areas such as radio technology, aviation, chemicals, and engineering, affected the way in which postwar Americans lived their daily lives. Broadcast radio, commercial air travel, and new concrete roads continued the process of integrating the country. By 1920, there were nine million automobiles; ten years later, there were almost thirty million. Americans were on the move.[209]

As for the survivors of the Lost Battalion, the nightmare in the Charlevaux Ravine never ended. Many came home to suffer from what is now known as Post Traumatic Stress Disorder, unable to get the haunting sights and smells out of their minds. George McMurtry returned to Harvard and became a Wall Street lawyer. He would later make millions in the stock market. Nelson Holderman never returned to action and spent the remainder of his life on a full commission in the California National Guard. Charles Whittlesey came home as a decorated war hero. He returned to the practice of law in New York, where he was beset with demands for speeches, parades, and honorary degrees. However, he could not shake the horrors of the Lost Battalion and the burden of suffering placed on his men. In November, 1921, after dining with the captain of a ship destined for Cuba, Charles Whittlesey jumped overboard. His body was never recovered, yet another sad tragedy of a terrible war.

209 Ibid., 435-436.

Bibliography

"100 Years of Naval Aviation." Air and Space Magazine, March 2011. http://www.airspacemag.com/military-aviation/100-years-of-naval-aviation-78995366/?no-ist

"1918 World Series." Baseball Almanac. http://www.baseball-almanac.com/ws/yr1918ws.shtml

"1st Reconnaissance Squadron." Wikipedia. September 17, 2016. https://en.wikipedia.org/wiki/1st_Reconnaissance_Squadron

"Aeronautical Division, U.S. Signal Corps." Wikipedia. September 23, 2016. https://en.wikipedia.org/wiki/Aeronautical_Division,_U.S._Signal_Corps

"Airship." Wikipedia. September 30, 2016. https://en.wikipedia.org/wiki/Airship

Alexander, Caroline. "The Shock of War." *Smithsonian Magazine*, September 2010. http://www.smithsonianmag.com/history/the-shock-of-war-55376701/?no-ist

"American Experience." PBS. http://www.pbs.org/wgbh/americanexperience/features/general-article/warletters-censorship/

Automobile Journal 66 (September 1918). doi: Google eBooks. http://earlyamericanautomobiles.com/americanautomobiles19.htm

Ayres, Leonard P. "Four Million Men." In *The War with Germany: A Statistical Summary*. http://net.lib.byu.edu/estu/wwi/memoir/docs/statistics/statstc.htm#1

"B-class Blimp." Wikipedia. June 5, 2016. https://en.wikipedia.org/wiki/B-class_blimp

Beringer, G. N. *They mutilate: for humanities sake enlist*, United States Army, 1918. Pritzker Military Museum and Library (https://www.pritzkermilitary.org/explore/museum/digital-collection/view/oclc/813230382)

Bottge, Adrian, and Dan Licklider. *Adrian Looks Back: An Historic Account Gleaned from Early Newspapers of Renville, Minnesota*. Renville: Historic Renville Preservation Committee and the *Renville Star Farmer*, 1988.

Bourke, Joanna. "Shell Shock during World War One." BBC. March 10, 2011. http://www.bbc.co.uk/history/worldwars/wwone/shellshock_01.shtml

Bryant, Joyce. "How War Changed the Role of Women in the United States." Yale-New Haven Teachers Institute, Yale University. http://teachersinstitute.yale.edu/curriculum/units/2002/3/02.03.09.x.html

"C-class Blimp." Wikipedia. September 5, 2016. https://en.wikipedia.org/wiki/C-class_blimp

"Camp Mills." Wikipedia. September 2, 2016. https://en.wikipedia.org/wiki/Camp_Mills

"Canal de Berry." Wikipedia. May 1, 2015. https://en.wikipedia.org/wiki/Canal_de_Berry

Canfield, Bruce. "The Model 1917 U.S. Enfield." American Rifleman. April 19, 2012. https://www.americanrifleman.org/articles/2012/4/19/the-model-1917-us-enfield/

Cavendish, Richard. "The Battle of the Cornflakes." *History Today*, February 2006. http://www.historytoday.com/richard-cavendish/battle-cornflakes

"Cemeteries and Memorials." American Battle Monuments Commission. https://www.abmc.gov/cemeteries-memorials#.WEyGN4WcHIU

"Chapter 26: 1918." Early American Automobiles. http://earlyamericanautomobiles.com/americanautomobiles19.htm

Clark, Rodney A. "The Milwaukee Electrification: A Proud Era Passes." *The Milwaukee Road Magazine*, July/August 1973. March 3, 2009. http://www.oldmilwaukeeroad.com/content/proud/complete_text.htm

Colon, Raul. "The American Air Effort." Century of Flight. 2009. http://www.century-of-flight.net/Aviation%20history/airplane%20at%20war/us_effort.htm

Colon, Raul. "The End of the German Air Offensive on the Western Front." Century of Flight. January 25, 2009. http://www.century-of-flight.net/Aviation%20history/airplane%20at%20war/germany_the_end.htm

Denfeld, Duane Colt. "Fort Lewis, Part 1, 1917-1927." HistoryLink. January 16, 2008. http://www.historylink.org/File/8455

"Detroit Electric." Wikipedia. September 30, 2016. https://en.wikipedia.org/wiki/Detroit_Electric

Dock, Lavinia L. *History of American Red Cross Nursing*. New York: MacMillan, 1922. https://books.google.com/books?id=WEmkrC51DdgC&printsec=frontcover&source=gbs_ge_summary_r&cad=0#v=onepage&q&f=false

"Dry State." Wikipedia. September 7, 2016. https://en.wikipedia.org/wiki/Dry_state

Duffy, Michael. "Life in the Trenches." First World War. 2009.
http://www.firstworldwar.com/features/trenchlife.htm

Duffy, Michael. "Trench Latrines." First World War. 2009.
http://www.firstworldwar.com/atoz/latrines.htm

"Early Twentieth Century Railroads." HowStuffWorks. May
19, 2008. http://history.howstuffworks.com/american-history/
early-twentieth-century-railroads7.htm

"Espionage Act of 1917." Wikipedia. September 4, 2016.
https://en.wikipedia.org/wiki/Espionage_Act_of_1917

"Eugene Burton Ely." Wikipedia. February 4, 2016.
https://en.wikipedia.org/wiki/Eugene_Burton_Ely

"Expanded Service 1898-1920s." Postal Museum. http://
postalmuseum.si.edu/mailcall/2b.html

"Federal Fuel Administration." Wikipedia. March 13, 2016.
https://en.wikipedia.org/wiki/Federal_Fuel_Administration

"Field Punishment Number One." Spartacus Educational
http://spartacus-educational.com/FWWfield.htm

Flores, Trudy, and Sarah Griffith. "Circle Theater and
Pershing's Crusaders." Oregon History Project. 2002. https://
oregonhistoryproject.org/articles/historical-records/circle-
theater-and-pershing39s-crusaders/#.V_FdtzvYPFI

"Forty and Eight Boxcar." Skylighters. http://www.skylighters.
org/encyclopedia/fortyandeight.html

Gilbert, Martin. *The First World War: A Complete History.* 2nd
ed. New York: Holt Paperbacks, 1994.

Grouch-Begley, Hannah. "The Forgotten Female Shell-Shock
Victims of World War I." The Atlantic. September 8, 2014.
http://www.theatlantic.com/health/archive/2014/09/world-
war-ones-forgotten-female-shell-shock-victims/378995/

Harries, Meirion, and Susie Harries. *The Last Days of Innocence:
America at War, 1917-1918.* New York: Vintage Books, 1997.
Hartwell, Joe. "Troopships, Battleships, Subs, Cruisers,
Destroyers." WWI Ships Histories. August 14, 2013. http://
freepages.military.rootsweb.ancestry.com/~cacunithistories/
ships_histories.html

"Henry Perky." Wikipedia. September 26, 2016.
https://en.wikipedia.org/wiki/Henry_Perky

Hillman, Jr., Rolfe L., and Douglas V. Johnson II, Soissons
1918, Chapter 8, Texas A&M University Press, Kindle, 1999
"Historic California Posts: Camp Kearny (San Diego County)."
California Military History. http://californiamilitaryhistory.org/
cpKearney2.html

History of the Fortieth (Sunshine) Division; Containing a Brief History of All Units Under the Command of Major General Frederick S. Strong, 1917-1919. Los Angeles: C.S. Hutson, 1920. September 2, 2008. https://archive.org/stream/historyfortiethoounkngoog/historyfortiethoounkngoog_djvu.txt

Holmes, Richard. *Acts of War: The Behavior of Men in Battle.* New York: Free Press, 1986.

Hurley, Edward N. *The Bridge to France.* Philadelphia: J.B. Lippincott, 1927. http://www.gwpda.org/wwi-www/Hurley/bridgeTC.htm#TC

Jett, Martha R. "Buster Keaton in World War I." The Doughboy Center. 2000. http://www.worldwar1.com/dbc/buster.htm

"John D. Rockefeller." Wikipedia. September 29, 2016. https://en.wikipedia.org/wiki/John_D._Rockefeller

Laplander, Robert J. *Finding the Lost Battalion: Beyond the Rumors, Myths, and Legends of America's Famous WWI Epic.* Waterford: Lulu Press, 2006.

Lindsay, Drew. "Rest in Peace? Bringing Home U.S. Dead," History Net, 9/18/2012 http://www.historynet.com/rest-in-peace-bringing-home-u-s-war-dead.htm

"List of German Weapons in World War I." Wikipedia. June 2, 2016. https://en.wikipedia.org/wiki/List_of_German_weapons_of_World_War_I

Livingston County, Michigan, Memorial library, Pam@MemorialLibrary.com

"M1903 Springfield." Wikipedia. September 27, 2016. https://en.wikipedia.org/wiki/M1903_Springfield

Meldrum, T. Ben. *A History of the 362nd Infantry*. Ogden: A.L. Scoville Press, 1920. https://books.google.com/books?id=XP1FAQAAIAAJ&printsec=frontcover&source=gbs_ge_summary_r&cad=0#v=onepage&q&f=false

McGrew, Clarence Alan. *City of San Diego and San Diego County: The Birthplace of California*. Chicago: American Historical Society, 1922.

"Miramar History." Miramar Air Show. http://miramarairshow.com/miramar-history

Morton, Desmond. "First World War (WWI)." The Canadian Encyclopedia. June 17, 2015. http://www.thecanadianencyclopedia.ca/en/article/first-world-war-wwi/

"Nichols and Shephard." Wikipedia. September 7, 2016. https://en.wikipedia.org/wiki/Nichols_and_Shepard

O'Hara, Thomas Q. Marine Corps Air Station Miramar. Charleston: Arcadia Publishing, 2005.

Olivia Times-Journal, May 30, 1918.

"Personal Hygiene." Army of Medical History. June 18, 2009. http://history.amedd.army.mil/booksdocs/wwii/PrsnlHlthMsrs/chapter2.htm

Pescador, Katrina, and Mark Aldrich. *San Diego's North Island, 1911-1941*. San Francisco: Arcadia Publishing, 2007.

"Prohibition in the United States." Wikipedia. September 28, 2016. https://en.wikipedia.org/wiki/Prohibition_in_the_United_States

"Renville, Minnesota." Wikipedia. July 10, 2016. https://en.wikipedia.org/wiki/Renville,_Minnesota

"Renville County, Minnesota." Wikipedia. July 3, 2016. https://en.wikipedia.org/wiki/Renville_County,_Minnesota

Renville Star Farmer, August 16, 1917.

Renville Star Farmer, May 23, 1917.

Renville Star Farmer, November 1, 1917.

Richards, Anthony. "Letter Censorship on the Front Line."

The Daily Telegraph, May 30, 2014. http://www.telegraph.co.uk/history/world-war-one/inside-first-world-war/part-ten/10863689/why-first-world-war-letters-censored.html

Rippley, La Vern J. "Conflict in the Classroom: Anti-Germanism in Minnesota Schools, 1917-1919." *Minnesota History Magazine,* Spring 1981, 170-83. http://collections.mnhs.org/MNHistoryMagazine/articles/47/v47i05p170-183.pdf

Rivers, W.H. "The Repression of War Experience." First World War. August 22, 2009. http://www.firstworldwar.com/features/rivers4.htm

"Robert Alexander (United States Army Officer)." Wikipedia. September 20, 2016. https://en.wikipedia.org/wiki/Robert_Alexander_(United_States_Army_officer)

"Sedition Act of 1918." Wikipedia. July 15, 2016. https://en.wikipedia.org/wiki/Sedition_Act_of_1918

"Smith & Wesson Safety Hammerless." Wikipedia. July 28, 2016. https://en.wikipedia.org/wiki/Smith_%26_Wesson_Safety_Hammerless

"Southern Transcon." Wikipedia. June 7, 2016. https://en.wikipedia.org/wiki/Southern_Transcon

"Shellshock." Spartacus Educational. http://spartacus-educational.com/FWWshellshock.htm

"St. Clair Tunnel." Wikipedia. September 7, 2016. https://en.wikipedia.org/wiki/St._Clair_Tunnel

Staley, R. "World War I Letters." http://www.u.arizona.edu/~rstaley/wwessay.htm

Stallings, Laurence. *The Doughboys: The Story of the AEF, 1917-1918*. New York: Harper and Row, 1963.

"The Grand Trunk Western Railroad." American Rails. http://www.american-rails.com/grand-trunk-western-railroad.html

The New York Times, January 6, 1918. http://query.nytimes.com/mem/archive-free/pdf?res=9806E2DC133FE433A-25755C0A9679C946996D6CF

"The Star-Spangled Banner." Wikipedia. September 27, 2016. https://en.wikipedia.org/wiki/The_Star-Spangled_Banner

"The U.S. Army in WWI, 1917-1918." In *American Military History: Volume II*, edited by Richard W. Stewart, 7-52. Washington, D.C.: Center of Military History, 2005.

"This Day in History: December 4, 1917." History.com. http://www.history.com/this-day-in-history/psychiatrist-reports-on-the-phenomenon-of-shell-shock

"This Day in History: May 24, 1917." History.com. http://www.history.com/this-day-in-history/british-naval-convoy-system-introduced

"Trading with the Enemy Act of 1917." Wikipedia. September 15, 2016. https://en.wikipedia.org/wiki/Trading_with_the_Enemy_Act_of_1917

Tucker, Kathy. "Shipbuilders Will Help." Oregon History Project. 2002. https://oregonhistoryproject.org/articles/historical-records/shipbuilders-will-help/#.V_FcIzvYPFI

United States Army Infantry Division, 77th, *History of the Seventy Seventh Division, August 25th, 1917, November 11th, 1918*, New York City, W.H. Crawford Company, 1919.

"United States Railroad Administration." Wikipedia. August 20, 2016. https://en.wikipedia.org/wiki/United_States_Railroad_Administration

"United States Shipping Board Merchant Fleet Corporation." Wikipedia. July 25, 2016. https://en.wikipedia.org/wiki/

United_States_Shipping_Board_Merchant_Fleet_Corporation
Wells, Gail. "Union Activity and World War I." Oregon History Project. 2006. https://oregonhistoryproject.org/narratives/the-oregon-coastforists-and-green-verdent-launs/unions-and-hard-times/union-activity-and-world-war-i/#.V_FdgjvYPFI

Wells, K.A. "Music as War Propaganda." Parlor Songs. 2004. http://www.parlorsongs.com/issues/2004-4/thismonth/feature.php

White, Thomas H. "Radio During World War One (1914-1919)." Early Radio History. http://earlyradiohistory.us/sec013.htm

"World War I." Wikipedia. October 1, 2016. https://en.wikipedia.org/wiki/World_War_I

"World War I Casualties." Wikipedia. September 27, 2016. https://en.wikipedia.org/wiki/World_War_I_casualties

World War 1 Letters – The Doughboys Uniform and Equipment, 2011 https://worldwar1letters.wordpress.com/sams-references-explained/the-doughboys-uniform-and-equipment/

"World War I Posters – Search Results." Library of Congress: Prints and Photographs Online Catalog. http://www.loc.gov/pictures/search/?sp=8&co=wwipos&st=grid

World War I: The "Great War", ©2006 The Teaching Company. LLC. Reproduced with permission of The Teaching Company, LLC, *www.thegreatcourses.com*

"World War I Casualties." Military Wiki. http://military.wikia.com/wiki/World_War_I_casualties

Wright, Christopher James. "The Impact of Anti-German Hysteria in New Ulm, Minnesota, and Kitchener, Ontario: A Comparative Study." PhD. diss., Iowa State University, 2011. http://lib.dr.iastate.edu/cgi/viewcontent.cgi?article=3032&context=etd

CPSIA information can be obtained
at www.ICGtesting.com
Printed in the USA
LVHW051023070723
751838LV00006B/161